D1104314

The Dominici Affair

The Dominici Affair

Murder and Mystery in Provence

MARTIN KITCHEN

Potomac Books
An imprint of the University of Nebraska Press

The illustrations in this volume originally appeared in the French tabloid *Détective*, published by Éditions Gallimard.

Library of Congress Cataloging-in-Publication Data
Names: Kitchen, Martin, author.
Title: The Dominici affair: murder and mystery in Provence / Martin Kitchen.
Description: Lincoln, Nebraska: Potomac Books, an imprint of the University of Nebraska Press, [2017] | Includes bibliographical references and index. | Identifiers: LCCN 2017011117 (print)
LCCN 2017026717 (ebook)
ISBN 9781612349886 (epub)
ISBN 9781612349893 (mobi)
ISBN 9781612349909 (pdf)
ISBN 9781612349459 (cloth: alk. paper)
Subjects: LCSH: Dominici, Gaston. | Drummond, J. C. (Jack C.) | Murder—France—Lurs—Case studies.
Classification: LCC HV6535.F7 (ebook) | LCC HV6535.F7 L875 2017 (print) | DDC 364.152/3094495—dc23
LC record available at https://lccn.loc.gov/2017011117

Designed and set in Garamond Premier Pro by L. Auten.

For Bettina

Contents

Acknowledgments

None of this would have been possible without the friendship of the late Jean-Pierre Hamer and of Dominique Lagenebre through whom I got to know Lurs and who introduced me to a number of people familiar with the Dominici affair.

Principal among them was Gérard de Meester, the present proprietor of La Grand' Terre, to whom I am most grateful for his valuable assistance and generous hospitality. In ten years of exceptional effort he has exorcised and transformed an abandoned ruin into a delightful family home.

I am most grateful to the valuable assistance of the archivists at Boots UK Limited who gave me valuable information on Sir Jack Drummond's work with the company.

My thanks are due to Martine and Roger Favre for their friendship, help, and encouragement.

Geoffrey Hamm gave me invaluable assistance tracking down archival material in the National Archives Kew.

I owe a special debt of gratitude to Vera Yuen from the Interlibrary Loans Department at Simon Fraser University for her incomparable skill in tracking down obscure bibliographical material.

Financial support from the university's Faculty of Arts is also gratefully acknowledged.

At the University of Nebraska Press I have been ably assisted by Tish Fobben, Natalie O'Neal, Sabrina Stellrecht, and Tom Swanson. Vicki Chamlee undertook the daunting task of translating my text into American English, thereby lending weight to Oscar Wilde's adage that "we have really everything in common with America nowadays except, of course, language." The faults that remain are entirely my own.

I received invaluable help from my agent Don Fehr and to his assistant Heather Carr.

Last, my thanks are due to Bettina, who has been there from the first time that we visited the site of the Drummond murders in July 1991.

Introduction

In the *Times* of 6 August 1952 amid news that discussions had taken place between the Egyptian prime minister and the British ambassador over the possibility of a defense scheme for the Middle East, that a peace treaty between Japan and Formosa had been ratified, that workers at the Grand Hotel in Birmingham had gone on strike, and that in county cricket Surrey beat Nottinghamshire thanks to A. V. Bedser's brilliant bowling, there was a notice of "Three Murdered on Holiday" near "the Alpine village of Lurs, on the right bank of the river Durance." Although no papers or identification marks were found, a label on a suitcase and the vehicle registration number identified the victims as the distinguished biochemist Sir Jack Drummond, his wife Anne, and their daughter, Elizabeth, aged about twelve.[1]

At first it was assumed that the motive for this crime was robbery, even though 100,000 francs (about $280) was found under a seat cushion in the Drummond's car. Police were said to be looking for the owner of a motorcycle with a sidecar that the farmer living close to the murder site had seen about the time of the crime. They were also searching for a deserter from the Foreign Legion, whose uniform had been found some 25 miles away. At first it seemed the case would soon be solved, and Commissioner Edmond Sébeille, a flamboyant, publicity-seeking character who led the police team, told the press that it would not be long before he made an arrest. His statement soon proved to be an idle boast. The initial investigation of the murder site was seriously compromised and vital pieces of evidence ignored. The bodies were moved before official photographs were taken; the site was not cordoned off, so a swarm journalists trampled all over the place; and the gendarmes, basking in the limelight of a sensational murder, allowed themselves to be distracted by their persistent questioning. Suspicion fell initially on the occupants of the nearby farm: Gaston Dominici (seventy-five years of age); his wife, Marie (seventy-three); their son Gustave (thirty-three); and his wife, Yvette (twenty-three). After more than two months of investigations, the police arrested Gustave and charged him not with murder but for having failed to seek assistance for little Elizabeth, whom he testified still showed signs of life when he saw her in the early morning of 5 August.

Part of the problem was that, as readers of Georges Simenon's novels will know, French murder investigations emphasize psychological factors and tend to overlook the tedious business of gradually accumulating physical evidence. The search for a motive is the prime concern. In this instance robbery was soon discounted as a possible motive, leaving Sébeille faced with a seemingly motiveless crime. A further complication was that although the commissioner prided himself for his understanding of the peasant mentality, he found himself confronting a wall of silence. There were a large number of unsolved crimes in the area, most of which had to do with settling wartime accounts between resisters and collaborators. Many local peasants possessed illegal wartime firearms, and there was a strong tradition of not getting involved in any police investigation. Months passed without making any progress.

The British press launched a campaign of bitter complaints concerning the French police's inability to solve a particularly brutal murder of three British subjects. The case has striking parallels with the disappearance of Madeleine McCann in Portugal in May 2007. Both cases have shown the striking differences between police methodologies and the legal systems in Britain and on the Continent. The implication in the press in both instances was that the British police and legal systems were superior; thereby they overlooked their own spectacular miscarriages of justice, such as the wrongful conviction of Timothy Evans for the 10 Rillington Place murders in 1950, or their own unresolved cases, such as the murder by thirty-six stab wounds of the teenager May Rebecca Thompson in County Durham on 15 February 1952. In 1952 Mahmood Hussein Mattan was hanged for the murder of Lily Volpert. In 1998 the court of appeal ruled that the case against Mattan was "demonstrably flawed" and awarded his family £750,000 ($1,245,000) for this wrongful conviction, thereby setting a precedent for compensating the family of persons hanged for a crime they had not committed. Both British and French courts have relied on confessions obtained under conditions that could reasonably be considered as duress. Timothy Evans and Gaston Dominici were convicted on the basis of confessions obtained under singularly dubious circumstances.

Much has been made of the lack of a presumption of innocence in French civil law, especially in contrast to its central place in Anglo-American common law.[2] The principle of "innocent until proven guilty" has a dual purpose: First, as a rule of proof, it obliges the prosecution to prove guilt. Second, it is intended to ensure that no punishment occurs prior to conviction. It is quite true that the accused was afforded little protection under the French legal system. Not until 1897 was the accused permitted to have counsel present when being questioned by the examining magistrate (*juge d'instruction*). The accused had the right to remain silent, but any refusal to respond almost inevitably resulted in pretrial detention. In 1958, some years after the Dominici trial, pretrial detention was found to be arbitrary and oppressive. It was henceforth only permitted in exceptional circumstances. This ruling did little to change the situation, because most cases were deemed to be exceptional; thus, most suspects had to endure lengthy periods of detention. In 1970 the terminology was tweaked, with "preventive detention" renamed "provisional detention," but this was a purely symbolic gesture. Suspects in police custody could still be interrogated for up to forty-eight hours without the assistance of counsel. In 1995 President Jacques Chirac, himself in trouble with the law, established a commission under Pierre Truche, the president of the court of appeal (*cour de cassation*), in response to frequent charges from the European Court for Human Rights: prisoners held in provisional detention were mistreated, lengths of pretrial detention were excessive, and suspects were publicly portrayed as guilty. The Truche report concluded that the presumption of innocence must be strictly respected as an essential and fundamental prerequisite for "human dignity and social harmony."[3]

Although lip service is paid to the central role of the presumption of innocence, it is in fact little more than a rule of proof that has little force before the trial. Appalling indignities still are inflicted upon the accused prior to trial. While in custody, little distinction is made between the treatment of the accused and the convicted, and for all the journalistic talk of "suspected murderers," there is a general assumption of guilt when an arrest is made. That compensation is often paid for wrongful imprisonment indicates the assumption of innocence is often an empty formula. New life urgently needs to be breathed into this cardinal principal of Anglo-American jurisprudence, especially as the rights of the accused are being steadily eroded in a dangerously exaggerated response to the threat of terrorism.

Much is often made of the differences between civil and common law. Those who prefer the confrontational system of common law argue that the accused has a better chance of acquittal, whereas proponents of civil law insist that their inquisitorial system is more thorough and better designed to discover the truth. In common law the judge is presumed to be impartial, whereas in civil law the judge plays an active role in challenging evidence, questioning witnesses, and even in some instances directing police investigations. Under common law the accused's chances of acquittal depend to a considerable extent on the skill of the defense counsel. Thus, the poor are far more likely to be convicted than the wealthy, as the socioeconomic backgrounds of death row inmates clearly indicate. The often painfully protracted investigations in civil law cases may result in less innocent persons being brought to trial, but the assumption of innocence easily goes by the board. At the end of the day, both systems have strengths and weaknesses, neither are perfect, and both are responsive to societal change.

That the Dominici case was exceptionally badly handled demonstrated the shortcomings of the French legal system in the 1950s, but it was soon reformed. There were comparable appalling miscarriages of justice in the British system at the time as well, so there was no cause for complacency. On the positive side these mishandled cases strengthened the argument for abolishing capital punishment. The guillotine was last used in France in 1977, and the death penalty was formally abolished in 1981. The last execution in Britain took place in 1973 for the capital murder of a British soldier in Northern Ireland, but the death penalty was not abolished for all instances, including treason, mutiny, and serious misconduct in action, until 1998. Both Britain and France are now bound by the European Convention on Human Rights, which forbids the death penalty in all circumstances.

The Drummond murders happened only a few years after the liberation of Provence, and there was still a great deal of unfinished business after the *guerre franco-française*. Frequent outbursts of violence, murder, and brigandage overflowed from the armed resistance and in the ensuing civil war. The Partie Communiste Française (French Communist Party [PCF]) played a leading role in the antifascist struggle and enjoyed widespread support in the region, a radical enclave in an area known as *le midi rouge* (the red south).[4] The South, anxious to prove its regional identity by staunch republicanism and laicism while remaining sharply critical of Paris, was traditionally left wing. As Cold War tensions grew, the PCF vied with other parties for rural support. The local party first championed the Dominicis as innocent peasants, entrapped by an oppressive judicial system, but it soon felt obliged to back away when public opinion turned against the family.

The involvement of the PCF with the Dominicis, combined with increasing Cold War paranoia, lent weight to a conspiracy theory that Sir Jack Drummond was a British secret service agent who had been assassinated at the behest of the Soviet Union. An alternative explanation for this seemingly motiveless crime was that Drummond had been parachuted into the area during the war with a large sum of money for the Resistance and had come back to pick up whatever remained of this hoard. That the first of these theories was shown to have originated in the fevered imagination of a deranged criminal in a German jail and that the second is demonstrably false—Sir Jack Drummond was never a secret agent and neither he nor any British agent was parachuted into the area during the war—do not deter those disaffected persons who, for whatever reason, remain stubbornly blind to facts. The century-old adage that, other things being equal, one hypothesis is more plausible than another if it involves a fewer number of new assumptions once again proves its mettle.

Conspiracy theories in the Drummond case still persist in large part due to a desire to assert Gaston Dominici's innocence. This in itself is a surprising development and is one of the most interesting aspects of the story. At the time of his arrest, he was almost universally regarded as a primitive sadistic brute, a violent patriarch who savagely mistreated his wife and children, and a heartless drunk given to uncontrollable fits of rage. During his trial, he had to be protected from a lynch mob by an extra detachment of police. On his release from prison, the local population fought tooth and nail to stop his taking up residence in his birthplace. Then over the years, his image gradually changed until he metamorphosed into an archetypical peasant, who by hard work and determination established himself as a proudly independent smallholder and maintained his family in modest comfort. The public image of Gaston Dominici thus went from one extreme to the other of the dual nature of the Provencal peasant as represented in the works of writers such as Marcel Pagnol, Jean Giono, and Pierre Magnan. Gaston Dominici could be sturdy, upright, and reliable, but he was also mean spirited, vindictive, and violent. At the time of the murders, he confirmed the urban Frenchmen's distrust and fear of their rural fellow countrymen. The murder of a distinguished English gentleman and his family by a savage peasant provided them with living proof that their fear of rural life was not the result of paranoia but based on harsh fact. With the passage of time this obsessive fear of rurality vanished, despite many other murders, with some of them being similar to the Drummond case. With the fear and anxiety gone, however, the "Monster of Lurs" was nostalgically transformed into the dignified patriarch of a bygone age. How did this change come about?

French society underwent a fundamental transformation between 1945 and 1973, when the oil crisis put an end to an unprecedented period of economic growth, which averaged an annual rate of 5.9 percent. In fewer than thirty years, the country had undergone a transformation from an essentially agricultural to an industrial and even postindustrial society.

French farmers had done relatively well in the immediate postwar years as food shortages drove up prices, but with the economic recovery, the steady drop in agricultural prices relative to industrial prices resumed, a trend that had begun as early as 1870, when grains and meat from the Americas began to flood European markets. This "scissors crisis" was partly offset by the subsidies granted by the Common Agricultural Policy, which came into force in 1962. This program relieved successive French governments from the burden of propping up a moribund sector of the economy. They could now concentrate on supporting industry against fierce competition, especially from Germany's "economic miracle." None of this did anything to help smallholders such as Gaston Dominici. Funds were concentrated on the large-scale sugar beet and grain producers in the north. Nothing was left over for subsistence farmers. They had no capital for mechanization and modernization and no possibility of entering southern France's already glutted markets for wine, olive oil, and fruit. The likes of Gaston Dominici were doomed to extinction.

Whereas at the beginning of this period 40 percent of the population was classified as farmers and peasants, now France is an industrial society with only 8 percent working on the land. The flight from the land caused serious problems of overcrowding in urban areas, one that was further exacerbated after France's defeat in Algeria resulted in the influx of European colonists (*pied-noirs*). Some of their forebears had originated as peasant farmers in France who, unable to make a living at home, had exploited the possibilities afforded by cheap land and labor in the colonies. These issues were compounded by the integration of Algerians loyal to France (Harkis). Mounting social tensions, racism, and inequality between the rich and the poor strained France's generous version of the welfare state to the limit, while entrenched interests rendered any fundamental reform extremely difficult.

Postwar France was growing economically at an amazing rate, but it faced a series of shattering defeats. The euphoria of liberation hardly outweighed the humiliation of defeat in 1940. Gaston Dominici's trial occurred in the same year that France was defeated in Indochina and that Algeria began its revolt, which also led to a shattering loss that left the country on the brink of civil war. The badly bungled Suez crisis in 1956 was a further embarrassment, and the Battle of Algiers that year marked a further escalation of the Algerian War. Charles de Gaulle's efforts to restore France's prestige failed to paper over the cracks in a society that had undergone fundamental changes and had not yet adjusted to a new reality both at home and abroad. Small wonder then that many hankered after the mythical good old days, thereby discounting many of the benefits of a consumer society and a rising standard of living for most.

In such an atmosphere it is hardly surprising that there was nostalgia for a past when many imagined life was simpler and less stressful, values were secure, and people were authentic. There arose a romantic vision of rural France, where pride in a peasant ancestry was the mark of being a true citizen of *la France profonde* (deep France). Both the Right and the Left saw a growing sentimental attachment to the rustic as part of a quest for a genuine, natural, and real sense of community. The harshness, brutality, superstition, and prejudice of rural life as depicted by Honoré de Balzac, Émile Zola, and Émile Guillaumin were forgotten. A new image gradually formed of the simple rural worker who embodied inestimable human values that were reflected in a robust civil society but had been lost amid the anomie of the modern world. A distorted version of the history of the French Revolution led to the claim that the peasants were the true heirs of the republic, thanks to the redistribution of landed property, making them more than any others truly French and genuinely republican.

Gaston Dominici, the man condemned for murdering the Drummonds, was first seen as a vicious, sadistic monster; however, over the years he has been transformed in the popular imagination into an honorable, hardworking peasant and the victim of an international conspiracy. In popular culture he has been presented as a sturdy symbol of a bygone age and an archetypical Frenchman as reincarnated by Jean Gabin in Claude Bernard-Aubert's 1973 movie *L'affaire Dominici*. The world of the Dominicis as portrayed in this film is alien and slightly threatening, but it is far removed from the reactionary, stiff, malicious, avaricious, hypocritical, and baleful portrayal of peasant life in Jacques Becker's

1943 classic movie *Groupi mains sales*, which he made in opposition to Vichy's attempts to emphasize the eternal values of peasant life. This extraordinary metamorphosis from fiend to innocent peasant, caught in an international conspiracy and wrongfully convicted by an intimidating legal system, is largely due to the transformation of postwar France from an essentially rural to a postindustrial society and the gradual romanticization of rural life.

The Dominici Affair

1   A Fatal Journey

An invitation from an old friend to spend a month's holiday in a villa on the Côte d'Azur was a tempting offer. In the austerity Britain of 1952, it was irresistible. The Festival of Britain, held the previous year in commemoration of the centenary of the Great Exhibition of 1851, was a joyful event that helped many forget the deprivations and dreariness of the immediate postwar years; but it soon served as a reminder of Britain's dismal decline since the heyday of the Victorian age. The hangover was painful. Postwar rationing, which was even more severe than it had been during the war, remained in full force until 21 February 1952.[1] Rationing did not finally end until midnight on 4 July 1954 when restrictions on the sale of meat and bacon were lifted. The general election in October 1951 had brought Winston Churchill and the Conservatives to power, even though they received more than a million *fewer* popular votes, but the prime minister was a spent force. His government, which concentrated on foreign affairs within the context of an intensifying Cold War, was unable to find a way out of the economic crisis.

Sir Jack Drummond, who received the holiday offer, had an additional incentive to escape to sunlit southern France. He had suffered a mild stroke at the beginning of the year and needed a long rest from his duties as director of research at the Boots Pure Drug Company in Nottingham. He had many fond memories of visiting France and had spent an enjoyable week in Paris with his wife the year before, as well as a visit to Hyères on the Côte d'Azur. He eagerly seized the opportunity offered by Professor Guy Marrian—his former student, old friend, and colleague—who, as he had done for several years, had rented a modest little house in Villefranche-sur-Mer between Nice and Saint-Jean-Cap-Ferrat for the month of August. Drummond agreed to share the rent. His ten-year-old daughter, Elizabeth, on whom he doted, was thrilled with the prospect and made him promise that they would camp out on occasion during their holiday. She thought up all manner of places to visit, so many indeed that her father jokingly remarked that it would take a great deal longer than a month to visit all of them.[2]

Foreign travel was exceedingly difficult for the British during the immediate postwar years. Precious few could afford it, and those who could were hampered by strict currency regulations. The Conservative Chancellor of the Exchequer Richard Austen (R. A. "Rab") Butler increased the allowance to £25 in sterling, or the equivalent in foreign currency. This amount worked out at less than £1 per day for a month's holiday—hardly enough to travel in much comfort. Any excess was liable to be seized by customs and forfeited.[3] The maximum amount the Drummond family would have been allowed was equivalent to about 75,000 francs, but like many others they had stowed away some additional funds, in this case about £50. This left them with about £125 for an entire month, hardly a princely sum for a family of three.[4]

Many travelers found it prudent to travel with camping equipment in case funds ran low, so Sir Jack was readily complied with his daughter's wish to sleep in the open air should a suitable opportunity arise. He had recently bought a Hillman Minx station wagon with sufficient space for camping equipment. With its 1265cc four-cylinder side valve engine, capable of a maximum speed of 73 miles per hour, it was a respectable mid-range vehicle costing about £700, one third of which was tax. He bought a couple of camp beds for himself and his wife Anne. Elizabeth was small enough to sleep in the back of the car when the back seat was folded down. They also had a small khaki-colored tent.

Armed with a route to Villefranche provided by the Automobile Association in collaboration with the French Tourist Office, the Drummonds set off from Nottingham at the end of July. The journey began inauspiciously as a stormy crossing from Dover to Dunkirk caused a seven-hour delay. They drove along the straight roads of Picardy, through the vineyards of Champagne and the valleys of Lorraine. With little Elizabeth's having a passionate interest in Joan of Arc, their first visit was to the cathedral at Reims before visiting her birthplace at Domrémy-la-

Pucelle. Elizabeth wrote a postcard to her maternal grandmother, Mrs. Wilbraham, from Domrémy, showing the room in which the Saint was born:

> I am having a lovely time. This is the birthplace of Joan of Arc. On the boat we were daylayed [sic] for seven hours and had to sleep the night in the car. I was 4th in exams with 71.1% present [sic].

> Tons, Cwts, Lbs, ozs of love
> Elizabeth

With Anne doing most of the driving, they then continued south through Burgundy, where Jack the wine lover must have cast a longing eye at the signposts pointing the way to the great vineyards at Gevrey-Chambertin, Vougeot, Vosne-Romanée, Nuits-Saint-Georges, Beaune, Pommard, and Mâcon. These vintages had been virtually unobtainable in wartime Britain. Passing through the Beaujolais, the family turned east to Aix-les-Bains, a small spa in Savoy on the shores of the Lac du Bourget. They arrived on 30 July and stayed at one of the better hotels.

The following day they drove on to Digne-les-Bains, a modest little town that is the departmental capital of the Basses-Alpes.[5] They stayed at the Grand Hotel, which despite its imposing name, was described by the *Guide Michelin* as being of "modest comfort." Having not made any reservations, with characteristic English suspicions of the French as congenitally disingenuous and out to swindle the hapless foreigner, they insisted on a "cheap" room.[6] They put the car in the garage and only brought in a small amount of luggage. They left the hotel at about seven o'clock, with Elizabeth asking for the key in halting French. They returned an hour and a half later.

Quite what they did during this hour and a half remains a mystery. Although this typical British family would have been immediately noticeable in a small, sleepy Provençal town, no one appears to have seen them. Presumably they went to find something to eat, but subsequent police inquiries at all the cafés and restaurants drew a blank.

The following day, 1 August, Elizabeth saw an advertisement for a humorous entertainment involving clowns and daring young men who ran in front of young bulls.[7] It was to be held the following Monday, 4 August, as part of Digne's annual Lavender Festival, which lasted from 1 to 4 August. Jack was sympathetic to his daughter's pleading. At the prompting of the hotel receptionist, Jeanine Roland, he went to Louis Chauvin's radio store and reserved three tickets.[8] The decision to return to Digne for this event involved a real sacrifice by Elizabeth's parents. They had been on the road for six days and were now in the dog days of August. That they were prepared to return to Digne and sit for hours in the blazing sun after only two days' rest on the coast, all for a rather mediocre event, is testament to their willingness to indulge their daughter. She had already persuaded her parents to take her to Reims and Domrémy-la-Pucelle; now she could boast to the Marrians that she had once again managed to get her way. It was a victory with fatal consequences.

The Drummonds left Digne at 10:30 a.m. on 1 August and headed for Villefranche. They did not arrive at their destination until 5:00 p.m. It is impossible to reconstruct the route they took, but that is of little consequence. That it took six and a half hours to drive nearly 103 miles is hardly surprising. The roads were poor, the route circuitous, and the landscape magnificent. They drove through the harsh, rocky landscape of northern Provence, with its barren mountains and ruined hilltop villages, to enter the luminous Riviera ablaze with the brilliant colors of bougainvillea, hibiscus, and oleander. A leisurely lunch, frequent stops, and difficulty in finding the house are adequate explanations.

The Drummonds spent two pleasant days in Villefranche with Phyllis and Guy Marrian and their two daughters, Valerie and Jacqueline, although the tiny bungalow set in a gloomy hollow with the hackneyed name of Le Beau Cyprès must have been something of a disappointment. Anne Drummond wrote a postcard to her mother from the Côte, notifying her of the address and telling her to add the name of the district—Vallon de la Murta—an appellation that she found entertainingly macabre. She thereby confused the word for myrtle with that for death (*mort*). Elizabeth played tennis with the Marrian girls, who were considerably older, and they went to the beach together. Jack stayed in the house and worked on a paper, the subject of which remains unknown. He had not published in any academic journals since he had resigned his professorship at London University in 1945 to join Boots Pure Drug Company; so it can be assumed that the paper was some internal document. His papers were later handed over to the British consul in Marseille, but there is no record of their subsequent whereabouts.

Their return visit to Digne on 4 August began at 6:30 am. For whatever reason, the Drummonds left their passports behind in Villefranche, along with Jack's driver's license and the contraband £50. They had already spent £20, almost half of which on gas. Given that they had paid their share of the rent in advance, they still had sufficient funds for the remainder of the holiday. They took eight £5 travelers' checks along, but they would have been of little use without proper means of identification. Since the banks were closed on Monday, they borrowed a "significant amount" of money from the Marrians to tide them over.[9] They took the road that Napoleon Bonaparte had followed on his return from Elba. Upon landing with eight hundred men at Golfe-Juan on 1 March 1815, the emperor and his men took eight days to wind their way through the barren mountains of Provence, trudging through Grasse and Digne, before reaching the valley of the Durance River. With the Hillman, the Drummonds would only need a few hours. Their start was therefore exceptionally early for a relatively short trip to attend an event that began late in the afternoon. They were unlikely to have moved as slowly as they had done three days before, and they had already seen all that was to be seen in the town. They were first sighted in Digne when they had lunch at 12:30 p.m. in La Taverne, whose proprietor Edmond Bizot was also chairman of the Lavender Festival Committee.

Earlier that morning they paid a visit to the beautiful hilltop village of Lurs. Founded under Charlemagne, it had been the site of the summer residence of the bishops of Sisteron. It is a picturesque, fortified medieval village, with a Romanesque church and a château. By 1952 it was partly ruined, with a population of about fifty, but was in the process of being restored, thanks to the efforts of the internationally renowned typographer Maximilien Vox. Jean Giono, a distinguished local author, had introduced Vox to the region, and they had just started organizing the Lure International Meetings, which are held annually in the village to discuss every aspect of book production.[10] Lurs is today—in large part because of its unsurpassed views of the Durance River, the hills of the Pays de Forcalquier, and the mountains of Montagne de Lure—a highly desirable address.

Francis Perrin, the village postman, noticed a green station wagon with Great Britain (GB) number plates driving down the hill from Lurs between 11:30 and 11:45 a.m. on 4 August. A man was driving. A little girl with shoulder-length, dark brown hair was sitting at the back. No one else in the village remembered seeing the car. The proprietor of the café suggested that perhaps the family had not driven all the way up to the village, because the Hillman was not a suitable car to tackle the only approach road, which was unpaved, steep, and badly rutted. The postman's brother, Aimé, claimed that he had seen a car with a GB plate on the main road between 10:00 a.m. and noon on either 3 or 4 August, but he was unable to give any more precise details. It was the first British car that he had seen that year.

The strange thing about the Drummonds' possible visit to Lurs is that they would have had to drive some 25 miles past Digne to get there. Driving from the southeast, it is impossible to see the village, which is hidden behind by a steep hillside. Furthermore, the access road is extremely difficult to find, even today. In 1952 there would have been no compelling reason to make such a detour. One possible explanation was that they were looking for the nearby monastery of Ganagobie, which is mentioned in Jack Drummond's copy of the *Guide Michelin*. It is a beautiful Romanesque church with some fascinating mosaics, but at that time it was virtually a ruin. Accessing it, up the steep hillside, would have been exceedingly difficult by car.[11]

Valerie Marrian later provided a more likely explanation for the detour. She said Jack Drummond had told her that they intended to return to Villefranche via Aix-en-Provence because the road was not so tortuous, and Anne was going to do the driving. There is no reason to doubt this statement, although the Drummonds had clearly underestimated the distance. They had agreed to meet the Marrians for a midday lunch at La Trinquette in Villefranche the following day. They would have had to set out from Lurs at a very early hour to arrive on time. Nevertheless, it seemed probable that having reached Digne in good time, the Drummonds then drove on to find a suitable spot to spend the night when the Perrin brothers saw them in the neighborhood of Lurs. Having found an appropriate spot, the family returned to Digne.

After lunch the Drummonds picked up the tickets for the *charlotade* (comic bullfight) from the Grand Hotel's reception desk and then went to the Bar du Soleil, where they waited until four o'clock for the spectacle to begin. Several witnesses noted that "the English" took a lively interest in the proceedings, but they left some twenty minutes before the end, at about 5:40 p.m., possibly because of the crippling heat or maybe because they wanted to avoid the rush to the exits.

Rose, the wife of the *patron* (owner) of La Taverne, claimed to have seen the Drummonds' car parked outside her establishment between 6:30 and 7:00 p.m. Elizabeth was reportedly playing with a dog while waiting for her parents. This testimony, however, contradicts that of a gendarme who later gave a detailed account of a curious encounter involving the Drummonds.

Émile Marque was a gendarme from Valensole, a town about 31 miles away, who had been detached to Digne for the festival.[12] He was on road patrol and had taken up position outside the Hotel L'Ermitage, which was situated a little outside the town on the main road to Nice. It hardly merited its four stars, but its restaurant was described as one of the best in the region. At about 6:15 p.m., Marque saw a gray-green station wagon with a GB plate entering the hotel's courtyard parking lot. Three people got out: a man, a woman, and a child. They went inside the hotel and stayed there for about an hour. When they drove out onto the main road, they stopped beside the gendarme. The man, who was at the wheel, asked in French for the directions toward Château-Arnoux. He said a few words in English to the woman, who was seated to his left, and Marque thought that he heard the word "Lurs" mentioned.

Marque said the man appeared to be about fifty years of age. He had a small mustache. His hair was sparse, and he was somewhat overweight. He was wearing a black jacket. The woman was smaller, hardly reaching his shoulder. She had an oval-shaped face, and her hair was dark brown. The little girl had short hair, but he could not remember what she was wearing. After the gendarme gave them directions, they drove back toward Digne.

About an hour later a car with right-hand drive, coming from the direction of Nice, pulled up outside the hotel. It was a small, box-shaped brown car, looking like a cross between a Renault 4CV and a Peugeot 203. It appeared to be an older model. A man and a woman were inside. The man got out and with a strong English accent asked the gendarme where they could get something to eat. He also asked whether an English car had passed by recently. Marque told them that he had indeed seen one and that it had driven off in the direction of Château-Arnoux. He also said that they could eat at the hotel. He saw the car drive into the parking lot, where both people got out. The man went into the hotel, while the woman remained standing by the car. The man emerged from the hotel about a quarter of an hour later in an agitated state. Both jumped into the car and drove off at considerable speed in the direction of Digne.

The man was about five feet nine, slim, around thirty years old, and bareheaded with pomaded hair. He was dressed in a white shirt and white trousers. The woman was about six inches shorter and dressed in black. She was thin, with short curly light brown hair. The car had a GB plate at the back on the left-hand side.

There are a number of problems with this story. Jack Drummond spoke no French and was not driving. He had left his license at Villefranche. It is somewhat curious that he had asked the way to Château-Arnoux, which would have been a slight detour had he been heading for Lurs. It is an attractive little town, but there is little there of particular interest, apart from a sixteenth-century château. Besides, it was also getting late. Although there was large chemical factory at nearby Saint-Auban, it would not have been of any professional interest to Sir Jack as it did not have a research laboratory and only produced standard chemicals.[13] It is unlikely that he would have wanted to pay it a visit the following day because that would have meant canceling the lunchtime appointment with the Marrians, and he almost certainly would have informed them that evening of any such change of plan. Marque's testimony implies that the Drummonds dined at the hotel, but we know from the post-mortems that their stomachs were empty. The mysterious "woman in black" appears at various points in the narrative, but she was probably Anne Drummond, who had black clothing in her bag and had changed her dress before settling in for the night.

Rather than setting off to Château-Arnoux or Lurs, the Drummonds indeed drove back to Digne and parked the car outside the Grand Hotel. The precise time of their arrival is uncertain. It is highly probable that Gendarme Marque, who testified months afterward, may have thought that the Drummonds arrived later than in actual fact. In any case, two reliable witnesses saw their Hillman outside the hotel sometime between 6:30 and 7:15 p.m. There is no indication why the family went back to the hotel. Was it to see if by chance there was a room available, to leave a message, or to make a telephone call?

They had obviously abandoned any possible idea of going to Château-Arnoux. Leaving Digne at about 7:30 p.m., they drove directly toward Lurs. About 9 miles from Digne, at the village of Malijai, they were noticed by a motorcyclist, who was extremely irritated because their car was driving so slowly. The Drummonds pulled up outside a small store, where Jack bought a bottle of Vichy water. Then they drove to Les Mées with its spectacular rock formations on the banks of the Durance. Known as the "Penitents," the sandstone columns that stand 164 feet high are said to be the petrified remains of monks from the Lure Mountain. Saint Donat had turned them into rocks for their having dallied with the beautiful Saracen maidens whom the local baron had brought back from the Crusades.[14] The formations would have looked particularly splendid with the setting sun casting deep shadows and giving them a warm glow.

Having crossed the Durance at Les Mées, they drove a few miles along what was then the main road to Manosque and Aix-en-Provence before stopping on the side of the road to set up camp, thus granting Elizabeth her special wish. It was, after all, not such a great hardship. The moon was full, and August is the month of falling stars, offering an extraordinary spectacle. Jack Drummond was a doting father, who found it hard to resist his daughter's every wish. Both father and mother were, by the standards of the day, elderly parents who could be excused for giving way. Besides, why shouldn't Elizabeth's wishes be taken into consideration? The Drummonds were determined that this trip should not be a typical nightmare family holiday, in which a child is treated as a tiresome impediment and a needless expense, with her wishes utterly ignored. Jack had inquired at the Grand Hotel whether a room was available for the night of 4 August but had been told that Digne was fully booked because of the festival. It would thus only have been possible to see the *charlotade* if they spent the night afterward, and they had come all the way from England fully prepared for such an eventuality. The Marrians' daughter Valerie told the police that the Drummonds had said that they would camp on the side of the road and that they were fully equipped to do so. As it was swelteringly hot during the day and the nights were still very warm, however, they had left their tent behind in Villefranche.

The spot where the Drummonds chose to spend the night was far from picturesque. It was on the then main road from Digne to Manosque and Forcalquier.[15] They parked on a level turnout covered with gravel that was used for vehicles doing repair work on the road and to deposit gravel and sand. It was one of the few places along the road where it was possible to park a car, and it had the additional advantage of offering relatively easy access to the river. Although the Durance River ran nearby, it was hidden from view by a clump of dwarf oak trees.

It was still light when they arrived, but the sun would have already fallen behind the steep hill on the other side of the road. A short distance away was a shabby yellow farmhouse, hidden from the road by a high wall in which was set the dilapidated remains of a door. Behind it was a flight of steps leading down to a courtyard, in which the farmer's family would sit on wooden benches to drink their homemade pastis and wine and occasionally welcome a neighbor or family member. Between the Drummond's campsite and the farmhouse were rows of vines and apricot trees interspersed with alfalfa. Not far was a stone bridge that crossed a railway line, and on the other side a steep slope led down to the Durance. What seemed from a distance to be an attractive riverbank along an inviting river was viscous black clay strewn with huge jagged rocks, uprooted trees, and sundry detritus, including the rotting remains of a sheep. It was not at all the place for a leisurely evening stroll. The river branches into several streams, some of which have impressive currents, and a number of stagnant pools of some depth. It was hardly an inviting place for a young girl looking to take a dip. Perhaps the Drummonds had deliberately chosen the spot, thinking that a nearby farm and a busy road offered them a greater degree of security than an idyllic and remote spot in the country.

The farmhouse, situated a few hundred yards farther down the road, was known as the Grand' Terre. It was a desolate property from which an elderly peasant, Gaston Dominici, managed to scratch a living. He lived there with his wife, Marie; his son Gustave; his daughter-in-law, Yvette; and his grandson Alain, who was ten months old. Relations between Gustave and his father had never been good, but they had recently reached the breaking point. They lived under the same roof but maintained separate households. They rarely spoke to one another except to quarrel. Things had grown even worse since April of last year, when Gustave announced his intention to set up on his own as a tenant farmer. Gaston had flown into a towering rage, denouncing him as a useless layabout who had proved himself inept in his attempt to run the Grand' Terre and who would be totally incapable of setting up on his own.

Gustave deeply resented that he was the only one of the nine Dominici children who had been compelled to stay at home. There had been no jobs available during the war and no possibility of finding an apprenticeship. Now he was thirty-three years old with a young wife, infant son, and a baby on the way, working for his board and lodging but with virtually no income. The sale of apricots brought in 72,000 francs that year, and the bank had advanced 65,000 francs in anticipation of the wheat harvest.[16] Precious little of this money ended up in Gustave's pocket. In short he was trapped by his seventy-five-year-old father, who needed him to run the farm but whom he loathed and feared. Gaston's death would be the only way of escaping from his tyrannical hold over Gustave.

Although there was a major fete in Digne, on the farm the fourth of August passed as usual. Gaston got up sometime between 3:00 and 4:00 a.m. to take his goats to pasture. He came back to the house for his midday meal, changed his boots for slippers, ate his lunch, and took his habitual siesta in an armchair. By 4:30 p.m. the heat had subsided suffi-ciently for him to venture out once more. As he led his goats out again, he noticed that a field of alfalfa, which was being watered, was in danger of flooding. He went back to the farmhouse and asked his daughter-in-law, Yvette, to turn off the water. The sluice gate was about 330 feet away from the house and about 98 feet higher. For whatever reason, possibly because she was pregnant, Yvette refused. Gaston then ordered his wife to do it for her. She replied with unaccustomed forcefulness: "Do it yourself!" Gaston raged at such insubordination, pointing out that he could not leave his goats alone because they would start nibbling at his barley. With great reluctance and after a significant pause, Marie went and turned off the water.

Meanwhile, Gaston went to the bridge across the railway, only a short distance from the farmhouse, to see the extent of the damage. Mud, shrubs, and undergrowth had slipped down the slope and had reached the gravel bed of the railway. He was therefore concerned that the landslide might continue during the night and block the railway so that the first train, scheduled for 6:45 a.m., would be unable to pass. He would then be faced with a hefty fine.[17]

Gaston was furious that his son was not at hand to deal with this awk-ward situation. He was away that day, helping his wife's maternal uncle with the threshing on his nearby farm. Gaston continued to graze his goats, while keeping an eye on the landslide, and returned to the house at about 7:30 p.m. On his way back across the bridge and along the path that led to the main road, he noticed the Drummonds' Hillman parked on the side of the road, a few yards to his right. Given Gaston's difficult dialect and the parents' poor French, it is unlikely that they exchange any words between them.

Gustave returned to the Grand' Terre soon after eight o'clock. He went almost at once to make sure that the railway line was free from any obstruction so that the last train of the day, scheduled at nine o'clock, could pass. On the way he also noticed the Hillman parked in the turnout.

Having seen that for the moment the track was free, Gustave had a quick supper. Then he went on his motorcycle to Peyruis, about 2 miles down the road in the direction of Digne, and reported the flooding incident to Faustin Roure, who was in charge of a gang of platelayers working for the French state railway Société nationale des chemins de fer français (SNCF). Roure and his wife, Rose, invited Gustave in for a drink just as the nine o'clock train passed through the station. He assured Gustave that he and his team from the Lurs railway station, situated 547 yards away from the Grand' Terre, would come and look at the landslide early the next morning and make sure that it was free from any obstruction.

On his way home, Gustave passed La Serre, a farmhouse on the edge of the road where his sister Germaine lived with her husband, Roger Perrin, and their sixteen-year-old son, Roger. Known as Zézé, he was Gustave's much loved nephew. Zézé later testified that Gustave honked his horn "as usual" as he rode past the farm. Gustave returned home shortly after nine o'clock.

Meanwhile, Anne and Elizabeth Drummond had taken a canvas bucket to the farmhouse and asked for water. Yvette filled it up at the outdoor pump. Elizabeth was well prepared for this task. Her last bit of homework for her French class at her boarding school before the end of term involved translating from French the following passage:

The girl gave the white hen to her mother.
Do you have any fine butter, Madame?
There is no milk in my bottle.
Please give me some.[18]

Elizabeth was considered reasonably proficient in French and had recently recited Jean de la Fontaine's fable "Le Corbeau et le Renard" to the satisfaction of her French teacher, Miss Hancock.

Jack Drummond spread out a tablecloth, and the family nibbled at some biscuits and cake. They placed the two camp beds parallel, hidden from the road by the car, and prepared a bed for Elizabeth in the back of the Hillman. A rug was hung over it to provide an added degree of privacy and some shade from the bright moonlight and the headlights of passing cars. The sun set that day at 7:55 p.m., but it did not get fully dark until 10:00 p.m. The moon rose at 8:21 p.m., and it would be full the following night. A full moon with clear, starlit skies in Provence in August is an impressive sight, providing unexpected visibility, deep shadows, and haunting luminosity. It would reach its zenith at 11:53 p.m. and set at 4:35 a.m.

Elizabeth and her father changed into pajamas, but her mother, who had not brought any nightclothes with her, simply changed into another dress without removing her under garments. Exhausted after a hectic day, they went early to bed and were soon asleep.

2   The Murder

Shortly before six o'clock in the morning of 5 August 1952, Jean-Marie Olivier was returning home to Oraison on his New-Map motorcycle, having finished the night shift at the chemical factory in Château-Arnoux-Saint-Auban. He was halfway home on the *route nationale* N96 when, on the left-hand side of the road, a man popped up "like a jack-in-the-box" from behind a vehicle parked on the side of the road and flagged him down.[1] Olivier, who recognized the man by sight, slammed on the breaks and pulled up about 98 feet farther down the road. The man ran after him and, after pausing to catch his breath, asked Olivier to go to the gendarmes in Oraison because he had seen "a dead body on the slope on the edge of the road." Without pausing to investigate the scene of the crime or to ascertain the precise location, Olivier drove off in the direction of Oraison. Just over 130 yards from where he had stopped, two women—one old, one young—were leaning motionless against a farmhouse wall.

While Olivier drove to Oraison, Faustin Roure left home on his moped at about 6:15 a.m. to examine the damage done by the landslide, as he had promised Gustave Dominici. On the way he overtook three men on bicycles: Gustave's brother Clovis, Roger Drac, and Marcel Boyer, who was also Clovis's brother-in-law. They were all were members of Roure's SNCF team.[2] Faustin arrived at the Grand' Terre at 6:35 a.m. Ignoring the car parked on the side of the road, he went directly to the bridge over the railway and examined the extent of the landslide. Crossing the bridge he turned left, walked parallel to the railway for a couple of hundred yards, then went down the slope to see whether any immediate action was required.

Boyer was the next to arrive on the scene. He pedaled past the parked British car without noticing anything untoward and went to join Gustave, who was standing on the road near the farmhouse. Gustave just had time to tell Marcel that there was a dead body nearby, when his brother Clovis arrived.[3] He noticed the general disorder around the parked car, with empty suitcases, cardboard boxes, pillows, and blankets strewn around. He remarked that the campers must have had quite a party. According to Boyer's testimony, Gustave replied that he had heard five or six shots at about five or six o'clock that morning. Gesturing with his arm in the direction of the Durance, he added that he had discovered "a dead body." Clovis and Boyer walked in the direction indicated. Boyer stayed at the top of the slope, while Clovis scrambled downward toward the Durance to have a closer look.

When Roure arrived after examining the landslide, Clovis asked him, "Have you seen it?" Roure, imagining that he was referring to the landslide, replied that fortunately he had seen nothing that would hinder the train's passage. Clovis then nodded his head in the direction of the body of a young girl lying in the tall grass a few meters down the slope. For whatever reason, whether out of indifference or an anxiety not to get involved in any way, neither Roure nor Boyer went to have a closer look. The three men then returned to the farm.

On their way back, they noticed the outline of another body, completely covered by a blanket, near the English car. On the other side of the road, they also saw an overturned camp bed. Again they did not take a closer look. Clovis and Boyer mounted their bicycles and pedaled back to the Grand' Terre to join Gustave; his young wife, Yvette; and his mother, Marie. Roure went back to the bridge, where he had parked his moped, and pushed it along to join the others.

Roure's detail was scheduled to begin work at the Lurs railway station at 7:00 a.m., so he ordered his men to move on. They all left, except for Clovis, who was anxious to find out what had happened on the family farm. Having given his men their orders, Roure headed to Peyruis to inform his SNCF superiors that all was well. He also told the telephone company (Postes, Télégraphes et Téléphones) that some branches had fallen on the telephone wires and that they needed to be removed.

Roure, who had been active in the communist partisans (Francs-Tireurs et Partisans Français [FTPF]) during the war and was the secretary of the Peyruis cell of the French Communist Party (Parti Communiste Français [PCF]), also reported the incident at the Grand' Terre to Roger Autheville, secretary of the Departmental Federation of the PCF and thus head of the party in the Basses-Alpes. He was also a journalist.[4] He had been the commander of the Fifteenth Company of the FTPF in Sigonce, a particularly violent outfit in which Gustave Dominici had served. Gustave's role in the Resistance was far from glorious. He joined on 15 August 1944, the day the Allies landed in southern France. He seems to have done little, apart from taking part in the victory parade in Forcalquier, where he proudly displayed his armband to a local photographer.

Autheville arrived on the scene of the crime very early in the proceedings, both in search of a good story and to keep an eye on the local party militants. Paul Maillet, the local secretary, was the Dominicis' friend. Yvette Dominici's father was a member of the party's Departmental Federation. Her brother-in-law Clovis was a member of the Peyruis cell as well.

All locally prominent figures in the Communist Party visited the Grand' Terre. They included Mr. Emmanuelli, the director of the communist newspaper *La Marseillaise*, and Mr. Bonnaire, alias "Noël," who was a former colonel in the FTPF. The communist Sunday newspaper, *Humanité-Dimanche*, sent a special correspondent to investigate. He later wrote, "Lurs has witnessed two scourges: the killer and the police. As a result two families have been afflicted: the Drummonds and the Dominicis."

The Communist Party had good reason to frustrate the efforts of the police. After the liberation of France, there had been a series of what the minister of justice had called "executions without a judicial guarantee," or executions in what amounted to something like a civil war between "collaborators" and "resisters." It has been estimated that roughly the same number of people, 160,000–170,000, were on each side, with the Resistance being minuscule until June 1944.[5] Contrary to legend, the Resistance concentrated more on killing other Frenchmen than on disposing of Germans. Regardless of whether the victims were compatriots or occupiers, the communists saw it all as part of a glorious "struggle against Fascism."

It is hardly surprising that we know very little about the Dominicis between the armistice in 1940 and the end of the war. This was a particularly troubled period in French history, a time of betrayals and shameful compromise, of extraordinary heroism and base opportunism, of the vicious settling of accounts, of cover-up and deceit. There were active resisters, collaborators, the indifferent, and those who waited to see which way the wind would blow. The lines were seldom clearly drawn and were often crossed.

Until the German invasion of the Soviet Union in June 1941, the PCF, true to the spirit of the 1939 Molotov-Ribbentrop Pact, offered no resistance to the Germans. Only in November 1942, when Vichy France was occupied, did it become active in the south. The local group based in Sigonce was then commanded by "Capt. Della Serra" (alias Manuel Lopez). The group's reputation was far from honorable, for it was generally regarded as an unruly bunch of robbers and assassins. This assessment was definitely not the result of intense anticommunist sentiment among conservative peasants. At that time the communists were extremely popular, and the party did everything it could to attract rural support. The FTPF's activities, however, rendered them so unpopular that the PCF sent Roger Autheville to try and bring them to order. He did his best, but his mission was unsuccessful. After the war Roger was a frequent visitor to the Grand' Terre. He and his friend Paul Maillet would both be expelled from the PCF, however, when the local leadership felt that their involvement with the Dominicis reflected badly on the party.

Another resistance movement, based on the Ganagobie plateau, was commanded by "Capt. Claude" Renoir, the youngest son of the painter Auguste and brother of the movie director Jean Renoir. Nicknamed "Coco," he often served as his father's model, notably in *Claude Renoir en clown*. He trained as a ceramicist and worked in the film industry as an actor, an assistant director, and a director. He was awarded the Croix de Guerre and the resistance medal for his wartime activities. His group comprised some twenty-five men; most were former policemen, army officers, or civil servants who refused to serve the Vichy regime. They were in direct contact with London and received parachute drops of arms and money, which were used to build up the resistance movement in southeastern France. At the Ganagobie monastery, Father Lorenzi gave them his enthusiastic support, helping to hide them when unwanted visitors arrived. The Germans never discovered their hideout.

A third group, the Secret Army (Armée secrète), was established in 1943 by the resistance hero Jean Moulin. It was the most highly disciplined and effective of all the resistance movements. In the south it was made up of the amalgamation of two groups, Combat and Libération Sud. On 1 February 1944 the FTPF theoretically joined them to form the Forces françaises de l'intérieur (FFI), and in June Gen. Marie-Pierre Koenig, the hero of the Battle of Bir Hacheim, took command. But cooperation was never close because of serious ideological differences.

That Gaston, who was already in his late sixties during the war, played no active part in the Resistance is hardly surprising. He tended his flock, dabbled in the black market, and kept his eyes and ears open and his mouth shut. He often hinted that he knew what Gustave had been up to while in the FTPF and that he would use it against him were that necessary; but quite what that was we shall never know. The Communist Party actively supported the Dominicis in the early stages of the murder investigation and did what they could to frustrate the efforts of the police, but here again the party's motives are obscure. Neither Gaston nor his son Gustave were ever party members.

In France after the Allies landed, some 10,000 people were killed in extrajudicial proceedings as "resisters" settled scores with "collaborators." Within a radius of nine miles of Lurs there were a number of such "executions," and Gaston and Gustave were certainly aware of them. One such instance was the assassination of the mayor of Peyruis François Muzy. A former gendarme, he had served as mayor for twenty-five years and was elected as departmental councilor. He was also a member of the Radical

Party, a staunch republican, and an outspoken anticommunist. His wife was a schoolteacher who worked for a time at the tiny school in Ganagobie. She knew Gaston, as did her husband, who had given him a Gras rifle.[6] Muzy was gunned down in his own home on 29 June 1944 by two young men who accused him of denouncing members of the Resistance. As a man who was widely liked and respected, his death came as a terrible shock.

A number of communists had been arrested at the beginning of the war on orders from the Édouard Daladier government. They were released after the armistice thanks to the Germans, who until 22 June 1941 were allied with the Soviet Union. The authorities in the Basses-Alpes asked Muzy to keep a close eye on the activities of two communists who had recently been released from a detention camp. Much to the disappointment of the prefect, the mayor absolved them of any defeatist sentiments.[7] In spite of Muzy's positive report, one of these men, Pierre Puissant, was arrested and eventually interned in Algeria, where he was liberated by the Allied forces in November 1942. He died fighting with the Free French at Monte Casino, Italy. The other, André Jouval, was seldom seen and soon joined the Maquis.

Muzy was certainly no hero but simply an ordinary man caught up in terrible times. On the one hand, he did nothing to help the Jews in Peyruis, even though rumors of their fate were circulating. They emanated from the mistress of the Gestapo boss in Sisteron. On the other hand, he helped save known communists from the Germans. One of these men was to become his successor.

With Muzy out of the way, Peyruis became the only commune in the Basses-Alpes controlled by the PCF. The elections of 1945 witnessed some bizarre maneuvers by the communists. Three candidates ran for the communal elections: a communist, a socialist, and an independent.[8] The communist failed to get an absolute majority in the first round of elections, whereupon the socialist withdrew from the race. The communist was duly elected councilor but soon afterward was found dead (presumably poisoned), and his house was burgled. It was widely believed that he possessed a list of fourteen people in Lurs who were to have been killed by the FTPF group of which Gustave was a member.

Della Serra's FTPF group was involved in a number of heinous crimes disguised as acts of resistance, and the members were determined to cover them up in the postwar years. Ten minutes after Muzy was shot, the local justice of the peace, Mr. Itais, was gunned down in his garden, with an entire magazine emptied into his body. His only apparent offense was that as a royalist and anticommunist, he was clearly in the reactionary camp. He had been involved in judging a murder case concerning a woman who was said to have been of German or Lorrainian origin and rumored to have been the mistress of a German officer. The murderers were never discovered, but it was assumed that they were from the FTPF. The case had been closed by the time of the justice's death. One link with the Dominicis was that the woman concerned lived about 100 yards from the farm owned by Gustave's father-in-law.

Also in Peyruis Mr. Amalrie, the local head of the FFI, which was also known as the "Fee-Fee," was gunned down. At Saint-Auban two brothers of a miller by the name of Queyrel were shot. This turned out to have been a mistake, obliging "Noël" to apologize to the unfortunate miller. Across the Durance at Mées, a young hairdresser, Miss Colette, paid the highest price for having offered comfort to the enemy. A married couple who ran a tobacco shop at Mallefougasse were killed, as were a farmer and his entire family in Pierrerue. An eighty-year-old antiquarian at Valensole, Jean Mille, was shot. At La Motte-du-Caire Dr. Ciamborrani was killed and his gold tooth removed.

The most spectacular of these murders in the neighborhood occurred directly across the Durance River from the Grand' Terre at the Château de Paillerol, where a married couple, the Cartiers, lived with their grandson and Monsieur Cartier's mother. They had a daily cleaning woman, who lived in the village, while a local peasant looked after the grounds. During the war they received regular visits from the Maquis, who demanded food and money. These demands were so excessive as to amount to extortion, so Cartier began to protest. One morning the cleaning woman, Miss Gal, arrived for work to find the door locked. The elder Mrs. Cartier was hanging out of a second-floor window, screaming for help. Some neighbors arrived on the scene and managed to break down the door.

They found Mr. Cartier lying on the floor, shot through the head. Mrs. Cartier's body was found on the first-floor landing. She had also been shot in the head. Their bed was unmade, and they had obviously been awoken in the middle of the night. Mr. Cartier's office had been turned upside down. His safe was open and empty.

The grandmother said that she had heard voices at about ten o'clock the previous evening. There had been a furious dispute and sounds of physical violence. The inquest concluded that since the door had not been forced open, the Cartiers must have known their assailants. The investigation was put into the hands of Commissioner Stigny from Nice. He had hardly begun his inquiries when he was rudely interrupted by FFI members while eating his dinner in his lodgings in Forcalquier. He was asked to follow them. His body was later found in a ditch a short distance from Paillerol.

It later transpired that a colleague in the Nice police department had denounced Stigny as a collaborationist. He had been executed on orders from "Serge," the departmental head of the FTPF, who in civilian life was a bookseller from Paris named Schulz. After the war Schulz was amnestied. Lamontre, the policeman who had denounced Stigny, was given a ten-year jail sentence but was soon set free. A direct connection between the murders of the Cartiers and Stigny was never established, but whatever the case, they were both the work of Della Serra and his men.

Another inexplicable murder was that of André Gras, a photographer from Forcalquier. He had not been a member of the Maquis, but he had rendered the FTPF service on a number of occasions. In August 1944 four young men entered the tobacconist's shop run by his parents and asked to see him. He was led away, and nothing was heard of him for two years. His bones were found in the cemetery in Forcalquier. His gold bridgework, wedding ring, and watch had been removed. Neither any apparent motive nor the murderers were ever found. A wall of silence surrounded the crime, as was the case in so many other inexplicable incidents during these troubled times.

Charles Tillon and André Marty, two militant communists who had been expelled from the party hierarchy in 1952 after being denounced as police spies, sought refuge in the region at Montjustin. They had been charged with being police informers and for ideological heterodoxy. Tillon had been a prominent figure in the FTPF and after the D-Day landings had tried to organize a communist revolution in France, but Joseph Stalin ordered the party's leader, Maurice Thorez, to rein in this headstrong revolutionary. Forced to undergo a process of intense self-criticism, he had retired to the Basses-Alpes, where his faithful henchmen kept the press and photographers at bay with clubs and rocks. Marty had been on the secretariat of the Communist International (Comintern) and had played a controversial role as the inspector general of the International Brigade during the Spanish Civil War.[9] In 1943 he represented the PCF in Charles de Gaulle's provisional government and soon rose to be number 3 in the party hierarchy after Maurice Thorez—whom he detested—and Jacques Duclos.

Jean Giono, the local writer and member of the Académie Française, said that the war and the Resistance had resulted in an appalling transformation of the region. With staggering exaggeration, he told a British journalist:

> During the war and during the liberation the people of the country, who were normally law-abiding and kind, in appearance at least, became beasts: women are known to have torn young boys who could have been their sons into pieces with their bare hands. A young man I know, who seemed quite harmless, after raping a woman, poked out her eyes, cut off her ears and otherwise mutilated her with a kitchen knife. His excuse was that she spoke with a German accent. She was in fact a Frenchwoman from Alsace. Practically all the population did something for which they could easily be blackmailed. That atmosphere still hovers over us. Their hatred of the Germans has now been turned against English speaking foreigners, particularly Americans.[10]

Giono seems to have forgotten that in 1942 he had told the German consul in Marseille that he had "more faith in the task of bringing France and Germany closer together, for which end I have been working ever since 1933," and that he had asked the well-known journalist Alfred Fabre-Luce, "What is Hitler—the man—if not a poet in action?"[11]

Thus, with still a lot of unfinished business, that the locals would be loath to talk or assist in a local murder investigation is not surprising. Most of them still possessed weapons they had obtained during the war, despite the authorities' efforts to collect them. The Dominicis were also known to be violent. One night in 1946 two truck drivers had stopped outside the Grand' Terre. Clovis had welcomed them with a burst of machinegun fire. He later told the gendarmes that he had thought they were burglars. Two years later Gustave had a pistol stolen. The robber, Sube by name, was arrested. He testified that he had seen a military weapon in the Grand' Terre. The gendarmes investigated and found a Mauser rifle. Gustave was fined 6,000 francs and given a suspended sentence.

Back at the Grand' Terre, the next person to arrive on the morning of 5 August was Jean Ricard. He was a thirty-six-year-old traveling salesman from Marseille who had been camping and visiting Father Lorenzi, a lone monk who lived in the nearby monastery at Ganagobie.[12] He came upon the scene of the crime shortly before 7:00 a.m. He had walked down from the hilltop on which the monastery is situated to catch the bus for Marseille. The bus stop was about 100 yards past the Grand' Terre. Noticing the incredible shambles around the car, which he saw had GB number plates, he assumed that there had been some sort of accident. Since there was no one around, the Dominicis having gone back into the farmhouse, he decided to take a closer look. He saw an overturned camp bed at a distance of between 5 and 7 feet from the car, with a person sleeping on the ground rather than on the camp bed; but anxious not to miss the bus, he did not stop to investigate further. The bus soon arrived and took him home.[13]

Meanwhile the motorcyclist, Jean-Marie Olivier, had arrived at the gendarmerie at Oraison at about 6:15 a.m. and reported the incident to the duty officer, Fernand Gilbert. Olivier told him that he had been stopped by a peasant, whom he knew by sight, on the main road near

Lurs. The man had told him to report to Oraison or to telephone the gendarmes in Forcalquier that he had discovered a dead body. The man had pointed in the direction of the Durance. Olivier claimed that the man, who turned out to be Gustave, had said someone who seemed to be dead was lying on the slope down to the river and that "there must be some other dead bodies." Olivier also stated that he had seen two women—presumably Yvette and Marie Dominici—on the lookout, standing near the farmhouse.

Gilbert immediately alerted the head of the Oraison station, as well as the gendarmes at Forcalquier under Capt. Henri Albert. The latter ordered two of his men to take a motorcycle with a sidecar and proceed at once to the Grand' Terre. On their way, however, they were stopped by Aimé Perrin, Germaine (née Dominici) Perrin's brother-in-law.

Aimé told a somewhat garbled story in his impenetrable dialect. His wife, who was already working in the fields beside the railway line, had been informed by Albert Bourgues, who worked for the SNCF under Roure, that there had been a "killing" at the Grand' Terre. Perrin had taken his moped to go and have a look and met Yvette on the way. She said there had been shots during the night and that Gustave had found a young girl's body on the slope leading down to the Durance and had asked for help in alerting the gendarmes. Since they had not yet arrived, she explained that she was on her way to a store at Giropey so she could telephone the gendarmerie and find out what was happening. When Aimé said he wanted to see for himself what was going on at the Grand' Terre, she begged him not to go, suggesting that he might go in her stead to call the gendarmes.

The gendarmes told him that they were already on their way to the scene of the crime. Thus, Aimé returned home and told his wife what had happened. He then went to the Grand' Terre.

No one seemed to think it was strange that Yvette, who was pregnant, was sent on a bicycle to fetch the gendarmes rather than Gustave, who had a motorcycle. Nor was she ever asked why she had been so insistent that Aimé should not go to the Grand' Terre right away. Was it because the Dominicis needed time to make some changes at the scene of the crime?

The two gendarmes, Sgt. Louis Romanet and Gendarme Raymond Bouchier, arrived at the Grand' Terre at 7:15 a.m. They were surprised to find the place deserted. Roger Perrin and his wife, Germaine, were the next to arrive. The gendarmes went up to the Hillman Minx station wagon. Just at the moment that they saw a body covered with a blanket, Gustave came up behind them. He then showed them another body, that of a man lying on the other side of the road, covered by an over-turned camp bed. Romanet immediately went to Giropey to telephone his superior officer, Captain Albert, as well as the mayor of Lurs Henri Estoublon. Bouchier remained at the Grand' Terre, where he took some photographs.[14]

No one attempted to cordon off the area because in those days the gendarmes were not provided with the yellow or orange tape now used for this purpose. The French police paid scant attention to material evidence. They concentrated almost exclusively on questioning witnesses in the hope of finding the motives behind the crime. It was an approach that later horrified the British police and did not prove very helpful in uncovering a seemingly motiveless crime.

Captain Albert, having been informed of the extent of the crime, called his immediate superior, Commandant Bernier, in Digne as well as the judicial police in Nice, which were responsible for the Department of Basses-Alpes. The court in Digne was also alerted.

At about 7:45 a.m. Gaston Dominici came back to the farmhouse with his herd of goats. At roughly the same time Roure returned to the Grand' Terre on his moped, followed shortly afterward by Roger and Germaine Perrin's son, Zézé, who came from his home at La Serre on a bicycle. Yvette told Gaston that bodies had been found nearby. He asked her where. She pointed the direction out to him. Accompanied by Gustave and joined by Zézé, he set off toward the Hillman.[15] No one seemed to find it strange that this was ostensibly the first Gaston had heard of the murders. His son had found a dead body on his property, yet neither Gustave nor Yvette had apparently seen fit to tell him what had happened until hours later.

Captain Albert arrived at the scene of the crime in his black Peugeot 203 shortly afterward. He was accompanied by two other gendarmes, Crespy and Rebaudo. They found Gaston, Gustave, and Zézé standing near the Hillman. Although Captain Albert was an experienced officer with an excellent reputation, he also did nothing to seal off the crime scene, which was rapidly becoming seriously compromised with the arrival of neighbors and curious passersby, who parked their cars along the main road. They were soon joined by sundry other officials and several journalists. Commandant Bernier, who arrived shortly afterward from Digne, also did nothing to rectify this lamentable state of affairs.

The attitude of Gustave and Yvette seemed incomprehensible to Captain Albert. He asked Yvette why she had not even bothered to have a look at the little girl. Her reply was curt: "I'm not a nurse! Anyway, I didn't want to get mixed up in this business." Albert then asked Gustave why he had not gone to check on Elizabeth's parents. He replied: "One can't think of everything." Albert was also intrigued by the precision with which all the Dominicis remembered both the arrival of a motorcycle with a sidecar at 11:30 the previous night and the sound of foreigners who chatted away and a woman laughing. This was in marked contrast to their hazy recollection of the events surrounding the murders. They admitted to having heard shots but claimed that they came from the other side of the river, from Peyruis, or even from the mountains. They claimed not to have heard any screams or any other suspicious noises. With the Hillman only about 170 yards from the farmhouse, this story was scarcely credible, especially on a hot night in August when they slept with the windows open.

At 9:30 a.m. Deputy Public Prosecutor Louis Sabatier, Examining Magistrate Roger Périès, and Clerk of the Court Émile Barras—all of whom were officials of the court in Digne—arrived in their official Peugeot. Hardly conducive to a cool-headed investigation of the crime scene, all this hullabaloo was the result of the intertwining of police, judicial, and local authorities entrenched in the French legal system, in which the definitions of fields of competence are liable to become blurred.

Under French law when a murder takes place, the public prosecutor (*procureur de la république*) opens the investigation. In the case of murder he or she is obliged to hand the conduct of an inquiry to a prosecuting magistrate (*juge d'instruction*). The prosecutor is attached to a higher court (*Tribunal de grande instance*), is appointed by the president of the republic, and is responsible to the minister of justice, whereas the prosecuting magistrate is fully independent and free from political control.

The prosecuting magistrate enjoys complete independence to initiate a judicial inquiry. He or she is responsible for coordinating the judicial inquiry within the limits set by the prosecutor. With authority over the police investigation, the medical-legal team, and other experts, the magistrate decides whether and when to give the judicial police the right to examine witnesses and to issue search warrants (rogatory permission.) He or she is obliged to take note of the defense lawyers and those acting on behalf of a civil suit. Additional responsibilities include overseeing the autopsy and keeping track of all the interviews conducted by the judicial police and the magistrates (*procès-verbaux*).

Next the examining magistrate decides whether the assembled dossier merits an indictment or whether the case should be dismissed (*non-lieu*). Upon indictment he or she is obliged to make the entire dossier available to the defense, but it is not given to the jury. The dossier is then sent to the local court of appeal (*cour de cassation*) for a pretrial hearing. If the judge supports the prosecuting magistrate's case, it is then sent to trial in an assize court (*cour d'assise*), the only court in France with trial by jury.

The powers of the prosecuting magistrates, an office instigated by Napoleon in 1811, are considerable and are the matter of intense debate. On the one hand, their independence from political control, plus the fact that they can start an investigation on their own initiative without first being ordered to do so by the public prosecutor, has enabled them to probe into the activities of such powerful politicians as Jacques Chirac, Roland Dumas, Dominique Strauss-Kahn, Dominique de Villepin, Nicolas Sarkozy, and Christine Lagarde; businessmen such as Bernard

Tapie; and banks like the Crédit Lyonnais. Eva Joly, a fiercely independent prosecuting magistrate, launched a spectacular investigation into a $325 million corruption scandal involving the oil concern Elf Aquitaine between 1995 and 2002, and thirty of the thirty-seven prominent accused were found guilty.

On the other hand, there have also been startling abuses, such as Fabrice Burgaud's investigation of pedophiles in 2002 that resulted in fourteen innocent Frenchmen being held on remand for up to three years. Relatively few cases are now investigated by the prosecuting magistrates, most of them dealing with terrorism, where the examining magistrates have proven relatively successful in their dual roles as detectives and judges. They are responsible for collecting inculpatory and exculpatory evidence. The danger that they are answerable to no one is offset by fears that if they were to be abolished, then the judiciary would be subjected to an unacceptable degree of political control.

An inquiry into penal procedure in France, conducted by Philippe Léger in 2009, recommended abolishing the office of examining magistrate. The commission's principle arguments were that the prosecuting magistrate was placed in an essentially ambiguous situation by being required to be both inquisitor and judge. Ninety-five percent of criminal cases were conducted by the Judicial Police, acting on behalf of the public prosecutor, without the intermediary of an examining magistrate. The system is time consuming and expensive, and it leads to a lengthy delay before bringing a case to trial. Further complications arise because a plea of guilty is inadmissible in a French court. A case as complex as that of Bernard Madoff, had it occurred in France, would have taken years rather than months to reach a final judgment.

The Léger commission's recommendations provoked a fierce debate, with the Left insisting that such changes would bring the judicial system under stricter governmental control and make prosecutions in cases of political corruption, public health abuses, and so on, less likely. Supporters of the reform proposal pointed out that a similar office in Germany (*Untersuchungsrichter*) was abolished in 1977, thereby greatly streamlining the judicial system without any noticeable ill effects. Opposition to the Léger proposals was so fierce that the system remained unchanged, and examining magistrates continued to uncover a number of spectacular cases of corruption.

Dr. Henri Dragon, a country doctor with no experience in forensic medicine, came to the Grand' Terre with the mayor of Lurs at about 8:30 a.m. Long before the criminal investigation team arrived from Marseille, he made a superficial examination of the bodies, and in the process, he moved them.[16] First, he crossed the road and removed the camp bed that was covering a male body, dressed in a white sweater, blue pajama bottoms, socks, and unlaced tennis shoes. He noticed two bullet wounds in the neck, but he did not say whether the entry wound was in the front or back. He then examined the female body, which was wearing a red dress with a floral print, vest, bra, and panties, lying partially covered on the ground behind the Hillman. The feet were bare. He turned the body over, cut the left strap of her bra and the right sleeve of her dress, but made no precise description of her wounds.

Last he went across the railway bridge to examine the body lying on the slope down to the Durance. It was that of a young girl wearing sky-blue pajamas and with bare feet. Her skull had been crushed by blows from a blunt instrument. Whereas the other two victims showed advanced signs of rigor mortis, the girl's body was still noticeably relatively supple. According to the doctor, the soles of the girl's feet showed no signs of abrasions even though the ground between the car and where she was lying was covered with pebbles, coarse grass, and prickly plants. This seemed to indicate that the body had been carried from the campsite and deposited out of sight in the long grass on the reverse slope. Dr. Dragon felt that the nature of the head wound indicated that the girl had been hit while lying down. These points in Dr. Dragon's report would later cause a fierce debate. The police report clearly indicates that there were traces of shingle on her feet. (Commissioner Edmond Sébeille stresses this detail in his account of the crime, admittedly written in self-defense eighteen years later.)

Having thus had a brief look at the three bodies, Dr. Dragon went to the Grand' Terre and asked Gaston Dominici, whom he knew well, for water with which to wash his hands. The old peasant appeared to be in a state of shock. All he could do was to repeat the words "some water, some water!" Instead of inviting him into the house, Marie filled a basin with water, but Gaston brushed it aside, complaining that the horses would smell the blood and would refuse to drink out of it. The doctor washed his hands under the outdoor pump. The Dominicis seemed determined to avoid letting the doctor enter the house. What could they have had to hide?

At about ten o'clock a police dog from Digne, a regional champion, arrived at the Grand' Terre with its handler, Legonge. The German shepherd bitch snuffled around in various directions but found no new clues. She did not show any particular interest in any of the Dominicis, nor did she follow the track leading from the little girl's body to the campsite. This too suggested that the girl might have been carried and had not run away in a desperate attempt to escape her murderer.

The murders were soon reported in the French and international press. The summer months were a bit short of news. A number of UFOs had been spotted in the United States. Before the television age, the Helsinki Olympics had not excited great interest. The epoch-making formation of the European Coal and Steel Community aroused little popular enthusiasm, and Col. Gamal Abdel Nasser's overthrow of King Farouk seemed of little concern, although details of the king's sybaritic private life was not without entertainment value. There was a lull in the fighting in Indochina. But although the murders provided excellent copy for a press hungry for lurid news, undoubtedly they caused real shock and dismay, particularly in France. As *Paris Match* wrote: "The horrible assassination of Sir Jack Drummond, his wife and daughter, is a matter for individual mourning for all the French. They were our guests, invited to share our *joie de vivre* and our sun."[17]

Meanwhile, the police in Forcalquier had duly informed the police in Nice of the murder, but being seriously overworked during the summer season, the Nice police told Captain Albert to refer the case to the regional service of the judicial police in Marseille. For this reason it was not until nine o'clock that news of the triple murder reached Commissioner Georges Harzic's office at the Marseille police headquarters, the Échêvé. Formerly the bishop's palace, it also housed the offices of the Ninth Mobile Brigade of the judicial police.[18] Harzic decided to give the case to Commissioner Edmond Sébeille. Albert warned Harzic that it was going to be a very difficult crime to solve. Harzic condescendingly replied that had this not been the case, there would have been no need for the gendarmes to consult the judicial police. Thus, from the outset the case was bedeviled by the rivalry between the gendarmes and the Judicial Police.

Commissioner Sébeille was just wrapping up a simple case involving an Arab who had been killed in nearby Berre and was looking forward to joining his wife and eighteen-year-old daughter, who were at their holiday home in the Aveyron. His holidays were to begin on 14 August. At 9:15 a.m. on 5 August, however, the telephone rang in his office at the Échêvé. Commissioner Harzic asked him to come immediately to his office. He read him the following message from the gendarmerie in Forcalquier:

Three corpses have been found today, 5 August 1952, at about six o'clock in the morning, on the territory of the commune of Lurs, at about 600 metres [650 yards] from the railway station of that locality. Preliminary investigation having been made it would seem that the motive for the crime was theft.

The victims (a man and two women) were killed by a firearm. No identity papers have been found on them. An English car was in the vicinity. Initial information has revealed that shots were heard during the night of the fourth to fifth of August at about one o'clock in the morning.

The gendarmerie from Forcalquier is already at the scene of the crime. The Digne bench has been informed.[19]

Harzic then asked Sébeille whether he was interested in the case. Sébeille, startled by this remark, replied that if he were not interested he would deserve to be dismissed from the force. He knew the region well, although he had never been all the way up the hill to the village. Harzic said that the case was tailor-made for him, because Sébeille was known as an expert in peasant affairs. Of the fourteen murder cases Sébeille had handled during his career, eight or nine had been in rural areas. He understood Provençal and could speak it reasonably fluently. He prided himself for being able to comprehend the peasant mind and claimed to get on well with country folk.

Appearing to feel little urgency, Sébeille took some time before he decided to set out to Lurs in an ancient Citroën *traction avant* (front-wheel drive), the classic French police car known colloquially as "the open tomb." First, he had to close the file on the Berre murder case, and then he had to get his team together. His assistant Henri Ranchin and driver César Girolami were at hand, but he was unable to contact the two other inspectors allotted to the case—Lucien Tardieu and Antoine Cullioli. Both men were engaged in investigations in Marseille and could not be contacted until they returned to headquarters. Next, they had to go home and collect some personal effects. Then they had to wait for twenty minutes behind a long line of military vehicles before the Citroën could be refueled. Being good Frenchmen, they almost certainly stopped for lunch. Although what time they eventually arrived at the Grand' Terre is not certain, it was unlikely to have been before three o'clock that afternoon.

Sébeille's team was given a cold reception by Public Prosecutor Sabatier, Examining Magistrate Périès, and Clerk of the Court Barras in Digne. They had been waiting impatiently for five and a half hours for the team and were not impressed by the commissioner's explanation for his late arrival. Another group of officials—including the sub-prefect and the mayor of Forcalquier, the mayors of Lurs and Peyruis, and the commanding officer of the gendarmerie in the Basses-Alpes—gave them an equally chilly welcome. The main reason for the officials' disquiet at the police's late arrival was that under ministerial circular number 32, the gendarmes were forbidden to touch anything on the murder site before the arrival of the police. Thus, a valuable eight hours were lost. Things were not improved by Sébeille's failure to greet Captain Albert on his arrival, itself testament to the intense rivalry between the gendarmerie and the police. Sébeille was outspokenly contemptuous of the work done so far by those whom he considered to be bungling amateurs.

A large crowd of onlookers was trampling all over the scene of the crime, and the atmosphere reminded Sébeille of a country fair as all manner of people arrived during the day. They wandered around, sought shade from the blistering summer heat, excitedly discussed the mystery of the murder, and had eagerly awaited the arrival of the criminal investigation team. Efforts by Captain Albert and his gendarmes from Forcalquier to control the crowd had proved singularly ineffectual.

Precisely what Sébeille did and at what time is somewhat unclear, prompting all manner of wild speculation. The records of the police, the gendarmes, and the examining magistrate do not give the exact time of his arrival at the crime scene. There is no compelling reason to doubt that Sébeille arrived in time to examine the bodies and have them photographed before they were taken to Forcalquier for a postmortem examination. He claims that he did, and the examining magistrate did not contradict his testimony. Had he arrived after the bodies had been removed it would have constituted a more serious infraction of due procedure that would have brought the entire case into question. Sébeille also claims to have gone to Forcalquier at five o'clock to assist at the autopsies, but there is no corroborating evidence that he was there.

One thing is certain: the scene of the crime had been seriously compromised before Sébeille's arrival. Contrary to due procedure, the gendarmes had rummaged around in the Hillman in an attempt to discover the victims' identity. In addition, Dr. Dragon had clumsily moved the bodies and had cut some of the victims' clothing.

Captain Albert showed Sébeille two cartridges that had been found—one, a few yards in front of the Hillman; the other, 2 yards behind it. He had also found two rounds that had not been fired. From this evidence Sébeille concluded that the weapon used was a semiautomatic gun and that whoever had fired the weapon was unfamiliar with its use.

Further confusion arises over who discovered a bullet mark on the right-hand side of the bridge and when this happened. Commissioner Sébeille claimed that he was the first to have noticed it and did so soon after his arrival on the scene of the crime. Pierre Carrias, Périès's successor as examining magistrate, insisted that it was not spotted until 16 November 1953, when Gaston Dominici pointed it out in the course of reconstructing the crime and claimed to have shot at little Elizabeth, who was "running away like a rabbit." There is no mention, however, of this astonishing and improbable confession in the police records. An employee of the ministry of transport also claimed that he was the first to discover it, but Captain Albert testified that he had noticed it during the evening of 7 August.[20]

Similar confusion exists concerning a second piece of important evidence—namely, a splinter of wood found on the ground near Elizabeth's head. On 6 August Gaston Dominici claimed in a statement to Commissioner Sébeille that he had found it about a foot from the girl's head at eight o'clock the previous morning, when he was covering up her body. He said he gave the piece of wood to one of two gendarmes, but he could not remember which one. Neither of them had any recollection of this ever happening. Months later two laborers claimed that one of their colleagues had found the piece of wood about four inches from Elizabeth's head and that it had been passed from hand to hand. The two men denied that Gaston had handed it over to the gendarmes. Much later Gaston's son Marcel claimed that he had found it, but he could not remember to whom he had given it.

This piece of wood came from the stock of the murder weapon, which had not yet been found. That Gaston showed such interest in this splinter clearly indicated that he knew that it had come from the weapon and that he knew that Elizabeth had been hit over the head with it. His motives for claiming to have been directly involved in bringing this important piece of evidence forward are obscure. Sébeille argued that it was to explain away any fingerprints that might have been on it, but this makes little sense. If Gaston's first version was true and assuming that he was indeed the murderer, then he would have disposed of this incriminating piece of evidence. Perhaps he invented the story to show that he was willing to cooperate fully with the investigation, but quite why he should cook up this story, which was flatly contradicted by the laborers' plausible testimony, is difficult to comprehend.

Even more perplexing than the question of the bullet mark and the piece of wood was a critical piece of evidence that was completely ignored. According to testimony given by Inspector Girolami, Sébeille's assistant, three years after the murders, at about 3:00 p.m. on 5 August he had seen a pair of well-worn corduroy trousers hanging on a clothesline outside the entrance to Gaston and Marie's part of the Grand Terre. The trousers were still wet, and no other garments were beside them. Girolami asked Gustave Dominici to whom they belonged. He replied that they were probably his father's, since they were certainly not his. The inspector then asked him who did the washing in the Grand Terre. Gustave replied that two of his sisters, either Clotilde Araman or Augusta Caillat, took the dirty washing home and brought it back dried and ironed. Girolami reported this to his superior, who promptly told him to get on with more important business.

Sébeille, who did not see anything exceptional about a pair of trousers hanging out to dry near a farmhouse, chose to ignore them, and it was not until the investigation was reopened in 1955 that they took on a central importance. The Dominici daughters confirmed that they did all the washing for the Grand Terre and stated that neither of them had done any washing around the fifth of August 1952. They also stated that their sister-in-law Yvette had read about these trousers in the newspaper account and had confirmed that they had been hanging out to dry that day. But she had added that they had been washed several days before and not because of any bloodstains. Given that the weather was particularly dry and hot in August, there could be no question of them being still soaking wet after several days; nor was there any reason why they should have been left out to dry for days on end.

In 1954 the sub-prefect of Forcalquier, Pierre Degrave, wrote to Captain Albert, the head of the gendarmes in the town, saying that on 5

August 1952 he had heard that another witness had seen a pair of blue work trousers while looking through the window blinds into Gustave's bedroom. Albert confirmed that on 3 September 1952 he had asked Gustave's wife about these trousers. She had replied that she had indeed washed a pair of her husband's trousers that day so that he could have a clean pair for the market in Oraison and had added somewhat truculently that she had a perfect right to do so if she wished.

It is indeed quite extraordinary that Sébeille should have totally ignored the deeply suspicious facts: two pairs of trousers, belonging to Gaston and Gustave Dominici, respectively, were hanging out to dry the same day three horrendous murders had been committed almost on their doorstep and that this was not the normal method of doing the washing at the Grand' Terre. The Dominicis later denied that this was true, but the testimonies of Inspector Girolami, Sub-prefect Degrave, and Captain Albert—and confirmed by Aimé, another Dominici son—removed any shadow of doubt that this was indeed the case. There are only two credible explanations why they had been either washed or hanging out to dry: First, it could have been that there were bloodstains resulting from the blow to Elizabeth's head or from moving her parents' bodies. Second, they could also have gotten wet while disposing the murder weapon in the shallow waters of the Durance.

Sébeille's astonishing reason for failing to take any notice of such pieces of evidence is that he believed that material evidence in such a case was of minor importance when compared with questions of motive. The case was eventually closed by Gaston Dominici's confession. In such circumstances, Sébeille argued, the question of whether the trousers were covered with blood or not was of secondary importance. By twisted logic the inspector excused his negligence by saying that if traces of blood had indeed been found on the trousers, they would have simply made Gaston the prime suspect. But since he was that already, the discovery would have made no difference.[21]

3   The Police Investigation

Given the slipshod nature of the investigation so far, it comes as no surprise that the autopsies were conducted in an amateur fashion. This was a remote and backward part of France, in the depths of *la France profonde*. The hospital at Forcalquier was small and ill equipped. The two doctors appointed by the court to conduct the autopsy—Dr. Nalin from Forcalquier and Dr. Girard from Digne—were competent general practitioners but had little or no experience in criminal investigations, even though Girard had the title of forensic scientist (*médecin légiste*). Girard had visited the scene of the crime the morning of 5 August and had made a perfunctory examination of the bodies. He had noticed a wound on Jack Drummond's hand and mentioned it to the examining magistrate, Roger Périès. Dr. Nalin did not go to the Grand' Terre. Neither doctor spoke to their colleague Dr. Dragon, who had first examined the bodies. It does not seem that they inspected the victims' clothes for evidence of rips or bloodstains. They took no photographs, and their conclusions, which were not ready until 17 August, were terse and contradictory. Their report did not enter the public domain until the trial.

The autopsy reports do not mention any powder marks on Jack and Anne's bodies, and that indicates the shots were fired at a distance of at least 5 feet. It is obvious that neither of the two doctors had any experience in examining gunshot wounds. There is no mention in their reports of the criteria used to establish entry and exit wounds. Nor were they able to establish exactly the angle at which the shots were fired.

A great deal of confusion also exists over the gashes on Jack's right hand.[1] One was diagonally across the muscle at the base of the thumb; the other, across the bottom joints of the middle and ring fingers. Girard associated these injuries with a small piece of flesh that had been found on the rear bumper of the Hillman, but he did not mention this in the autopsy report and assumed that it was the result of a gunshot. During the trial Dr. Nalin insisted that he knew nothing about the piece of flesh that had been found at the murder site. His colleague Girard had died before the trial began, so it was no longer possible to pursue the matter any further. Sébeille kept this piece of flesh in a matchbox, and it was never produced in evidence.

Since there is no mention in the autopsy report of any powder marks or burns on Jack's hand, it is safe to assume that he was not shot at close range. The alignment of the wounds is such that they could only have been caused when the hand was closed, in which case a gunshot would have caused considerably more damage. It is therefore highly unlikely that this was the result of him grabbing the rifle in self-defense, as the prosecution argued. Nor was the damage done some time before the murder, because in that case it would have been bandaged. The most probable explanation is that he stumbled and grasped hold of the Hillman's rear bumper while trying to avoid his assassin.

Jack was hit in the back by two bullets. The first went through the right shoulder blade and the right lung, causing a massive hemorrhage, and the exit wound was to the right of the sternum. The shot was fired at a certain distance when the victim was in an upright position. The second bullet entered the body at the waistline, damaging the first lumbar vertebra; went through the liver, causing a further major loss of blood; and exited through the cartilage of the sixth right rib, some 2.0–2.4 inches from the first shot. This indicates that at the time of impact, the body was leaning forward at about thirty degrees. These were mortal wounds, but death would not have been instantaneous. An important conclusion that was not drawn in the report was that the injury to the lumbar vertebra would have damaged the spinal marrow and made it virtually impossible for the victim to remain standing for long. His stomach was virtually empty, indicating that he had not eaten that evening. There was no hint of any alcohol. His bladder was empty, and that finding explained why he was wearing shoes.

Certain preliminary conclusions can be drawn from the nature of these wounds. Jack was clearly shot from behind. The assassin must have been somewhere to the rear of the car. A pool of blood near a sump, about 2 yards behind the Hillman and directly across the road from where the body was found, indicated that perhaps Jack had collapsed there. Traces of blood on the road suggested that Jack had managed to stagger across the road, but after such a traumatic injury and massive loss of blood, would he have been able to cross the road on his own? The most likely scenario is that Jack had gone among the oak trees behind the Hillman to relieve himself. Walking back toward the car he saw a man, probably with his back to him, threatening his wife and child. He rushed forward to protect them, thus overtaking the assassin, who shot him twice in the back, firing from the hip. Jack fell forward as a result of the second shot and grabbed ahold of the Hillman's rear bumper to steady himself. Rapidly losing consciousness and incapacitated by the gunshot wounds, he stumbled along the side of the road and collapsed in the vicinity of the sump. He had then managed to drag himself across the road. There is no compelling reason why the assassin should have moved the body to the other side of the road.

The autopsy of Anne's body presents even greater problems than those of her husband's. Apart from the gunshot wounds, there was no evidence of any injury or signs of violence, nor was there the slightest evidence of a sexual assault. Her stomach was also empty. The autopsy report says that there were seven bullet wounds, but it did not distinguish between entry and exit wounds. She appeared to have been hit by four bullets, but the mystery remains why no bullet was found in the body. The autopsy concluded that Anne had been shot while lying down or possibly in a sitting position. The doctors were unable to determine the position of the assassin relative to her body.[2]

The inconclusive nature of the autopsy report, given the uncertainty about which were exit and which were entry wounds, as well as the alignment of the shots and the fact that the bodies had been moved gave rise to all manner of conjecture and speculation.[3] One such argument is that the difference in the diameter of two of the supposed entry wounds in Anne's body suggests that a second weapon, probably a handgun, was involved. If so, there might have been two assassins. This theory, propounded fifty years after the murders and based on a most unsatisfactory autopsy report, is hardly convincing.

The autopsy report on ten-year-old Elizabeth stated that the body was completely rigid, so it was assumed that she died at the same time as her parents. This clearly indicates that Girard and Nalin did not consult Dr. Dragon, who had examined the bodies the morning of the murders at about nine o'clock. He had noted that whereas Jack and Anne's bodies were "as stiff as a board," Elizabeth's was not yet affected by rigor mortis. Dr. Girard had visited the murder site that morning, but he obviously had not examined the bodies with due care.

Elizabeth received a blow to the head that had severely damaged the area around her right ear. The doctors considered that this wound— probably caused by a blunt instrument, although possibly by a large-caliber bullet—would have been sufficient for Elizabeth to have lost consciousness but would not have been mortal. Her death was caused by two massive blows to the head by a blunt instrument that formed a V shape just above her nose. These blows are described as having been extremely violent and delivered by a very robust attacker while Elizabeth was lying down. All three doctors agreed that Elizabeth likely would not have lived for more than an hour after suffering such severe damage to her skull, but this is contradicted by the statement in the autopsy report that her cerebral matter had not been affected. Blood had oozed from her nose and ears, so it is possible that Elizabeth, who was lying on her back, might have died not from the blows to the head but from blood flowing from the nasal cavity into the bronchi, causing asphyxiation.[4]

Elizabeth was found barefoot. The autopsy report makes no mention of any marks on the soles of her feet, suggesting that she had not run away from the campsite across rough terrain. There is, however, a possibility that like her parents, she might have been wearing shoes. Only one pair of her sandals was found, but they were carefully packed away and thus were unlikely to have been the ones that she had been wearing that day. But if she had been wearing shoes, it is difficult to see why her murderer would have removed and disposed of them. The police report clearly states that there was grit on the soles of her feet. An experiment conducted later with a girl of Elizabeth's weight and build showed that it was possible to run along the same path without leaving traces on the soles of the feet.

It would seem highly likely that Elizabeth had been killed where she was found. The piece of wood from the murder weapon was discovered nearby, and a pool of blood was on the ground under her head. Although it is impossible to know the precise sequence in which the blows to her head were delivered, the most likely order would be that she first received a blow to the ear that rendered her unconscious and lying on her back. This injury was then followed by two blows to the skull.

Inspector Sébeille left the Grand' Terre at about 5:00 p.m. on 5 August, ostensibly to attend the postmortem examination. It is uncertain whether he actually did, but whatever the case, he returned to the scene of the crime some two hours later. During his absence two of his assistants, Antoine Cullioli and Henri Ranchin, ably supported by Mr. Chapart from Agence France-Presse, carefully examined the area around Elizabeth's body. Wading in the shallow waters of the Durance, they found the stock of a rifle floating next to a sheep's rotting carcass amid a mass of detritus forming a small dam. It was about 20 yards downstream from where Elizabeth's body had been found. The rest of the weapon was buried in the sludge 30 yards upstream.

The weapon, an American M1 carbine with the serial number 1.702.864, was produced by the Rock-Ola Manufacturing Corporation. It was a semiautomatic weapon with a fifteen-round magazine. The caliber was .30 (7.62 mm). More than six million M1s were produced by ten different companies, including General Motors and Winchester. This particular weapon had a metal plate with the initials RMC, which caused all manner of confusion. It was suggested that they might stand for Régiment de Marche Coloniale, but this particular unit had long since been disbanded. On 19 August Aimé Dominici wrote to his brother Gustave and suggested that they were the initials of René-Marcel Castaing, a neighbor in Lurs who had died in 1946. Aimé said that on the day of Castaing's burial, his neighbor Paul Maillet had taken all his guns and later took over the Castaing farm. On receipt of this letter, Gustave Dominici jumped onto his motorbike and took it to Sébeille, who was singularly unimpressed. He had already concluded that RMC stood for the name of David Cullen Rockola's company, the Rock-Ola Manufacturing Corporation or the Rock-Ola Music Corporation, which also made the famous Rock-Ola jukeboxes. In fact, lengthy investigations by Interpol established that the weapon had once been the property of the Royal Military College in Kingston, Ontario.[5]

Aimé's letter seemed to be confirmed by an anonymous letter claiming that Maillet had stolen Castaing's American weapon on the day of the funeral. The gendarmes quickly discovered the woman who had written the letter. She claimed that in 1950 she had seen the rifle hanging on Maillet's kitchen wall, but it was without the magazine. Maillet, a railway man who lived with his wife and five children at a smallholding known as La Maréchale, at first seemed like a prime suspect. He had been active in the Francs-Tireurs et Partisans Français, rising to head a group in Mirabeau in the Vaucluse. He was also known as an expert poacher, as well as a sturdy hiker, so the gendarmes assumed that he could very well have been on the prowl for wild boar the night of the murders. Further, he had a quick temper and was of a nervous disposition.

On 29 August the gendarmes made a surprise visit to Paul Maillet's smallholding in an attempt to uncover the ownership of the presumed murder weapon. His wife, Ginette, and their older son, age ten, claimed never to have seen the gun, but their two younger children, ages nine and six, were not quite so sure. Young Paul, aged two, and the baby were not questioned. Having searched the house, they discovered that Maillet was stealing electricity from the main and that his bicycles had no license plates. They also found a couple of Sten guns with ample supplies of ammunition.[6] Sébeille and the public prosecutor in Digne, Louis Sabatier, agreed that they would not press charges on any of these offenses in the hope that they could use Maillet to break through the Dominicis' defenses. Meanwhile, all they got out of him was that in the afternoon of 4 August, while he was working on the railway line, he had heard a rifle shot.[7] Further investigation revealed that it had been fired by Aimé Perrin, Germaine Dominici Perrin's brother-in-law, who lived at Giropey. He had tried to scare away some crows. The gendarmes were surprised that he had used a rifle, a Springfield that he should have handed over in 1945, against magpies. He explained that he had chosen it because of the noise it made. The gendarmes took the illegal weapon and let the matter drop.

The area was bristling with army weapons collected in summer of 1944 as the Allies swept through the area. After the war it was strictly forbidden to own such weapons, particularly automatics like the Sten or semiautomatics such as the M1. Few were willing to hand them over, though, and the authorities did not ask too many awkward questions.

Paul Maillet, along with his wife, his father, and his mother, was interrogated at length at the town hall in Forcalquier. Their testimonies established his complete innocence. Maillet, mindful that the police had a hold over him for the possession of illegal weapons and stealing electricity, promised Sébeille that he would do everything he could to help him in his investigation.

The weapon that Sébeille's assistants found was in an appalling state of repair, which explains why the stock had become detached from the barrel. It had been held together with bicycle brake cable and a Dural-umin band. The piece of wood found near Elizabeth's body fit perfectly to the stock, clearly indicating that it was the weapon that had been used to kill her. That the carbine had been patched up in such an amateur fashion showed that it came from the neighborhood. Further evidence that it was owned locally was that the Duralumin strip was similar to ones frequently used to attach the obligatory plates to mopeds and bicycles that showed the owner's name. Extensive investigations revealed that this metal band had been sold in Lurs by Joseph Chauve, a tinker based at 16 Impasse de la Cité in Marseille. He could not remember to whom he had sold it so many years ago.

Regardless of ownership, the rifle was definitely not a weapon that a professional killer or hired assassin would have chosen. It remained to be seen whether it was capable of being fired and, if so, whether it had been used in the other two murders. Before any such investigation was even undertaken, Sébeille told the press that evening that "the weapon will talk" and would do so loud and clear. He maintained this rifle was a local weapon. The murderer had acted on his own and came from the vicinity of the Dominici farm. He had shot the two adults and, having run out of bullets, had clubbed Elizabeth to death with the butt. The commissioner, having leaped to a series of all too hasty conclusions, seemed to have imagined that the case would soon be solved. It was not long before he began to regret this display of self-confidence as the investigation dragged on for month after frustrating month, and the pressure weighed heavily on him to bring it to a satisfactory conclusion. The police investigation, which began on 5 August 1952, lasted until 16 November the following year.

In possession of this "talking" weapon, Sébeille implied that an arrest would be made within a matter of hours. Captain Albert from Forcal-quier, who unlike the commissioner was fully conversant with the peasant mind and milieu, was less sanguine. Shrugging his shoulders, he said they would "need a couple of hours, or perhaps a couple of years." His wry skepticism was fully justified. Sébeille would soon come up against not only the stubborn resistance in which peasant suspicions of the outsider were combined with an unwillingness to get involved in any way with this unpleasant affair but also the initial determination of the Communist Party to protect the Dominicis from the police.

At about 7:30 p.m., as Sébeille was going to leave the Grand' Terre, Gaston Dominici approached him. Pointing to a mulberry tree, he said that Lady Drummond had fallen there, adding that he was certain that she had not suffered. This was a very odd remark, because he knew full well that Anne had died close to the Hillman, or about 10 yards from the mulberry. In saying that she had not suffered any pain, he was merely repeating what Dr. Dragon had openly said. A day or two later he would say that the little girl started screaming as she ran away from the mulberry tree and attempted to escape.[8] Gaston also told Commander Bernier in front of a witness that "when someone shot at the little girl—" but was then interrupted by some hasty question. It is not at all clear what game

Gaston was playing here. Was he attempting some cunning ruse, or was this an exercise of his customary self-importance? No one bothered to question him further.

Just before calling it a day the gendarmes discovered a foreign legionnaire's uniform in a thicket near Aiglun, some 18 miles away, giving rise to speculation that the murderer was a deserter. An identity card in the name of Cesarino Donati led to the apprehension of a man with a cast-iron alibi. All told, a few pieces of evidence had been collected, including what appeared at first sight to be the murder weapon; the victims' bodies had been taken to Forcalquier; and the Hillman was stored in a garage in Peyruis. (It was left unsealed and later moved to Digne, where it was left in care of the clerk of the court's wife. Long before the trial took place, it was sent back to England, where it was auctioned off by Sir Jack's heirs. In a ghoulish coda it was bought by a circus proprietor, who exhibited it in Blackpool, complete with crudely fashioned wax figures of the Drummond family.) Still nothing had been done to cordon off the murder site, and it seemed that the perfunctory search for material evidence had come to an end. Sébeille concluded this first day of his investigation by announcing that the crime site had nothing more to tell.

Although Sébeille talked frequently to the press, the story that emerged was often wildly speculative. *Combat* reported that Sir Jack and his wife had been machine-gunned (apparently with a Winchester), that Elizabeth (said to be aged twelve) had been brutally clubbed to death, and that another young woman had managed to escape and was wandering about the countryside in a state of shock. The murderer was a deserter from the Foreign Legion who had killed the Drummonds to get some civilian clothes. The British press also printed the horrific story of a multiple murder all for the sake of a suit.[9]

The behavior of the Dominici family on the first day of the investigation was remarkable. They claimed to have heard some shots but assumed that they were caused by poachers. They denied having heard any screams and appeared to be indifferent toward the victims. Both Gaston and Gustave admitted that they had got up during the night, but it was very strange that neither of them saw fit to see how the campers were doing. Gustave claimed to have found Elizabeth's body when he went to see whether any further damage had been caused by the landslide, but when Sébeille asked why he had not gone to tell her parents, he gave the absolutely unbelievable answer that he had been far too scared to do so, because he imagined that the parents had killed her. The commissioner then asked why, after Gustave had told Jean-Marie Olivier that he had found Elizabeth's body, he had gone to look after his animals rather than examining the campsite. Gustave also claimed that when he had hailed Olivier he had not seen Anne's body, even though according to his testimony he had been standing only a few paces away. (Olivier claims to this day that Gustave had not stopped him, but he had halted because Gustave popped up from behind the Hillman.[10]) Gustave would then have been beside Anne's body. Jack's body was also just across the road, so it is impossible to believe that Gustave had not seen it. Sébeille also inquired why he had sent his pregnant wife, Yvette, on a bicycle to telephone the gendarmerie rather than going himself on his motorbike. Gustave was unable to give any satisfactory answers to such questions and appeared to find them very difficult to understand.

The Dominicis stuck to their version of events. The previous evening Gustave had gone to Peyruis to report the landslide to Roure. The family had gone to bed at the usual hour. They had been awoken at about 1:00 a.m. by the sound of gunfire. It had crossed their minds that it might have had something to do with the English campers, but they had seen no reason why they should bother about them. Gaston had gotten up as usual at 4:30 a.m. to take his goats to pasture. Gustave had gotten up two hours later, as was his habit, and went immediately to look at the landslide to see whether the railway tracks were free. It was then that he had seen the body of the little girl. After Olivier had stopped and Gustave had asked him to inform the police that he had found a dead body, Gustave had returned to the farmhouse. None of the Dominicis had seen fit to go and see the little girl or to ascertain whether the English campers needed any assistance. They simply had waited for the gendarmes to arrive and told them they knew absolutely nothing of the events that had occurred so close to their home.

Even given the notorious Provençal reluctance to have anything to do with matters that might possibly prove to be unpleasant, under the motto "Qui de rien ne se mêle, de rien ne se démêle" (Get involved, nothing solved), the attitude of the Dominicis is truly astonishing. Their subsequent variations on their original story, their obfuscations, and their recantations only served to prove that they had something they hoped to conceal. Whatever their original intentions might have been, the sudden appearance of Olivier on his motorcycle caught Gustave, who claimed ignorance, at the scene of the crime.

Commissioner Sébeille's father had been a famous detective who had solved a number of celebrated cases. Among the most spectacular was a multiple murder at Valensole in 1929. The Richauds, a farming family with two sons aged ten and three and a servant named Amaudric, were brutally murdered by their eighteen-year-old former farm laborer, Joseph Ughetto, and Stephan Mucha, his sixteen-year-old Polish lover. Mucha was saved from the guillotine thanks to his youth and given a twenty-year prison sentence, but Ughetto paid the ultimate penalty in Digne in January 1930. His father had gruesomely argued in court that he deserved to be executed. Ughetto's was the last execution in the Basses-Alpes.

Robert Sébeille had been the chief inspector of the Ninth Mobile Brigade in Marseille. The mobile brigades were elite police units formed in 1907 by Georges Clemenceau, who at that time was president of the council and minister of the interior. They were known as the Tiger Brigades, after Clemenceau's nickname, which was earned by the ferocity with which he treated his opponents whether in peacetime or war. As French society underwent a profound social change, the brigades were designed as a dramatic response to an alarming increase in criminality that was only partially disguised behind the glittering *belle époque* facade. Police methods in France were hopelessly antiquated, having scarcely changed since the days of François Vidocq, a scintillating figure who had abandoned the life of a habitual criminal to become a highly successful, if singularly unconventional, policeman and who had served as a model for Honoré de Balzac's sinister character Vautrin. In 1906, 106,000 crimes were left unsolved. Bands of brigands roamed the countryside, attacking isolated farmhouses, holding up trains, and acting as highwaymen. The most notorious of these gangs was the Chauffeurs de la Drôme, whose name came from their habit of applying flames to the soles of their victims' feet so they would confess where they had hidden their money. Theirs was the stuff of pure fiction: by day they worked as honorable artisans and craftsmen; by night they were transformed into ruthless criminals, who between 1905 and 1908 terrorized the area between Valence and Romans-sur-Isère.

Twelve mobile brigades formed an elite force that not only mastered such modern techniques as finger printing, anthropometrical indexing, and the scientific techniques of the criminologist Alphonse Bertillon but also were kept in top physical condition and trained in martial arts as well as the use of conventional weaponry. From the outset they were spectacularly successful in combating crime, and banditry soon disappeared. Having fulfilled their original mission, they were renamed the *police judiciaire* (judicial police) and charged with determining the violations of the penal code, collecting evidence, and finding criminals. On being informed of a crime, the public prosecutors would call upon their specialized services. A task force would then be formed that would concern itself exclusively with the crime in question.

Robert Sébeille was a member of the Tiger Brigade in Marseille from the beginning, having been posted from Avignon in February 1908. During his long and distinguished career, he had earned the reputation of being a model policeman: wise, evenhanded, and having the common touch. Edmond, although he greatly admired his father, was determined to step out from under his shadow by swiftly solving the Drummonds' hideous murders, which had already gained widespread notoriety. He had found what he was convinced was the murder weapon. He felt that there was nothing more to be learned from the murder site. Above all he prided himself for having a unique understanding of the Provençal mind that would enable him to get at the heart of the matter in next to no time. But he would soon find himself lost in a labyrinth of half-truths, lies, contradictions, and surly silences that would leave him disheartened and frustrated.

Greatly flattered by the attention afforded him by the hordes of journalists that descended upon the Grand' Terre, he rapidly decided to groom himself to be a media star. He cut a striking figure with his recently purchased cigarette holder and dashing foulard. He made the mistake of spending far too much time in the company of journalists over aperitifs at the expense of more humdrum police work. For their part the journalists talked at length with the Dominicis, who were every bit as flattered by their attention as was the commissioner. At first there were some fifty of them, but soon there were more than eighty, seriously hampering the police investigation. It got to the point that even the publicity-hungry Sébeille began to get irritated.

Already considering himself a celebrity, Sébeille was obliged to live very modestly while working on the case. With a per diem out-of-town allowance of a mere 1,500 francs ($4.30), he could not afford a hotel room. He found lodgings in a large gloomy house at Peyruis, on the main road, run by two elderly sisters. His four assistants shared the two other available bedrooms and were obliged to sleep together in double beds. They took their meals at the home of the redoubtable Madame Geoffroy. As Sébeille remarked, they could not afford to get very thirsty.

Convinced that he had found the murder weapon, Sébeille set out on 6 August to find its owner. First, he went up the hill to the village of Lurs and visited the mayor's office. He received a frosty welcome. It was no warmer at his other ports of call in the vicinity. Even if anyone had known the owner, no one was going to admit it, for that would amount to the denunciation of a neighbor. Sébeille's much-vaunted understanding of the peasant mind had been put to the test and had been found seriously wanting. Followed by a horde of insistent journalists, he went from farm to farm, but his inquiries were shrugged off in mute incomprehension or met with sullen silence.

Later that day the commissioner, with the carbine wrapped in news-paper under his arm and accompanied by Inspector Henri Ranchin, came across Gaston Dominici's eldest son, Clovis, who was working on the railway line near the abandoned railway station at Lurs. When Sébeille showed him the weapon, Clovis became extremely agitated, falling to his knees and refusing to answer any questions. After having partially regained his composure, he insisted that he had never seen it before and that he did not have the faintest idea who might be the owner. Sébeille said he was unable to pursue the matter on the spot, because he was sur-rounded by a crowd of journalists and onlookers. He later claimed to have taken Clovis to Peyruis and to have cross-examined him for two hours, but there is no evidence that this was the case.[11] It would seem more likely that he failed to follow up this valuable lead, as he was forced to admit during the trial. Clovis's explanation of his extraordinary behavior—that he knelt down because that was his normal working posture—can hardly have convinced anyone. Clovis's wife, Rose, later testified that her husband changed completely after the murders. He suffered from acute insomnia, became extremely nervous, and appeared to be deeply depressed. She admitted that she hoped that her father-in-law would commit suicide and leave a note telling the entire truth.[12]

After his meeting with Clovis, Sébeille returned to the Grand' Terre to talk to the Dominicis. He was immediately struck by the fact that Gaston had buttoned his shirt at the collar and rolled down his sleeves so that his tattoos were no longer visible. He never showed them again and refused to say where he had gotten them. None of the family knew.

Since the examining magistrate had not given the commissioner the authority to cross-examine witnesses and place them under police custody, Sébeille could only treat the Dominicis as simple witnesses. They sat around the kitchen table with Gaston holding forth, confi-dently addressing the commissioner with the familiar *tu* (you) form. He announced that he knew very little, having simply heard a few shots in the night. He then said that when he brought his goats back to the farm at about 7:30 the previous evening, he had seen the Drummonds camping, but he had not spoken to them. When Gustave came home at about 8:00 p.m., Gaston had ordered him to clear the landslide, which Gaston had noticed as he walked along the railway embankment. Blaming Gustave and his own wife for having watered the alfalfa field too copiously, he went off to bed at 8:30 p.m.

About three hours later Gaston awoke when a motorcycle with a sidecar stopped beside the house. Gaston hung out of his bedroom window to see what was going on. The driver asked him something in a language he did not understand. Gaston yelled at him to go away, whereupon the man left.[13] He heard laughter as the motorcycle drove off. Gaston went back to sleep and was awakened again at 1:00 a.m. by some gunshots. He counted five or six. The first two were spaced; the remainder were in rapid succession. He imagined that they came from a military weapon used by a poacher hunting along the banks of the Durance. He denied having heard any screams and did not get out of bed.

He woke up at his usual hour of 4:30 a.m., but contrary to his usual practice, he led his goats in the opposite direction to the campers. Questioned by Sébeille on this somewhat suspicious deviation from his normal routine, Gaston mocked the commissioner for his lack of understanding of country life. From time to time goats are given the salt they need for their health. Salt makes them thirsty. He had given them salt that morning. Therefore, he had taken them along a different path, which allowed them easier access to the Durance, where they could slake their thirst.

When he returned to the Grand' Terre at about 8:00 a.m., he found Faustin Roure, who had come to say hello to Yvette. She told him that Gustave had discovered the body of the little girl. Gaston immediately went to have a look. Sébeille asked him if he had not noticed the gendarmes and the crowd that was already forming around the campsite. Gaston replied that he had, but he "had no time to lose." He covered the girl's body with a blanket because red ants were crawling over her.

Gustave confirmed his father's story. He added that after he had shoveled the earth away from the railway tracks and was returning to the Grand' Terre, he was shocked that Lady Drummond and Elizabeth were preparing to go to bed in full view and without embarrassment. After supper Gustave went to Peyruis to report the landslide to Faustin Roure, who had said there was nothing to worry about as the last train of the day had already passed. Roure then suggested that Gustave should get up early to make sure that all was well.

He went to bed shortly after 9:30 p.m. but was awoken a couple of hours later by the motorcycle with a sidecar. Gustave claimed that when he leaned out of his bedroom window, he saw a man walking toward him, while a woman and a child remained on the motorcycle. He could not understand a word the man said. The man then went into the courtyard muttering a load of "gobbledygook." Then the stranger rode off in the direction of Manosque, laughing loudly. Gustave and Yvette were awoken at 1:00 a.m. by the sound of gunfire, and once again he repeated virtually word for word what Gaston had said. Gustave claimed to have thought that the campers might have been attacked, but he was far too frightened to go and have a look. Unable to get back to sleep, Gustave got up as usual at 5:30 a.m. and went immediately to check the landslide. It was then that he saw the little girl lying on the bank that led down to the Durance. Assuming she was dead, although not bothering to make sure, he ran back to the main road. A motor scooter passed by, but since it had a foreign number plate he did not bother to try and stop it. Shortly afterward, as he was walking toward the Grand' Terre, he spotted Olivier and asked him to report that a body had been found.

Sébeille then asked Gustave to retrace his steps and describe how he had first seen Elizabeth Drummond's body in the early morning of 5 August. Gustave walked across the railway bridge. Instead of turning immediately to the left so he could take a closer look at the state of the railway line—and going in this direction, he would have been unable to see Elizabeth's body—he walked straight to the head of the slope. It took the commissioner several weeks to realize that this was evidence that Gustave already knew where the body was. Gustave could have seen that all was well from the middle of the bridge. Had he wanted to take a closer look at the landslide, he would have cut the corner as he turned left. It will be remembered that when Faustin Roure went to the site of the landslide on the morning of 5 August, he had not seen Elizabeth's body. Clovis had pointed it out to him on his way back to the Grand' Terre.

Yvette was the next to be questioned. She merely repeated what the others had said. Old Marie said that she had seen nothing, had heard nothing, and had slept soundly through the night. All the Dominicis were adamant that none of the Drummonds had come to the farm to ask for food or water.

Sébeille found a number of anomalies and implausibilities in the Dominicis' initial statements. Gaston could not have possibly seen a motorcycle from his bedroom window, which was on the back of the house. It was most unlikely that Gustave could have seen anything because the stables blocked the view from his bedroom window. Extensive investigations produced no evidence that the motorcycle ever existed. But why would the Dominicis invent such a story, especially as the shots were apparently fired two hours after the motorcycle had driven on toward Manosque?

Even more improbable was their claim not to have heard any screams. They admitted to having slept with their windows open, and the Drummonds were camping a mere 175 yards away. A farmer by the name of Dabisse, who lived more than a mile away and on the other side of the river, claimed to have heard the shots and screams. Then there was the indubitable fact that Gustave could not have seen Elizabeth's body by pure chance.

Sébeille now called it a day. He went to Digne, intent on obtaining a warrant to search the Grand' Terre and to cross-examine the Dominicis.

He returned to the Grand' Terre armed with the necessary authority at three o'clock the next afternoon, 7 August. A preliminary search of the farmhouse and outbuildings revealed nothing. He found Gustave in bed with a note from Dr. Paul Nalin, whose father had conducted the autopsies, claiming that he was suffering from nervous exhaustion as a result of persistent harassment by the journalists. Gustave invited the press into his bedroom, where he lay on the bed fully clothed, his eyes closed, and his face contorted into a pitiful expression. His pretty young wife stood beside him, a comforting hand on his shoulder. Sébeille did not believe a word of this nonsense, but there was nothing he could do about it. Angry at having been outwitted, he ordered Gustave to report the next day to Peyruis and warned him that if he failed to comply, he would be taken there by force.

Sébeille then turned to Gaston and asked him what language the stranger on the motorcycle had spoken. With a sly grin he replied that it was Italian. The commissioner pointed out that he had previously stated that he had no idea what language the man had spoken. Gaston flew into a violent rage, waving his cane at Sébeille. The commissioner, seeing no point in staying any longer at the Grand' Terre, hurried off to Forcalquier for the Drummonds' funeral.

The *campo santo* (graveyard) where the ceremony was held is a remarkable space consisting of a terraced maze of immaculately tended yew hedges. Built in 1835 it was listed as a historic site in 1946. The funeral service, conducted by a Protestant minister from Digne, was attended by a considerable crowd. The sub-prefect, the mayor of Forcalquier, a deputy mayor of Marseille, and the British consul from Marseille were among the dignitaries. Boots Pure Drug Company sent a delegation to attend the ceremony. The Drummond family was represented by Jack's only nephew, James Austin-Smith, who was also his godson. Their friends the Marrians, with whom they had been staying in Villefranche, were also present. Sébeille learned from the Marrians why the Drummonds had decided to go back to Digne. Having examined the contents of the Hillman, they were convinced that nothing had been stolen.

The following day, 8 August, Gustave seems to have made a remarkable recovery. He underwent four hours of grueling questioning in Forcalquier without showing the slightest sign of strain or fatigue. Apart from denying that he had ever said that Faustin Roure had ordered him to look at the railway line early in the morning of 5 August, he stuck to his story, offering no reasonable explanation why he had been in a position to notice Elizabeth's body, how he could have been sure that she was dead, and why he had not seen fit to check on her parents. His answers were staggeringly inept. He repeated that he had not wanted to touch Elizabeth for fear of leaving his fingerprints. He had not wanted to talk to her parents because he imagined that they had killed her and had fled the scene of the crime. When asked why he imagined that Jack and Anne had departed when the Hillman was still there, he replied that he had supposed that they had gone on foot.

Scarcely able to contain his rage, Sébeille drove him back to the Grand' Terre, where a large crowd of journalists had assembled. After three days of inquiry, the commissioner had only been able to establish one fact: Gustave was a liar. A frustrated Sébeille gave the following statement to the assembled journalists:

> Even though there are several contradictions in the statements made by Monsieur Gustave Dominici, these could be ascribed to his emotional state. . . . In any case we have no new evidence that might cast suspicion on the farmer.[14]

At this point the Communist Party began a concerted effort to mobilize support for the Dominicis. The mayor of Peyruis became extremely agitated when he heard that a truckload of FTPF veterans, intent on demonstrating against police harassment of the Dominicis, had arrived in his village. He rushed off to warn Sébeille, who was far less concerned about Gustave's wartime comrades making such a gesture of solidarity than he was about criticisms from his superiors.

Vincent de Moro-Giafferi, the president of the Justice Committee in the National Assembly, had written to Minister of Justice Léon Martinaud-Déplat, complaining about the treatment of the Dominicis. Moro-Giafferi was of Corsican origin and might well have thought that the Dominicis were his compatriots. He was a brilliant jurist, who at age twenty-four had become the youngest person ever to be admitted to the Paris bar; was an outstanding trial lawyer; and was an outspoken socialist deputy. He had defended the "French Bluebeard," Henri Désiré Landru, who was executed for murdering eleven lonely widows, as well as Georgi Dimitrov, the secretary general of the communist World Committee against War and Fascism, who was accused of complicity in the Reichstag fire of 1933. He was also chosen to defend Herschel Grynszpan, whose murder of the German diplomat Ernst vom Rath was used as an excuse by the Nazis to launch the pogrom of 9–10 November 1938 inappropriately known as the *Kristallnacht*, or "Night of Broken Glass." Moro-Giafferi was a lawyer of such eloquence that many began to question whether the jury system was an appropriate means of delivering justice.

Maurice Garçon, another brilliant lawyer, also leaped to the Dominicis' defense. He was well known for his defense of Violette Nozière, who was accused of murdering her sexually abusive father and whose cause was championed by the surrealists. He was also on the defense team for Herschel Grynszpan and had defended the publishers of the Marquis de Sade's *L'Histoire de Juliette* against a pornography charge. He was a distinguished man of letters with a taste for the occult who was elected to the Académie Française in 1946, along with Paul Claudel, Marcel Pagnol, and Jules Romains. Garçon wrote a savage letter to *Le Monde*, which tempted Sébeille to abandon the case, but Georges Harzic, his commanding officer in Marseille, persuaded him to continue the investigation. Faced with such criticism and with his investigation frustrated at every turn, the commissioner was beginning to reach the end of his tether. He kept himself going by chain smoking and drinking countless cups of coffee, which only served to worsen his insomnia.

The Drummond murder quickly became a political issue. The local Communist Party cell organized a support committee for the Dominicis, and their innocence was heralded by the Communist Party daily newspaper *L'Humanité*, which defended the Dominicis with hammer and sickle. The party's local newspaper *La Marseillaise* also supported their cause. According to *Le Dauphiné Libéré*, a daily paper founded by members of the Resistance but without any communist affiliation, members of the PCF met every evening at the Grand' Terre. Right-wing newspapers such as *L'Aurore*—another product of the Resistance that used the famous name of the newspaper that published Émile Zola's rousing defense of Alfred Dreyfus in "J'Accuse" and that by 1952 was controlled by the industrialist Marcel Boussac—were sharply critical of the Dominicis. The journalist Gabriel Domènech, writing for *Le Méridional*, consistently defended Commissioner Sébeille against his critics.[15] The British popular press, however, denounced the incompetence of the French police, with the *Sunday Dispatch* offering a reward of 500,000 francs ($1,440) for anyone who solved the crime. Not to be outdone, *Samedi-Soir* offered an equal sum. Gaston Dominici offered a further 10,000 francs ($29), prompting Sébeille to remark: "He would have helped us a great deal more if from the start he had told us clearly and openly everything he knew, everything he had seen and everything he had heard."[16]

L'Humanité, the Communist Party's national newspaper, pounced upon an article in Lord Beaverbrook's *Daily Express* saying that Sir Jack Drummond had gone behind the enemy lines in the final stages of the war. For *L'Humanité* it was darkly suspicious that "while the Soviet Army marched to victory" and when the horrors of the Belsen concentration camp were known, Sir Jack could have been complicit with the Nazis.[17] Rumors were already circulating that Drummond was a secret service agent, and the Communist Party was anxious to counter the suggestion that Soviet agents were involved in the murders by reviving improbable stories of sinister dealings during the war between the British and the Germans at the expense of the Soviet Union.[18] *L'Humanité* repeated the insinuations that Drummond was involved in several secret missions of dubious intent. The newspaper also made the wild claims that Lady Drummond had been in the Admiralty's secret service during the war, that Sir Jack was an expert in modern weaponry, and that the Drummonds had been followed by a second Hillman with British number plates. It reported the fact that the Drummonds had left before the end of the *charlotade* on 4 August as evidence that he was late for a rendezvous, presumably with the mythical "other Hillman."[19]

The conservative daily *Le Figaro* counterattacked by suggesting that their assassin could very well have been a member of the communist resistance, which had been involved in a series of summary executions. *L'Humanité* expressed its outrage at the suggestion that members of the Resistance, who had executed "traitors," could be thus considered murderers. The same paper reminded its readers that *Le Figaro* was in favor of the Federal Republic of Germany's joining the North Atlantic Treaty

Organization, which amounted to the reconstitution of the Wehrmacht under the command of "Nazi war criminals."

As the case wore on, Patrick Reilly, the British minister in Paris, was particularly anxious to scotch the rumors that Sir Jack was an intelligence agent who had been parachuted into the Lurs area sometime between 1943 and 1944. He suggested that the Foreign Office hire a lawyer to defend Drummond's interests and put an end to the absurd rumors, vigorously encouraged by the French Communist Party, that there were political motives behind the crime.[20] A copy of this letter was sent to the British consul in Marseille. The Foreign Office investigated this rumor thoroughly and was unable to find a single shred of evidence that Sir Jack had ever been an intelligence agent. The Ministry of Food assured the Foreign Office that he had been employed as the scientific adviser to the ministry until 1946, at which time he had moved full time to Boots.[21]

The fifteenth of August—the Feast of the Assumption, Napoleon's birthday, and the date of the Allied landings in southern France in 1944—is a holiday in France. The village of Peyruis celebrated in in grand style, for the holiday was its patron saint's day. It was also Gustave Dominci's birthday. Sébeille decided that it would not be prudent to continue the investigation in such a festive atmosphere and mingled with the crowd. In a corner of the village square where the locals played *boules* (bocce), he noticed Gustave and Yvette dressed in their Sunday best. Yvette was looking particularly attractive in an elegant dress, with her coiffure in the very latest fashion, and smiling continuously. They were very much the center of attention—*Paris Match* published a full-page photograph of Gustave and Yvette with their son in her arms—but the commissioner was unable to decide whether the attention paid to them was due to curiosity or genuine sympathy.[22] He found their behavior somewhat bizarre, particularly when he learned that this was the first time that the couple had ever gone to the annual fete at Peyruis. He also noticed that Yvette was far more at ease than her husband, who seemed to be on edge and continually looking to see whether Sébeille was watching him. The commissioner concluded that Gustave's furtive behavior indicated that he knew a great deal about the murders and held the key to their solution.[23]

Discouraged by the barrage of criticism and frustrated by the obdurate intractability of his potential witnesses, Sébeille seemed to have begun losing interest in the case. The autopsy reports were completed on 17 August, but he showed little interest in them. Further, he never bothered to ask any questions about the position of the bodies relative to the line of direction of the shots, and that information might have thrown some light on the sequence of events.

The following day Sébeille received a telephone call from Marseille announcing that a man named Aristide Panayotou claimed to have witnessed the assassination of the Drummond family and said that he would be able to recognize the person concerned. He was a thirty-five-year-old traveling salesman of cheeses and tarts. He claimed to have the *Légion d'honneur* (Legion of Honor) as well as the resistance medal and to have been mentioned twice in dispatches. He boasted that he was a descendant of the higher Greek nobility and that he drove a 1948 Lincoln. He had recently been diagnosed with multiple sclerosis and was rapidly losing weight. He spoke in a loud voice with a strong Marseillais accent, which served to accentuate his extreme nervousness.

Commissioner Harzic brought Panayotou to Lurs, through which he said he had been driving home to Marseille from Grenoble on the night of the murders. His headlights were not working properly. He stopped near the Grand' Terre to relieve himself. Modestly he opened both doors so he could go about his business as privately as possible. It was then that he heard screams and shots. Panayotou saw a man cross the road, where he bent over someone who was lying on the ground and then retraced his steps. The man wore light-colored trousers and was in his shirtsleeves. He had prominent cheekbones. Panayotou claimed that he noticed that the time was just after one o'clock in the morning.

Sébeille was at first enormously impressed by this new witness and felt that he had found the key to the whole affair. He confidently announced to the crowd of journalists that followed his every footstep that he would solve the case within eight days. Commissioner Harzic also said that a major step forward had been made.[24] But then things began to unravel.

Panayotou insisted that his identity be kept absolutely secret because he wanted to avoid any publicity and to prevent his wife from finding out where he had been that night. His wife later told the press that it did not matter to her where her husband was or what he did. He was also concerned that he might be charged with failing to give due assistance to a person in trouble. He flatly refused to go with Commissioner Fernand Constant to the Grand' Terre and see whether he could recognize one of the Dominicis.

The police, who could not understand why Panayotou had taken so long before stepping forward, quickly concluded that he had made up the entire story. His claims to be a highly decorated aristocrat were shrugged off as a further product of his fruitful imagination. Sébeille suggests that it might well have been that Panayotou was after the 500,000 franc rewards offered by the *Sunday Dispatch* and *Samedi-Soir*.[25] This idea was taken up by the communist press, which painted him as a money-grubbing mountebank. Professor André Ollivier, a psychiatrist who was director of the police laboratory in Marseille, pronounced Panayotou a fantasist.

Panayotou was not the only dubious character to appear on the scene. Soon the Grand' Terre was infested with dowsers, tarot card readers, fortune tellers with crystal balls, spiritualists, and fairground charlatans, all of whom plagued the police with their advice. For some the murderer was tall and thin; for others, short and fat. He came from nearby or he came from afar. He was acting on behalf of a foreign secret service, or it was a personal vendetta. A host of different motives were suggested, none of which threw any light on the case.

4   Gaston Denounced

The Lurs affair attracted the attention of a number of experts who offered their assistance to the police. Scotland Yard was bombarded with notes from psychics who were anxious to help the investigation. Ella Squire had a vision of a man in a Tyrolean hat. Lady Knollys had a nice chat with the Drummonds, who told her that Gaston Dominici had protected them from the murderer, "who had been following them around." A. L. dreamed that it was the old farmer. The "Bournemouth Tramp" asserted that it was the work of the "Secret Stalin Society." Mino de Miribel, the premier medium of France, knew that Gaston killed the parents, while Gustave murdered Elizabeth. H. J. Smith, a somewhat predisposed clairvoyant, thought that the murderer was a black American, but unfortunately he did not have time to pursue the case because he was after a Jew in Lowestoft who was rigging the slot machines at a funfair.[1]

One dowser claimed that the murderer was a poacher who had crossed the Durance, shot a fox, and dumped it in the well before killing the Drummonds. The gendarmes were skeptical but decided to examine the well. Gaston asked them what they were doing. When they told him, he said, "So you're looking for the fox my son killed a few days ago?" Gendarme Rebeaudo went down the well and recovered the putrefied carcass of a fox. Gustave said he had killed it with number 6 shot. An autopsy proved him to be correct.[2]

Only one of these practitioners of the occult was of any use to the police. According to the police reports, one Jean-Claude Coudouing and his assistant Gaston Beucherie, specialists in "astro-rhabdomancy" from the Institut des Hautes Etudes d'Astrologie, 42 Rue des Marais in Paris, visited the Grand Terre on 1 September. A policeman asked them to look for bullets. They took off with their pendulums and within an hour came back with a bullet that they had found on the slope down by the railway. Commissioner Constant announced to the press later that day that the bullet that had nicked Elizabeth's ear as she ran away had been found, but he did not say where or by whom. That he could so confidently assert, without any forensic investigation, that it was indeed the bullet in question is a further example of the astonishingly wild assumptions made by the police that are characteristic of the case.

The bullet was sent to Professor Ollivier at the police laboratory in Marseille. His report was submitted on 4 September, showing that the bullet had indeed been fired from the presumed murder weapon, so Constant avoided any embarrassment. It was a useful piece of evidence but not one that threw decisive light on the affair, beyond showing up the exceptionally slapdash police work in the preliminary investigation of the murder site. Almost four years after the murders, two gendarmes patrolling the road near the Grand' Terre found an American cartridge that could well have come from the murder weapon as well.[3] The police do not seem to have been embarrassed, however, that the shoddiness of their initial investigation of the murder site was thereby revealed.

Since Sébeille considered Gustave to be the prime suspect, he decided to reconstruct the scene when Gustave had stopped Olivier in the early morning of 5 August and had asked him to inform the gendarmes that he had found a body. Both men stuck to their original versions of events. Olivier insisted that Gustave had emerged from behind the Hillman and was standing in front of the hood. Gustave claimed that he had been standing behind the mulberry tree about 16 yards from the car and that he was about to return to the farmhouse. He flatly denied having been at the scene of the crime.

The police were waiting for Gustave on 3 September when he returned to the Grand' Terre on his bicycle. He had been out hunting. A fox and a rabbit were tied to the carrier behind the saddle.[4] According to a report in Le Monde, the police had been hampered in their work by a group of locals; thus, they had taken Gustave to the gendarmerie in Forcalquier for further questioning. Sébeille, who was suffering from nervous exhaustion and lack of sleep, let his colleague Fernand Constant and Commissioner Noël Mével, the deputy head of the judicial police in Marseille, conduct the cross-examination; but they were equally unable to get Gustave to change his story. The gendarmes took a break for lunch at one o'clock, and while seated at a table at a nearby inn, they were accosted by Yvette Dominici, who demanded that her husband be released. Captain Albert, the head of the Forcalquier gendarmerie, led her away and questioned her until six o'clock to no effect.

Gustave was questioned throughout the afternoon. He finally admitted that he had seen two camp beds: one was on the left-hand side of the Hillman covered by a blanket; the other, across the road, was turned over. He insisted that he had not gone to take a closer look and that he had not seen the bodies. The gendarmes, finding this scarcely credible, decided to detain him overnight and continue their questioning the next day.

The next morning, as Gustave began to show signs of breaking down, the gendarmes received a telephone call from Sabatier's superior, Orsatelli, the public prosecutor in Aix-en-Provence, who called for Gustave's immediate release on the grounds that grilling a simple witness for hours on end was unacceptable. Examining Magistrate Roger Périès and Deputy Pubic Prosecutor Louis Sabatier, both from the district court in Digne, had gone to Forcalquier the evening of 3 September to see whether the gendarmes had managed to glean any information from Gustave. Out of courtesy they had informed their superior, Orsatelli, who was resting nearby at Castellane and recuperating from an accident. He evidently decided that for the moment nothing more could be gained from Gustave and that it was pointless to continue holding him for questioning. Furthermore, it was problematic under French law to hold a simple witness so long for questioning. Gustave was driven back to the Grand' Terre, where a tearful Yvette flung herself into his arms.

Gustave complained to the press that he had been mistreated by the police during this grueling cross-examination. Commissioner Constant, fixing him with his piercing blue eyes, had reportedly said, "You are an assassin. We're going to arrest you and your wife. As for your kid, he'll be handed over to Public Assistance. If you don't want that to happen, you'll have to talk. Tell us what you know." Gustave told the press Olivier's statement that he had appeared from behind the Hillman was a fabrication. Gustave repeated that he had been standing on the main road about 15 yards away. He also flatly denied having seen the bodies of Jack and Anne Drummond.[5]

The press now presented Gustave as a victim, his name unjustly synonymous with "false witness." The entire community of Lurs, feeling that it was under suspicion, rallied around Gustave and denounced the policemen from distant Marseille for their ignorance of local customs and mentalities. From Manosque the famous Provençal novelist Jean Giono magisterially announced that contrary to Sébeille's conviction, the assassin was not from the immediate locality but had come from far, far away. With astonishing disregard for his own denunciation of the bestiality displayed in the settling of wartime accounts, he boldly proclaimed that a Provençal peasant would never commit such a dreadful crime and certainly not a peasant from a close-knit community such as Lurs.[6]

A letter appeared under Gustave's name in the communist newspaper *Ce Soir*, founded after the liberation by the writer Louis Aragon. It read:

> I am neither a murderer nor a coward, indifferent to the fate of respectable people who were struck down in a mad fury, when I could have gone to their help. Nor am I so lacking in all moral sense that I would protect a monster from the wrath of all decent people. I have therefore decided to seek redress without regard for the rank of those who have done me this unpardonable wrong, whatever their functions or motives . . . my attitude has been above criticism since the tragic events of which we all know. . . . My one misfortune is to have notified the local police. . . . My conscience and my courage have upheld me throughout. I ask no more than the attainment of my aim, that justice shall restore my honor and my peace of mind in the eyes of all.[7]

This was clearly not written by the barely literate Gustave but was probably the work of his lawyer, Émile Pollak. This prominent Marseille lawyer and Communist Party member had shown a lively interest in the case from the outset.[8]

Sébeille racked his brains to find a possible motive for the crime. Persistent rumors claimed that Sir Jack Drummond had parachuted into France during the war with a large sum of money and that he had come back to collect the rest. Extensive inquiries revealed that there had been such drops in southern France; however, not only were they miles away in the Aveyron but also the British Special Operation Executive officer who acted as the liaison was Lt. Col. Sir Walter Stansfield, known as "Commander Hubert Choeur."[9] Another preposterous rumor suggested that Lady Drummond had played a prominent part in the murder of Adm. François Darlan, the head of the Vichy French armed forces, in December 1942.[10]

It was further suggested that a meeting of former members of the Resistance, all of them members of the Communist Party, had taken place on 4 August at the Grand' Terre, where it was decided that the troublesome foreigners should be removed. One whimsical suggestion was that the meeting was part of a communist conspiracy to smuggle weapons to the Algerian Liberation Front. But this made no sense at all. Jack had not been in contact with the Resistance during the war. There was no evidence that a meeting had ever taken place on 4 August at the Grand' Terre. If this murder was a contract killing, it would have hardly been done with a broken old weapon by someone who did not even know how to use it.

Moreover, that the murder was the consequence of a family feud was out of the question. There was no evidence whatsoever of a crime of passion. It was also obviously not the work of a sadistic or sexual maniac. All those in the region who were suspected on either count had been questioned, and their alibis were found to be watertight. Was it perhaps an act of villainy committed by a chance passerby intent on theft but who ran away before robbing his victims because of heavy traffic? This scenario was highly unlikely but still possible. Was the murderer perhaps a poacher who came across the campers by chance? Sébeille's team interviewed all the local casual laborers, tramps, poachers, snail collectors, and jailbirds, as well as a deserter from the Foreign Legion, but all to no avail.

Some days previously Commissioner Constant had told the reporters that they now knew the appearance of the assassin but didn't know his name. His statement seemingly implied that the murderer was not someone from the Grand' Terre, an impression that was strengthened by the testimony of Henri Chastel, a truck driver from Orpierre in the Hautes-Alpes. He told the police that he had driven past the Grand' Terre at ten minutes before midnight. He saw a man leaning over the Hillman, peering inside. The man was 5 foot 11, about forty years of age, and sturdily built with tousled hair. Chastel's testimony was confirmed by Lucien and Georges Duc, truck drivers from La Roche-de-Rame.

The Duc brothers had been driving their truck to the Cavaillon market during the night of the crime. They passed the Grand' Terre about half an hour after Chastel had. They saw a man standing near the Hillman at about one o'clock. They gave a similar description and noted that he had a full head of hair and wore a shirt with rolled-up sleeves. Standing motionless in the headlights, he appeared to be trying to conceal something in his left hand. Lucien had remarked to his brother Georges the man had an ugly face, and Lucien didn't want to stop if the man wanted a ride.

Could this man have been Gustave? Or was it one of the local road menders, a lonely bachelor whose rotten teeth and equine visage matched the description given by Duc? The poor man, who was obviously mentally defective, was subjected to a lengthy grilling, but his alibi was perfect. Anonymous letters also accused Gustave Dominici, but their author was never found. Sébeille finally concluded Gustave was psychologically incapable of such a crime. Sébeille's suspicions fell instead on the quick-tempered, violent, and egotistical Gaston, but they were not shared by his colleagues in the judicial police. Commissioner Georges Harzic agreed with Giono, saying that a simple peasant from the Basses-Alpes could not possibly have committed such a monstrous crime. Examining Magistrate Périès, who was familiar with incidents of violent crime in the region, was more sympathetic toward the commissioner's hunch.

Meanwhile, Henri Conil from Peyruis claimed to have seen a shadow behind the Hillman at 2:15 a.m. Far more significant was the testimony of a Marceau Blanc from Sisteron. He was driving his delivery truck past the Grand' Terre at about 4:00 a.m. when he saw a camp bed 3 or 4 yards in front of the Hillman. He thought this extremely odd. An hour and a half later another witness claimed to have seen a camp bed on the other side of the road from the Hillman. He also noticed that a blanket covered the windows of the Hillman. By the time the police arrived, it had been removed.

The press, both in France and England, soon began to lose interest in the case. There were other more pressing issues to address such as the vexing question of German rearmament, which met with fierce opposition in France, and the war in Indochina. The British press made much of Anthony Eden's marriage to Churchill's niece, Anne Clarissa Spencer-Churchill, a colorful character with a wide range of friends from all walks of life. The marriage at Caxton Hall attracted a crowd almost as large as that at the marriage of Elizabeth Taylor and Michael Wilding a few months earlier. There were some acid comments from predictable sources about Eden's divorce and remarriage to a Roman Catholic.

By this time Sébeille, frustrated at every turn, was rapidly heading for a nervous breakdown. His nights were sleepless. He was virtually unable to speak. Priding himself on his unique ability to read the peasant mind, he had been confident that he would solve the case before going on leave on 14 August. He decided to postpone his plans, determined to make some major breakthrough beforehand, but it did not happen. The communist press was jubilant. The man whom with biting irony they dubbed the "Maigret of Marseille" or "our very own Sherlock Holmes" had failed to cast any suspicion on the "honest Dominici family," and his boast that he knew who the assassin was had proven empty.[11]

Sébeille refused to hand over the case to another but agreed that Commissioner Fernand Constant should take over while he joined his family in the Aveyron. He remained on holiday throughout the month of September. On his return his superior suggested that he should hand the case over to Commissioner Constant, but Sébeille protested vigorously and remained formally in charge. He stayed at his desk in Marseille, where he perused the dossier, while Constant continued the investigation in Lurs. The two men had very different approaches to police work that stemmed partly from their backgrounds. Sébeille was from Marseille and showed little understanding of the peasant mentality, despite his extravagant claims to the contrary. Constant, who was from the small town of Manosque, was a typical Provençal and fully familiar with the milieu. Sébeille charged in head first, engaging all concerned in lengthy questioning. Constant played his cards close to his chest, listened carefully, never got involved in relentless questioning, and, unlike his colleague, kept the journalists at a distance. Sébeille with his cigarette holder, Lacoste shirts, and marked Marseille accent was jovial and familiar. Constant, who spoke without a local accent, never smiled, and never unbuttoned his jacket, exuded an air of cultivated restraint.

Constant's approach soon proved fruitful. The Dominicis' neighbor, Paul Maillet, who worked with Clovis on the railway and was also secretary of the local Communist Party cell, told Constant that Gustave had said that the little girl was still alive when he discovered her in the early morning of 5 August. Maillet had always been shocked that Gustave had never sought help for Elizabeth. In early September he had gone to the Grand' Terre and had a chat with Gustave. He was dumbfounded when Gustave admitted that he had seen Elizabeth move that morning. He was also given another piece of important information on that occasion that, for the moment, he had decided to keep secret. Shortly afterward Maillet, while taking an aperitif in his kitchen, confided in Émile Escudier, who had a grocery store in La Brillane, that Gustave had seen Elizabeth Drummond move in the early hours of the morning. It was Escudier who had persuaded Maillet to give this information to the gendarmes.

The gendarmes did not question Gustave on this score until the early hours of 15 October. He was then taken to Digne for further questioning, along with his brother Clovis and Paul Maillet. After a lengthy interview, Gustave admitted that because he had heard a moaning sound while he was crossing the bridge over the railway, he had looked and discovered Elizabeth's body and had seen her left arm move. He also stated that he had told both his mother and Yvette what he had seen. Clovis confessed that he had advised his brother to keep mum. The gendarmes were appalled that none of them had thought either of seeking help or of informing the girl's parents. At two o'clock in the morning on 16 October they placed Gustave in police custody.

The following day Sébeille arrived from Marseille and went immediately with Constant to the Grand' Terre, where Sébeille questioned Gaston and Yvette while Constant dealt with Marie. All three stuck to their stories, with the two women denying that Gustave had told them that Elizabeth was still alive. Constant had already consulted the two doctors who had conducted the postmortem and Dr. Dragon, who first inspected the bodies at the murder site. They all insisted that had Elizabeth been attacked at the same time as her parents, she could not possibly have lived until five thirty in the morning. This meant that Gustave must have gotten up during the night shortly after she had been hit on the head. Uncomfortably aware of this contradiction, Sébeille made no mention of it in his account of the case. Subsequent advances in neuroscience have proved that she could well have still been alive, even if she had been attacked at the same time as her parents.

Examining Magistrate Roger Périès charged Gustave with failing to give assistance to a person in danger.[12] Périès also ordered that Gustave be kept in the Digne jail pending his trial, doubtless in the hope that the shock of incarceration would prompt him to be somewhat more garrulous. Gustave's lawyer, Émile Pollak, assisted by a colleague from Marseille, Pierre Charrier, was unsuccessful in his attempt to secure his client's release from prison. Périès was sympathetic, but Public Prosecutor Sabatier launched an appeal against any such decision. The appeal was upheld by the court in Aix-en-Provence.

Gustave, whom the communist paper *La Marseillaise* described as a hostage, remained stubbornly silent. On Gustave's arrest Yvette left the Grand' Terre and went to stay with her parents, François and Louise Barth, at their nearby farm.[13] Rumors began to spread that Gustave and Yvette's marriage was on the rocks and that she was terrified of her husband. But her explanation for the move was fully convincing. She was in an advanced stage of her pregnancy, and unlike the Dominicis, her father had a car ready for a quick dash to the hospital. She also did not particularly relish the idea of staying alone with her quarrelsome parents-in-law. Clovis went to live at the Grand' Terre and gave his father a hand during Gustave's absence. It was a generous move because relations between father and son were very strained since Gaston had accused Clovis's wife, Rose, of being a slut. Yvette went every day to visit her husband, but Gaston stayed at home, claiming that if he went to see his son in prison it would only make them both cry.

Gustave's trial was held on 12 November 1952. When the examining magistrate asked why he had kept quiet about Elizabeth's having shown signs of life, he replied that Clovis had warned him not to say anything so as not to get involved in the inquiry. Dr. Paul Jouve, a distinguished surgeon, confirmed the opinion of the postmortem team by suggesting that there might have been a time difference between the attacks on Elizabeth and her parents. He also stated that even if help had been available, she would not have survived. The examining magistrate argued that Elizabeth had shown signs of life after she had been seen by Gustave. He cited Dr. Dragon's statement, that she had been lying on her back with her arms stretched out, whereas Gustave had described her as lying with her left hand on her stomach. Here once again confusion and conjecture resulted from sloppy police work at the murder site as photographs of Elizabeth show her in both positions.[14]

Gustave's defense team of Pollak and Charrier argued that the law under which he was charged had been inserted into the French code by the Vichy government to force the French to assist any Germans who had been wounded by the Resistance; therefore, the law was no longer pertinent. Furthermore, they asked why Aristide Panayotou had not been charged under the same law. Neither argument impressed the court. According to the *Times* this case was the first time that section 63 of the criminal code had been applied.[15]

Sentencing was set for a week later, and Gustave was denied a temporary release from jail. He could well have received a three-year sentence for this offense but was given the singularly lenient punishment of two months for "behavior contrary to fraternal charity." Since he had already spent thirty-five days in protective custody, he only had to spend one month in prison. His connections with the FTPF and the Communist Party doubtless played a significant part in persuading the court prudently to opt for clemency, as it was relatively soon after the war, the Resistance was still surrounded by a nimbus of patriotic glory, and the Communist Party was still a powerful political force despite its grimly Stalinist leadership under Maurice Thorez. It was a dramatic scene. Gustave burst into tears and fell into his father's arms. Yvette, on the verge of collapse, flung her arms around him and moaned that he would die. When the magistrate asked whether he had anything to say, Gustave muttered "Merci," presumably in gratitude that he had managed to get off so lightly and would not be absent from the Grand' Terre when his father needed his assistance.

Meanwhile, there had been intensive investigations of various claims, rumors, and scraps of evidence. One of the most persistent stories concerned the existence of a second Hillman, which a number of people claimed to have seen, giving rise to the theory that the Drummonds had been killed by mistake.[16] On 3 October Adrien Queyrel, a miller from Les Mées, told Commissioner Constant that he and his cousin Paul Gilles had trapped crayfish in a stream near Peyruis on 1 August. When they arrived between 8:15 and 8:45 p.m., they spotted a British Hillman with a man who appeared to be in his fifties, a younger woman, and a little girl about ten years old. The family hastily packed up their belongings, including a tent, and sped off. The woman wished the bemused cousins "good night." These people could not possibly have been the Drummonds, however, because they were in Villefranche with the Marrians.

Apparently Constant immediately notified the Sûreté Nationale (National Police) in Paris, which wrote on the same day to Scotland Yard and asked it to trace a vehicle similar to the Drummond's Hillman that had been seen in the area with a man, woman, and young girl. The French stressed, "It is believed that these people were being sought by the murderer and that he killed the Drummond family in error."[17] A reporter from *Paris Match*, who had heard the theory of a "second Hillman" from Professor Marrian, had already alerted the Sûreté; and Marrian had independently informed Scotland Yard. Interpol also asked the Criminal Investigation Department (CID) to find the second car. Scotland Yard immediately began a meticulous search for any such vehicle. Rootes Group, the manufacturers of the Hillman, reported that it had supplied the domestic market with fifteen hundred Hillman Minx station wagons of the same year and model as the Drummonds'. The license plate numbers of all these cars were found, and the constabularies throughout Great Britain were ordered to interview all the owners. At the same time the police checked the records of all British ports servicing ferries to the Continent and listed all vehicles leaving the country between 1 July and 5 August and those arriving between 5 August and 5 September, as well as the name of the driver, nationality, registration number, chassis number, and the number of passengers, respectively. The Automobile Association reported that four similar cars were traveling on the Continent during this period. The police in Lancashire, Blackpool, Cheshire, and Aberdeen went off to interview the surprised owners, but all had cast-iron alibis.

Jack Shedley of Westcliff-on-Sea received a visit from the Southend police and much to his alarm was asked whether he had any reason to fear for his life. He had imagined that the visit was to inquire about the accident he had had in his Hillman Minx coupe at the Gorges d'Ollioules northwest of Toulon on 7 August. As far as he was concerned, the theory that the Drummonds had been mistaken for him and "killed by mistake" was baseless. He could prove that he was in Alassio, Italy, at the time of the murders.

Cecil McIntyre, his wife, son, and his son's girlfriend had been traveling in France in a Hillman saloon, but they had run out of money and had to go home before they reached Provence. Carlo Plezner, the Austrian-born principal of the Rudolf Steiner School in Blairs, Kincardineshire, had a Hillman estate car and had been traveling in France at the time but nowhere near Lurs. Frederick Catling of Belfast had traveled down the road from Lyon to Cannes in a Hillman Minx estate car, but he was back in England on 30 July. George Henry Kennard from Warwick told the police that he had a mist green Austin A40 Countryman and had been in the vicinity at the time. He had not seen any similar vehicle in the area. Among those questioned was the thriller writer Eric Ambler, whose wife had driven to Cap Ferrat with Edgar Wallace's daughter, Mrs. Patricia Frere of the Albany in Piccadilly, London. They were unable to shine any light on the matter. The *Daily Express* also appealed to its readers for information on the "second Hillman."[18] Various people came forward, but no valuable information was gleaned. Sundry other motorists received surprise visits from their local constabulary, but despite this intense search, no trace of a second Hillman was found. The theory can thus safely be discounted.

The French police, meanwhile, followed up another lead involving a Triumph sports car, whose GB plate began with the letters KJ, that was seen in the vicinity of the crime. KJ was a Maidstone designation. The local police began their inquiries and discovered a number of vehicles with KJ plates, including an Austin 7, a Standard 9, a Ford two-ton truck, and a Singer saloon. None of this was in any way helpful. Then a Triumph sports car with the number plate KJ9944 was found in a garage in Lyon. It belonged to a Canadian by the name of George K. Johnston. When interviewed by the police, he could prove that he was nowhere near Lurs at the time of the crime. Robert Corne, a baker at Saint-Sorlin-en-Bugey in the Ain, reported that he had seen two Canadians at the beginning of August. They had an army rifle on the front seat of their car that they had tried to conceal. This tip led nowhere, and Johnston and his companion were clearly not implicated. The communist *L'Humanité* placed great emphasis on the story of the Triumph sports car to take the pressure off the Dominicis. The paper added a nice touch to the story by saying that the car had been driven away by one Peter Martin, accompanied by a "ravishing young girl." They were most alarmed to find the vehicle surrounded by the police.[19]

The Sûreté Nationale then suggested the rumors that a British car had followed the Drummonds indicated some personal motive might be behind the crime, and it asked the CID to investigate the private lives of the Drummonds with this in mind. Norman Henry Burton, a waiter in the Chilton Court Restaurant in Baker Street, had seen photos of Lady Drummond in the press and already told Hampstead police that she had regularly met a man of about forty-five in the restaurant over the last couple of years. He claimed that they appeared to be having an affair. Hampstead police passed this information on to the CID, and a chief inspector contacted the Nottingham constabulary with the following note: "This is a very delicate matter, but the information cannot be disregarded." The Nottingham police made inquiries and concluded that Lady Drummond was not the type of woman to have such a relationship. The Drummonds were a devoted family, with Anne frequently accompanying her husband on his many visits to London, where they liked to dine in Soho. The photos in the newspapers were taken many years ago, so it would have been impossible to recognize her from them. Assistant Commissioner Howe of Scotland Yard therefore wrote back to Biget at Sûreté Nationale: "My Dear Friend, I can assure you that the family had a most excellent reputation in every way and we are certain from our enquiries that there was never any scandal nor could they possibly have been the victims of an act of vengeance."[20]

Yet despite this exhaustive investigation, rumors of another British station wagon with a man, woman, and little girl persisted. Barthélémy Borgna, Jérôme Cicheddu, Roger Gaze, and Francis Perrin all testified that they had seen such a vehicle. Borgna, Cicheddu, and Gaze said that the car was gray; Perrin said it was green. They all claimed that the girl, unlike Elizabeth Drummond, was wearing a red dress. There may very well have been another British station wagon similar to the Drummonds' Hillman in the area with a man, woman, and young girl on board, but since this was obviously not a contract killing or a planned murder, its existence was beside the point.

Sébeille visited the Grand' Terre while Gustave was locked away. He pointed out to Gaston that Marie, Yvette, and Clovis all knew that Elizabeth had shown signs of life that morning, yet he persisted in saying that he had heard nothing. Gaston flew into a terrible rage at the insinuation, waving his cane at his wife, yelling that "the old bitch" and "sardine" knew all about it and had told him nothing. She continued to feed the pigs with apparent indifference toward such familiar abuse. Sébeille asked him what he would have done, had he known. With a sly grin and a dismissive shrug, he coolly replied that he would have ordered Gustave to tell the police.

By this time the Grand' Terre presented a bizarre spectacle. The murder site was knee-deep in cigarette butts, waste paper, sardine tins, and empty bottles. Up to five hundred vehicles per day stopped to have a look at this macabre scene. Strange figures with wands and pendulums ambled trancelike through the detritus. With more than ten thousand visitors to the site, a businessman offered a substantial sum for the Grand' Terre with the intent of turning it into a hotel.

Sébeille left Lurs, sorrowfully announcing that the affair was not over but simply in "a period of hibernation." He remained in Marseille from mid-November until the end of December. Assisted by Inspector Ranchin he worked his way through piles of transcripts of hundreds of interviews, hoping to pick up a lead. He also discussed the case with his father, an experienced police officer, who, as noted previously, had specialized in rural crime. Robert Sébeille became so familiar with the case that it soon looked as if he were in charge and his son was merely his assistant. Sébeille senior reinforced his son's conviction that the answer to the crime lay in the Grand' Terre.

At first Robert thought of Paul Maillet, the passionate poacher who possessed a number of military firearms, but after his denunciation of Gustave, Sébeille was convinced that he was in no way involved. For Sébeille the key was why Elizabeth had not run in the direction of the farm. It suggested that she recognized her assassin, a point that was strengthened by the Dominicis' adamant denial that any of the Drummonds had come to the farm to ask for water. The Dominicis' claim to have been deaf and blind to the brutal murders committed only a few yards from their home was blatantly absurd. Sébeille senior felt that little could be obtained from either Marie or Yvette. Both seemed to have been well instructed as to what to say and would not alter their stories. Marie would continue to deny that she had heard or seen anything. Yvette, who appeared to be the most intelligent of the Dominicis, would be very difficult to break. Gustave, however, was a somewhat pathetic figure. He was weak willed, passive, unable to break free from his dominating father, and subservient to his wife. He might well be privy to the crime and certainly showed signs of trying to cover up something, but he was unlikely to have played a leading role.

Thus, Robert Sébeille's suspicions concentrated on Gaston, the violent-tempered patriarch, who had shown a complete lack of interest in the crowd of gendarmes, officials, and onlookers who were already at the campsite when he returned with his goats to the Grand' Terre on the morning of 5 August. He had always tried to intervene whenever the commissioner had discussed the affair with Gustave. He had the cheek to treat a police officer with defiant disdain, and his protestations of the total innocence of his entire clan merely strengthened the suspicion that he had a great deal to hide. Sébeille considered Gaston to be the prime suspect. His son Edmond dutifully agreed.

Robert also strongly suspected Zézé Perrin, the "smiling liar," as Edmond had called him. Robert argued that Zézé appeared to be totally relaxed, ready to answer any questions, always with a smile. He appeared to be immature, irresponsible, stupid, and incapable of understanding the consequences of his actions—a moral cretin. Robert felt that he might very well have been involved in the murders. Edmond did not agree with his father on this point, and they argued the pros and cons of Zézé's involvement in the crime at great length, without reaching a conclusion.

Sébeille senior ruled out Clovis Dominici as a suspect. He did not live at the Grand' Terre and was at home that night. His reaction at the sight of the murder weapon was further evidence in his favor. Whereas Gaston and Gustave had shown total indifference when shown the carbine, Clovis had been genuinely shocked—an indication that he knew that something terrible had happened that directly involved his family.

The question of a motive remained. Robert Sébeille felt it was a senseless crime, of a type not unknown in peasant circles. He did not attach much importance to the fact that the campsite had been ransacked, attributing it to a deliberate attempt to mislead the police investigation into looking for some ingenious motive.

Upon his release on 16 December, Gustave announced to the press that he had no idea why he had been treated so harshly and added that he felt it grossly unfair that he should be made to pay for others' crimes. No one bothered to inquire who these others might be. On his return to the Grand' Terre, the clan gathered to celebrate his return to the fold in great style. Yvette, who had left the Grand' Terre to stay with her parents, came home to welcome him. Clovis was still staying at the Grand' Terre. His sister Augusta Caillat, who was part of the welcoming party, went on the offensive. She told the press that her brother was *fada* (nuts) and an idiot who was quite incapable of defending himself. She claimed that if the police had "knocked on the right door" instead of harassing the Dominici clan, then they would have solved the crime long ago. No one pursued the question of where this mysterious portal might be found. In his frustration Gaston Dominici reportedly said to his grandson Zézé: "What arseholes [*couillons*] those English were! Why didn't they get themselves killed somewhere else?"[21]

The Dominicis, who had hitherto maintained a solid front behind a wall of silence, began to show signs of discord. The stonehearted clan was beginning to fall apart. Money was the cause. At a gathering of the clan, Gustave's father-in-law, François Barth, proposed that the family should share the cost of the trial in equal parts. There was full agreement among those present, but when Germaine Perrin, one of the daughters, heard what had been decided, she flatly refused to pay her share. The rest of the family resented this attitude, but later, when Germaine's son Zézé became implicated in the case, the family rift became acute.

More serious was the rupture between the Maillets and the Dominicis. The two families had been linked for more than fifty years as they moved from Brunet to Ganagobie and then to Lurs. Paul Maillet and Clovis Dominici worked together and were comrades in the Communist Party. Paul was equally friendly with Gustave. Paul had a strong dislike for

Gaston, who had always been patronizing toward his father and boasting of his success as owner of the Grand' Terre, while the older Maillet was a poverty-stricken sharecropper, now living in penniless retirement. Paul had been genuinely horrified when he learned of Gustave's failure to seek help for Elizabeth, to the point that he denounced his friend and saw him sent to jail. He had told the court that "dishonor hovers over honor," but for the moment he still withheld another damaging piece of evidence, which would dramatically change the direction of the investigation.

Paul Maillet had become something of an embarrassment to the Communist Party. The police had a hold on him because of his possession of illegal weapons and for stealing electricity from the grid. He had denounced Gustave, even though the local party was trying to defend the Dominicis and win support among the French peasantry. He was overly talkative and sought attention. Gustave had served in the FTPF under Roger Autheville, who was now the party's departmental secretary in the Basses-Alpes. Autheville was anxious to protect his former comrade, but he was concerned that the press might use the discovery of Maillet's cache of arms to suggest that the party was planning an armed uprising. It was therefore decided to dismiss him from his post as party secretary in Lurs. Maillet was suspended at the end of September and dismissed two months later. Clovis Dominici took his place as the party's candidate in the local election and was duly appointed to the municipal council. Autheville, in turn, would soon receive the party's opprobrium. He was dismissed as the party's departmental secretary in 1953 and thrown out of the party the following year. He was charged with being too compliant with the police, with lacking vigilance, and with having sold photographs and information to two popular magazines.[22]

Dismissal was a bitter blow for Paul Maillet. He had been banished from the tightly knit circle of the Communist Party and even experienced an attempt on his life. Returning to his farm one evening, he was knocked off his motorcycle by a wire that had been stretched across his path. Fortunately he was going slowly enough that he did not suffer serious injury, but it was a painful reminder of his ostracism. The Dominicis mounted a concerted campaign against him and spread the rumor that he was the owner of the murder weapon. Gaston's daughter Augusta Caillat nicknamed Paul Maillet "Sébeille." People in the village gave him the finger. He was ostracized at work. His children were tormented and his wife fell ill. One day Gaston Dominici came up to him and without saying a word pointed his cane at him like a rifle and made a gesture as if he were pulling the trigger. Maillet also received a number of anonymous threatening letters warning him to keep his mouth shut.

The campaign against Paul Maillet further convinced Sébeille and Constant that the answer lay somewhere in the Grand' Terre. Their suspicions were strengthened by some fresh evidence. First, while Gustave was locked up in Digne, a woman from Marseille told Constant that she had seen an extremely sinister-looking man at the far end of a shed at the Grand' Terre. Then Yvette's fifteen-year old brother, Jacky Barth, had heard her say something about giving someone some money; otherwise, they would get into serious difficulties. It was also reported that Yvette had said someone called Jo had spent the night at the farm, and cash had changed hands.

Further information reached Constant that someone had seen Clovis Dominici and Jacky Barth talking to someone called Jo, who was somewhat strangely dressed in overalls and a raincoat, near the Grand' Terre's shed at about five o'clock on a Saturday afternoon in early September. Marie Dominici was said to have been very perturbed about this man and had insisted that he be given money, or he would cause the family a great deal of grief. The description of this mysterious Jo, although very vague, roughly matched that of Marcel Chaillan, an agricultural laborer in Brillane who worked on a farm close to that of Yvette's parents, the Barths. He was known to have occasionally slept overnight in the shed.

Émile Pollak had visited the Grand' Terre on 8 September at Gustave's behest to discuss the possibility of taking legal action against certain newspapers. He had arrived with Pierre Charrier, a lawyer from Marseille and a Communist Party activist, who was interested to see the scene of such a notorious crime. Also in the party were Pollak's mistress Nelly

Leroy and their six-year-old daughter. While the two men examined the murder site, the little girl saw Gaston with his goats, herding them into the shed. She asked her mother whether she could go and have a closer look. Her mother took her daughter in her arms, because her leg was in a cast, and walked toward the shed. They were stopped by an agitated Jacky Barth, who said they should go not go into the shed because the goats were covered with fleas. There was some talk on this occasion of another man present who had terrible teeth and a face distorted in a rictus.

In what Constant labeled "Opération Bergerie" along with Sébeille and Examining Magistrate Roger Périès, a series of interviews were conducted to discover what had really happened. Gaston confirmed that he had seen Pollak, the little girl, and her mother, as well as another lawyer. Mother and child had peeped into the shed, but no one else was there. Gaston said that he neither knew a man named Jo nor anyone with frightening dentition. Marie Dominici said that Yvette had been there as well as her young brother Jacky Barth. According to her version of the story, Pollak had shown the goats to his daughter, not her mother. She could not remember having seen Charrier and professed not to know anyone by the name of Jo. Yvette's father, François Barth, had also been at the Grand' Terre that day. He confirmed the story that the mother had shown the goats to the little girl, but he claimed not to have seen the two men they had encountered. He too knew of no Jo and could not think of anyone with alarming teeth. Yvette stated that no outsider had been hired to work on the farm, even when Gustave was in jail. Gustave was equally unforthcoming. The only additional information he offered was that Francis Perrin, the local postman and his sister Germaine's brother-in-law, had also been there.

Francis Perrin had a much clearer recollection of that Monday. He claimed that a journalist had also been present. This was confirmed by Charrier, who said it was Lucien Grimaud, a reporter from *La Marseillaise*. Charrier also said that Francis's father had passed by and that someone had come to borrow a spray. No one asked Francis any questions about either Jo or the teeth. Francis's father, Louis Perrin, said that he had stopped off on his way home at the Grand' Terre, where he had seen

Nelly Leroy and her daughter by the shed talking to Jacky. Predictably, he knew of no one called Jo, but when asked about the teeth, he pulled back his lips to reveal a startling array of metal teeth and a decayed stump.

On 12 November, the day of Gustave's trial, it was the turn of Nelly Leroy. Apart from the Dominicis, she could only remember having seen Jacky, but on further questioning she admitted that she might have seen a man with metal teeth near the shed. She had not heard Marie Dominici say anything about paying off Jo to get him out of the way.

A few days later Périès questioned Yvette again. This time she remembered that Louis Perrin had been present and expressed surprise that the police were "looking for him." Périès interviewed Gustave in jail but got nothing more out of him. Gustave professed that he did not know that Francis Perrin and Pierre Charrier had been at the Grand' Terre that day.

Marcel Chaillan—a man with a grim appearance and a bizarre set of teeth and, as noted earlier, who was known to have occasionally slept in the shed at the Grand' Terre—was also submitted to intense questioning. He lived in a house belonging to his brother Louis and shared it with his nephew Fernand, a disabled veteran. Louis lived in a hotel in La Brillane, which he owned. The police thoroughly searched both places. Fernand testified that on the night of 4–5 August his uncle Marcel had dined as usual at his father's hotel and slept that night in the house. He testified that it would have been impossible for Marcel to have left the house without being heard. Sébeille was inclined to believe Marcel's brother and nephew. Constant, however, felt that Marcel Chaillan was singularly taciturn, even by the standards of the locals, and that he might well have something more to say. Poor Marcel was known in the neighborhood as dim witted, and the press heavily criticized Sébeille for persisting in questioning this hapless man until he eventually realized that he was on the wrong track.

Some also chuckled when Sébeille announced that the murderer was a local man, about 5 foot 9. He asked Gustave's father-in-law, François Barth, to provide him with a list of possible suspects. With 1,200 males in the Lurs community, it was estimated that about 350 men would fit the description, but Gustave Dominici, Paul Maillet, and Marcel Chaillan would have to be omitted from the list. Certain newspapers denounced Sébeille's team from another angle, accusing them of leading a witch hunt against men "whose sole crime was to have risked their lives in the struggle against the occupying power."[23]

The mysterious Jo was never identified. Possibly he never existed. Why was it that the mention of his name caused such a kerfuffle among the Dominicis? Who was the woman from Marseille who first told the police about him? Was he perhaps an imaginary figure planted by Pollak to lead the gendarmes on a wild goose chase? Was he involved in some illicit operation, such as distilling without a license—still a common practice in the region? Was Jo the code name of one of Gustave's comrades in the Resistance? Was he the person some witnesses saw near the scene of the crime during the night of 4–5 August? What hold could he have had over the Dominicis? Many such questions were asked. None found an answer. "Jo" disappeared from the dossier.

Commissioner Sébeille did not officially return to his duties until the end of January 1953. He was vexed by the vicious attacks by the communist press and annoyed that Constant had managed to wring a confession out of Paul Maillet that had sent Gustave, once his principal suspect, to jail. All the more determined to solve the crime, Sébeille decided that a drastic change in tactics was necessary. Bullying and intimidation had only caused a virtually impenetrable wall of silence in a remarkable display of peasant solidarity. Taking a leaf out of Constant's book, he realized that more could be gained by listening, cajoling, and slowly accumulating minute pieces of evidence until the moment came to strike. Above all, the press, with whom he had been far too open, had to be kept in the dark. Stealth must take the place of bravado. The nagging problem was that this case appeared to him to be a motiveless crime of exceptional barbarity, the outcome of some unfathomable peasant drama.

Sébeille went first to the Grand' Terre. Gaston acted somewhat surprised to see him, grunting that he had assumed that he had dropped the case. Gustave appeared to be a changed man. He had lost weight. His relationship with Yvette seemed to be strained. He no longer smiled. Whenever Clovis visited the farm, the atmosphere was charged with tension.

The commissioner dropped in at the Grand' Terre virtually every day. At first Gaston greeted him civilly, offering a glass of wine, which Sébeille consistently refused. Then he became increasingly irritated, to the point of complaining to the mayor of Peyruis that he was being subjected to police harassment. Getting nowhere with this tactic, the commissioner decided to pursue another tack.

Forgetting his fresh resolve to go softly, Sébeille went to see Paul Maillet shortly after his return to Lurs. He reminded him of the deal they had made on discovering Maillet's Sten guns. Why then did he pass on the information about Gustave's confession that Elizabeth Drummond was still alive to Constant and not to him as principal investigator? This was petty minded of the commissioner. After all, Constant was on the scene at Lurs, while he was far away, desk bound in Marseille. Maillet's offense was compounded in Sébeille's eyes, moreover, when he heard that Maillet had given even more important information to a couple of gendarmes from Forcalquier, making it seem that the case was slipping out of the hands of the "Maigret of Marseille."

Paul Maillet now claimed that sometime between the end of August and the beginning of September he had gone to the Grand' Terre to buy some potatoes. While Yvette went to fetch them, Gustave had suddenly cried out, "If you had seen it—if you had heard those terrible screams—I didn't know what to do!" Maillet asked him where he was at the time. Gustave replied, "Over there," pointing in the direction of the field of alfalfa.[24] Yvette came back with the potatoes immediately after this exchange, so there was no time to pursue the matter any further. Maillet was somewhat distressed to find that Yvette had charged him for 24 pounds of potatoes but had only given him 13 pounds. Gustave refused to discuss his confession during subsequent conversations with Paul.

From this moment Sébeille's suspicion that Gaston was the murderer and that Gustave was probably merely a witness was confirmed. Since the scene of the crime was not visible from Gustave and Yvette's bedroom window, he could have heard but not have seen the murders. Therefore, if Maillet was telling the truth, then Gustave's statement that he did not leave the house that night was obviously false.[25]

The investigation dragged on for months. A series of false leads were pursued. Anonymous letters piled up. The press was full of wild speculations. Criticism of the police grew ever shriller. The people of Lurs remained obdurately silent and uncooperative. The Dominicis were questioned over and over again, but they stuck to their stories. Sébeille's investigation seemed to have ground to a standstill.

Then, at the beginning of July 1953, Sébeille was granted a rogatory commission; in other words, he was given the same rights and powers as the examining magistrate when questioning witnesses. Shortly afterward he was invited to a ceremony by a friend, a primary school teacher from Martigues, who was to receive the Légion d'honneur. At the reception he was introduced to Minister of Justice Léon Martinaud-Déplat, who was also a member of the Chamber of Deputies for the Bouches-du-Rhône.[26] The minister asked Sébeille how the investigation was progressing. Sébeille could not have given a very encouraging reply. He had precious little to show after almost a year. Having been singularly lax in collecting material evidence, much to the disgust of British commentators, he had had come to rely almost exclusively on oral testimony. But here he had met with mulish reticence. The minister gave him every encouragement, however, telling him that he should not have listened to Orsatelli, who had ordered him to stop cross-examining Gustave in September 1952. Martinaud-Déplat also assured Sébeille that he would give him every support. That a minister should get so closely involved in a case that was not his direct responsibility is perhaps surprising, but Martinaud-Déplat was a hard-line conservative who was determined to fight the Communist Party at every turn. The party's close involvement with the Dominici affair was reason enough to arouse his suspicions and his interest.

This meeting marked the beginning of the final stage of the investigation, but it was not apparent for several months. Zézé Perrin; his mother, Germaine; Yvette; Gustave; and Gaston Dominici were questioned again and at length in May, but precious little new was revealed. The exception was that Zézé stated that Anne Drummond and her daughter had come to the Grand' Terre to ask for water. Further, Gaston, Marie, and Yvette were there when they arrived. Yvette had filled up the Drummond's bucket at the pump. Anne could speak no French, but Elizabeth had managed quite well. Yvette confirmed this story, mentioning that the Drummonds had a canvas bucket and that Gaston had shown his goats to Elizabeth.

Asked when he had first heard of the crime, Zézé replied that Faustin Roure had stopped at La Serre at about 7:00 a.m. on his way back from the Grand' Terre, where he had been to check the landslide, but Roure denied that he had told Zézé about the murders. Zézé claimed that he went to the Grand' Terre, looked at the dead bodies, and was told that Gaston had gotten up at 3:00 a.m. and Gustave at 3:45 a.m. He claimed that Gustave, having discovered Elizabeth's body, had told Yvette and had then gone to look at the campsite. He also stated that his grandfather had said that when he heard the shots in the night, he thought that the campers might have been attacked.

Germaine Perrin confirmed her son's statement that Anne and Elizabeth had gone to the farm to get water. Thus, it was reasonable to assume that Elizabeth had seen Gaston. It was also highly likely that Gustave had been at the murder site several times during the night, long before the time he initially claimed to have gotten out of bed.

In mid-May Jean Ricard, the man who had been camping at Ganagobie and had passed by the Grand' Terre at about 7:00 a.m. on 5 August, was questioned by Sébeille in Marseille. He added some important details. Even though he was on foot, he claimed not to have seen the overturned camp bed by the gorse bushes on the other side of the road from the Hillman. Nor did he notice the trail of blood across the road. He said that his eyes were fixed on the car and the "incredible mess" at the campsite. Not seeing anyone around, he went and peeped inside the car. He noticed nothing out of the ordinary. He saw an empty camp bed placed parallel to the car, and lying on the ground alongside it was a "human form" covered in a blanket, with the head facing away from the farmhouse. The person was lying on his or her back, fully covered except for the feet, which were pointing in the air. Ricard thought it an odd way to be sleeping, but being anxious not to miss the bus, he went back to the road and caught the bus about 100 yards beyond the Grand' Terre. Amazingly the gendarmes did not bother to question the bus driver, nor did they track down any of the other passengers. Ricard said that he saw no one at the farm, but Yvette said that she had seen someone with a rucksack walking along the road. He had turned around frequently and then took the bus.

Sébeille had met Ricard the previous August, at the beginning of his investigations, when he had gone to Ganagobie to talk to Father Lorenzi. He had asked Ricard a few questions but incredibly had neither taken any notes nor interrogated him in any detail even though he was clearly a key witness. Even more extraordinary Sébeille did not see fit to question him again for nine months.[27] Ricard's evidence was critical. He had found Anne lying on her back, with her uncovered feet in the air, parallel to the Hillman. The police had found her lying face down among the tall grass, fully covered, and at some distance and an angle to the car. There was a seat from the Hillman pressed against her left leg and a khaki-colored blanket under her legs. This difference clearly indicated that the body had been moved between about 7:00 a.m. when Ricard saw it and 7:15 a.m. when the two gendarmes arrived.

To make absolutely sure on this point, Sébeille returned to Lurs a few days after seeing Ricard to check Faustin Roure's testimony. It will be remembered that Roure had visited the Grand' Terre on the morning of the crime to look at the landslide on the railway line. He repeated the testimony that he had seen Anne's body lying beside the Hillman, but he was unable to say which way it was lying because it had been fully covered by a blanket.

Sébeille concluded from these two testimonies that the body had been moved twice. The first time was in the roughly fifteen minutes between when Roure's party left to go to work and Ricard's arrival at the scene of the crime, when the feet were uncovered.[28] Next, after Ricard left, the body had been turned over and moved into the tall grass before the gendarmes arrived about fifteen minutes later.

On 9 July Sébeille once again questioned Zézé Perrin, with whom he had not spoken since early May. He brazenly admitted that although no one had asked him to do so, he had lied to both the judicial police and the gendarmerie, but his new version of events was equally implausible. He now claimed to have gone to the Grand' Terre on the morning of 5 August on a bicycle belonging to his cousin Gilbert, Clovis Dominici's son. He had parked it beside Gustave's bicycle, which was propped against the mulberry tree. When asked why no one had seen it, he gave the unsatisfactory answer that he had moved it into the shade at 11:00 a.m. (A gendarme noted that the spot indicated by Zézé would have been in full sunlight an hour later.) He also now claimed that Gustave Dominici had sounded the horn of his motorbike as he passed the Perrins' farm at about 8:30 the evening of 4 August. His mother, Germaine, had left the farm on her moped at 9:00 p.m. to go to La Cassine, near Peyruis, where her husband was a tenant farmer. Zézé then claimed that Gustave had returned to La Serre, having met Germaine on the way, and told him about the landslide.

Sébeille suspected that Zézé might have then gone with Gustave to the Grand' Terre, but this he hotly denied. He insisted that he had stayed home alone and gone to bed at 9:15 p.m.

Sébeille interviewed Germaine Perrin the next day. She confirmed that she and her son had had dinner together, but she denied having met Gustave as she rode toward Peyruis. She added that had Gustave gone to La Serre, he would probably have taken Zézé with him to the Grand' Terre as the two were very close and the boy had often slept overnight at his grandfather's farm. It might therefore have been possible that Zézé Perrin had been at the Grand' Terre during that fatal night in August.

The Dominicis' attorney, Pollak, meanwhile protested vigorously that Sébeille had no need for rogatory authority, because no new evidence of any consequence had been produced for several months. Indeed, the investigation seemed to be getting nowhere. In fact, Sébeille and Examining Magistrate Périès were planning their final assault but felt they needed time for further thought and reflection. Their reasons for delaying action beggar belief. They decided that the idyllic summer in Provence should not be disturbed by an intensified police investigation. The roads would be packed by traffic, the beautiful hilltop villages teeming with happy tourists. The crops would be harvested under the blazing sun. It would be far too hot to think straight, and the bistros would be awash with pastis. Then came the wine harvest, which should not be interrupted by anything other than an act of God. Clearly then it would be inappropriate and unpatriotic not to wait until after the celebration of Armistice Day on 11 November. Regardless that they had not found such compelling reasons for taking time out during the previous summer, Périès and Sébeille decided to suspend the inquiry until 12 November. Then they were determined to attack in full force, break down the Dominicis, get a confession, and secure a conviction.

By this time the investigation was no longer a subject of much interest in the newspapers. So many issues of great import were taking place: the disastrous defeats in Indochina, the armistice in Korea, the trial of those involved in the June 1944 massacre at Oradour-sur-Glane, the spectacular act of parricide with an ax on Îsle Saint-Louis in Paris, the death of Stalin, the conquest of Mount Everest, and the coronation Queen Elizabeth II.

In the Dominici family, life seemed to be getting back to normal. Gustave's wife, Yvette, gave birth to her second child in May. There was a wedding in the family. In September Gaston took part in the opening ceremony of the road to the abbey at Ganagobie. He was politely but reservedly greeted by most of the local dignitaries, but the prefect of the Basses-Alpes refused to shake his hand.

The inquiry's final dramatic stage began on 12 November 1953 with another visit to the crime scene. At 6:00 a.m. the gendarmerie closed the road past the Grand' Terre by the order of Commandant Bernier from Digne and Captain Albert from Forcalquier. Commissioner Sébeille arrived forty minutes later. At 7:00 a.m. the Hillman was taken from a garage in Peyruis and parked where it had been on that fatal night in August the previous year. The camper Ricard and the SNCF workers— Roure, Boyer, and Clovis—were brought to the scene of the crime. The motorcyclist Olivier and Dr. Dragon arrived shortly afterward.

Despite the roadblocks, a large crowd of locals had collected. Some thirty journalists and an equal number of press photographers were present. Film crews from Les actualités V and Fox Movietone were on hand to record the proceedings. A peanut vendor did a brisk trade.

The arrival of the police prompted a violent reaction from the inhabitants of the Grand' Terre. The normally passive Gustave broke into a furious rage. Yvette, by now a mother of two and already pregnant with a third, threw herself onto her bed and began to sob bitterly. The habitually mute old Marie hissed through her toothless mouth: "Why take it out on us? Why don't you ask that motorcyclist? One day I'll kill him!" Only Gaston remained calm and collected.[29]

The first question addressed was the position of Lady Drummond's body. Boyer, Roure, and Ricard said that she lay parallel to the car, on her back, about 2 yards away. As they had previously stated, Roure insisted that the blanket covered the feet, while Ricard was adamant that the feet were uncovered. Clovis first said that the body was lying face down, diagonal to the car, at some distance; but then he changed his testimony to concur with that of Boyer and Roure. Gustave insisted that he had found the body in the position as his brother had first stated. Faced with this obvious contradiction, he finally admitted that he had moved Anne's body.

Gustave was then ordered to stand where he had flagged down Olivier in the early morning of 5 August. Gustave stood slightly more than 50 yards from the car and on the edge of the main road. Olivier was then ordered to drive past. Once again he flatly denied that Gustave had been standing there, insisting that he had emerged from behind the Hillman.

At 10:00 a.m. the road was reopened for traffic, and Gustave was taken to the law courts in Digne along with his brother Clovis. They left behind a hysterical Yvette, a weeping mother, and a raging Gaston. Roure, Olivier, Ricard, Paul Maillet, Zézé Perrin, and his mother, Germaine, were also taken to Digne, while Gaston, Marie, and Yvette Dominici remained under police surveillance at the Grand' Terre.

Sébeille first questioned Gustave alone in the library at the Digne courthouse. Gustave was seated, while Sébeille walked back and forth, firing questions at him. After a few moments Maillet was brought into the room. He calmly repeated what Gustave had told him: Gustave had seen the murders and had heard screams. At first Gustave denied this, then he admitted to having heard some cries but only for a very short time. He flatly denied having seen anything and insisted that he had not gotten out of bed.

Gustave was then confronted with Zézé Perrin, who also stuck to his story. He had been told not only that Anne and her daughter had come to the Grand' Terre and asked for water but also that Gustave had gotten up at 3:00 a.m., had seen Elizabeth's body, had then told Yvette, and afterward went to look at the campsite. Gustave admitted that his wife had told him that the Drummonds had come to the farm when he was not there. He had been working for Yvette's uncle, Jeannot Girard, and returned to the Grand' Terre at about 8:00 p.m. He was now prepared to admit that he got up at about 4:00 a.m. and not at 5:30 a.m., as he had previously stated. It was then that he had seen Elizabeth, who was still breathing but with great difficulty. She was lying on her back with her arms outstretched. Although he had then seen the Drummonds' bodies, he had not gone to the campsite until 5:45 a.m. and now claimed that he had *not* touched them. He insisted that Anne's body was perpendicular to the car. Sébeille then asked what he had done between about 4:30 a.m. and 5:50 a.m., when he stopped Olivier and told him to inform the gendarmerie. Gustave claimed to have looked after his livestock.

By this time Gustave was beginning to fall apart. Red in the face, trembling, and scarcely able to talk, he finally admitted that he had gone back to the campsite "to get a better idea of what had happened." When asked why he had not told the truth before and why he had not sought to help the little girl, he mumbled something about being afraid of getting involved in what was clearly a very nasty business.

Gustave's interrogation by Sébeille lasted until 7:00 p.m. Meanwhile, the examining magistrate Périès questioned Ricard, Roure, and Olivier. All three stuck to their original versions of the story.

Gustave's grilling resumed at 8:30 p.m. Sébeille immediately went on the attack, insisting that Ricard, Roure, and his brother Clovis had all testified that Anne was lying on her back with her feet in the direction of the Grand' Terre and that she must have therefore been moved between 7:00 a.m. and 7:15 a.m. Gustave was trapped. After repeatedly spluttering that he knew nothing, he finally broke down. He said that after Clovis and Ricard had left for work, he had taken Anne by the ankles and turned her over, dragging her to where the gendarmes had found her. He claimed that he had done so to ascertain whether she was still alive. Finding this explanation totally implausible, the commissioner decided to call it a day and resume questioning in the morning. It was now a few minutes before midnight, but Gustave claimed that two inspectors continued to grill him until the early morning. In fact, he spent a sleepless night in an armchair in the library, with two gendarmes keeping a close eye on him.

Gustave's cross-examination resumed next morning at seven thirty, while Périès ordered the gendarmes to bring Yvette, Germaine, and Zézé to Digne for questioning. Although claiming not in any way to be superstitious, Sébeille could not help noticing that it was Friday the thirteenth. For whom was it to prove an unlucky day? Yvette flatly denied that any of the Drummonds had visited the farm on the evening of 4 August. She refused to change her testimony even when she was told Gustave had admitted that she had said they had been there. Germaine and Zézé stuck to their original testimony. Yvette also remained adamant.

Oddly Sébeille did not keep a record of his examination of Gustave, which lasted until 10:00 a.m. He told Gustave that it was unthinkable that he had taken such risks moving Anne's body, simply to make sure that she was dead. Gustave then said he had done it to see whether there were any cartridges or bullets that had come from the farm. He said that he could not find any and therefore assumed that there was no connection between the Grand' Terre and the murders.

Périès took over from the commissioner at 11:00 a.m. From the minutes of this meeting, we learn that Gustave merely repeated what he had earlier said to Sébeille.[30] He claimed never to have seen the murder weapon. Gustave also told Périès that after he was released from prison in December 1952, his brother-in-law Jacky Barth had told him that Gaston had found four cartridges at the murder scene. Périès, however, did not even see fit to mention this revelation either to Sébeille or to the gendarmes.

Getting no further, Périès decided to hand back the interrogation to Sébeille. The commissioner realized that he was on the point of getting a confession. He began to feel a certain pity for Gustave, who appeared to him like a cornered beast, waiting for the deathblow. Within minutes Gustave broke down in tears. Resting his head on the commissioner's shoulder, he blubbered that his father had admitted to him at 4:00 a.m. on 5 August that he had committed the crime.

Sébeille went to get Périès at 4:30 p.m. They returned to the library with the clerk of the court. Gustave made a full confession, punctuated only by his sobs and the remorseless hammering of the typewriter as the clerk took down his statement. He testified that he had heard his father get up at about 1:00 a.m. Thinking this very strange, Gustave also got up to find out what he was doing. Assuming that Gaston had gone to have a look at the landslide, Gustave walked toward the bridge. When he reached the edge of the orchard, he heard the shots. He had then gone back to bed. When his father got up in the early morning of 5 August to tend his goats, Gustave got up earlier than usual to ask him whether he had heard the shots during the night. Gaston said that he had, adding that he had fired them. Gustave said that after being awoken by the shots he had been unable to go back to sleep. He had heard no further sounds in the house until he heard his father's footsteps at four o'clock. The implication here was that having fired the shots shortly after one o'clock, Gaston must have stayed outside for about three hours; otherwise, the sleepless Gustave would have heard him entering the house.

Gustave asked his father if he had gone mad. Gaston replied in the negative. When he asked him what had happened, Gaston merely said that he had met the English people who had come to the farmhouse the previous evening, then he left with his goats. On further questioning Gustave said that his father had gone hunting that night and had walked along the road in the direction of Peyruis. He stated that the carbine belonged to his father. Gaston told him that he had come across a man near the campsite and opened fire. He admitted to having killed the entire family. When asked what sort of a weapon he had used, he replied that it was a carbine that he had kept hidden. Upon further questioning, Gustave stated that his father had said that he had shot the man first, but he had not said how he had killed the little girl. Gustave also said that his brother Clovis knew what had happened, but they had not talked about it because their father had ordered them to keep absolutely silent. When Périès suggested that his earlier testimony of having crossed the bridge to look at the landslide was clearly false, Gustave admitted that his father had said that he had killed the little girl on the slope leading down to the river.

Gustave claimed that his first concern was with the little girl and that it was for this reason that he went to see her first. When he heard her groaning, he realized she was still alive. He did not go close to her but went back to the campsite, where he saw the bodies of her parents. He then went back to the Grand' Terre, where Yvette and his mother were in the courtyard. He told them what he had seen and that Elizabeth was still alive. By this time it was between 4:30 and 4:45 a.m., when day was dawning.

He then tended to his animals and returned to the campsite when the light was better to see if anything was lying about that belonged to his father. He noticed some cartridges behind the Hillman, but he did not bother to pick them up. At that time Olivier had passed by on his motorcycle. Gustave could not remember why he had moved Lady Drummond's body.

He told Périès that he had tried to get some further details from his father, but Gaston had told him that he did not wish to say anything more about it. When asked about the attitude of his father toward him when he returned from serving his prison sentence in Digne, Gustave said that he could not care less how many months he spent in jail. Later he had told Clovis everything that had happened.

At the end of this cross-examination, Gustave begged Périès not to let either the press or his family know that he had denounced his father. But Périès gave no such assurance. He was only interested in hearing Clovis's testimony, which he hoped would strengthen the case against Gaston.

Clovis was brought to the law courts at Digne at 6:30 that evening. As in the case of his brother, he was first questioned by Sébeille rather than by the examining magistrate, going against the more usual procedure. He was dumbfounded when he heard of Gustave's confession, at first refusing to believe it, but he soon began to change his tune. Gustave was then brought into the room. He was a shadow of his former self. His eyes were bloodshot, his face tense. Leaning on his brother's shoulder, he admitted that he had said that their father was the assassin. The two brothers fell into one another's arms, sobbing like small children. Fifteen months of bottled up emotions were suddenly released.

Clovis was then questioned alone and at length. He confirmed Gustave's confession by stating that while he was staying at the Grand' Terre during his brother's time in prison, his father had admitted to the crime. He could not remember the exact date but claimed that the remark had been made after dinner, at about nine or ten o'clock at night. Gaston and Marie were having one of their all-too-familiar arguments, and Clovis told them to be quiet and stop squabbling. A drunken Gaston flew into a terrible rage, threatening his son with his fist and yelling, "N'ai fa péta très, n'en ferai péta un autre!" (I've already killed three, and could kill another!) He then continued to yell, "I'm afraid of no one!" When Clovis asked him whether he was talking about the campers, he replied, "I killed the English!"[31]

Clovis tried to get some further details from his father, but all Gaston said was that he had gotten up at one o'clock to look at the landslide and made the curious remark that if it had been any worse there would not have been three dead but twenty or thirty in a serious train accident. He had taken his rifle with him. When questioned about the rifle, Clovis said that Gaston had used the word "carbine," but he had assumed that his father was referring to the Gras rifle, which he used when hunting wild boar.[32] He did not ask his father why he had taken a rifle with him, even though it was only a few hundred yards from the farmhouse to the site of the landslide. His father claimed that he had gone to have a look at the campsite and had a row with the Englishman. When it came to blows, Gaston had used his weapon. He then said, "I killed all three of them."[33]

Clovis did not question his father about the little girl, admitting that he was scared of his father. Although he was almost fifty years old, his father yelled at him as if he were a worthless little boy. Clovis therefore had no idea whether Gaston had killed Elizabeth at the campsite or at the site where her body had been found. All Gaston said was that he had killed the man and the woman. Clovis did not ask him what he had done with the rifle. He claimed never to have seen the gun before it was fished out of the river on 6 August. He attributed his violent reaction when Sébeille showed him the murder weapon a few days later to his thoughts about the atrocious nature of the crime.

At this point Périès observed that Clovis had just stated that he thought that his father was referring to the Gras rifle, even though he had been shown the M1 on two occasions. Clovis admitted that he had been somewhat confused and said that what he meant was that at the time of the crime he had not known that his father owned another rifle. Périès did not bother to follow up this line of questioning and asked what Gaston had said after having admitted to the murders. Clovis said that he had told him to keep his mouth shut and tell no one. He added that he was amazed that his father showed no signs of emotion or regret. When asked whether he had told Gustave about this confession, Clovis replied that he had told him about it later, after Gustave had finished his prison sentence, while they were chopping wood together at Saint-Pons. Gustave had admitted that he already knew.

Possibly worried what Gustave would tell Sébeille, Clovis blurted out that he would now tell the whole truth. He admitted that he recognized the carbine when Sébeille showed it to him as the one that was kept on a shelf in the shed. He said that on the evening of 5 August he had gone to check if the gun was still there. Seeing that it was missing, he was convinced that it was the murder weapon, but he had imagined that it was Gustave who had used it. He could not imagine that an old man like his father could possibly have committed such a dreadful crime. He had asked Gustave whether he had noticed that the weapon was missing. Gustave had said that he had. When Clovis asked point blank whether he had used it, he replied that he had not. Clovis found this difficult to believe and suspected his brother until the moment that his father confessed to the crime. When shown the murder weapon, Clovis stated categorically that it was his father's gun and that it was kept on a shelf in the shed. There could be no doubt about its identification, because the hand guard was attached to the barrel by wire and a Duralumin collar.

Périès now ordered that Gaston Dominici be brought to Digne. Meanwhile, in quite an extraordinary deviation from normal police procedure, Sébeille allowed Gustave and Clovis to sit together in a room at the law courts without a witness. Clovis had asked if they could stay there and avoid being questioned by the horde of journalists waiting outside the law courts. They also had grim forebodings about the reaction of the Dominici clan to their confessions. They stayed in Digne until the next morning.

5 Confession

Back at the Grand' Terre life continued as normal, although the atmosphere was undoubtedly tense. The Dominicis waited anxiously for Gustave to return. In the late afternoon of 13 November a journalist told Gaston that his son had admitted that he had left the house three times during the night of 4–5 August. He was both shattered and furious when he heard the news, exclaiming, "He said that? In that case he's fucked!" Gaston went away muttering and shaking with rage.[1]

Commandant Bernier of the Digne gendarmerie detachment went in person to the Grand' Terre to collect Gaston. They arrived at seven o'clock that evening back at the law courts, where a crowd of journalists was waiting. Gaston was taken to the library. He pretended to be casual and relaxed, browsing through the books, gazing at the ceiling, rolling his eyes, and whistling. Then he grew impatient, took his hat and cane, and announced that he was going home, "because you're starting to piss me off!" Sébeille and his assistant Henri Ranchin forced him back into his armchair, and Gaston calmed down somewhat when Sébeille hammered on the table, forcefully reminding him that he was now in the law courts and must show due respect. Ranchin also told him that they knew where he had hidden the carbine. It was on a shelf in the shed.[2]

According to the official record they gave Gaston a bowl of soup, which he ate with gusto. Wiping his mouth with the back of his hand, he calmly announced that he now intended to smoke his pipe. This was too much for Sébeille, who said that he was accused of murder, having been denounced by his sons Gustave and Clovis. Gaston muttered that they were both liars and calmly puffed his pipe. The commissioner saw no point in continuing the cross-examination. He left at 10:30 p.m., leaving him in the custody of his associates, Inspectors Ranchin, Antoine Cullioli, and Lucien Tardieu.

Having spent the night together, without any supervision, it was hardly surprising that when Gustave was questioned the next morning, his replies were identical to those of his brother. He said that he immediately recognized the carbine, adding that it had been in his father's possession for a number of years and that he had probably gotten it from some American troops. He claimed never to have used it himself. His father used it quite often when hunting wild boar. He thought there were two magazines that Gaston kept loaded. On 5 August he had noticed that the gun was no longer on the shelf in the shed, so he realized that his father had used the weapon to commit the crime. His father never told him which gun he had used.

Abel Bastide, a mason and expert truffle hunter from Lurs, also had suggested that Gaston might have obtained the gun from American soldiers. He had been working on the roof of the Grand' Terre when some American soldiers stopped at the farmhouse in 1944. They had shown how the gun worked by firing a few rounds. At this point Bastide had climbed down from the roof and was thus unable to see whether anyone handed it to Gaston.

When questioned on this point, Gaston admitted that Bastide had repaired his roof but claimed that the story about the carbine was simply village tittle-tattle. He said that Bastide was something of a crackpot. He lived alone, inhabited a fantasy world, and was considered by the villagers to be a simpleton. As a hopeless alcoholic, his testimony was deemed to be so threadbare that he was not called as a witness during Gaston Dominici's trial. It was also suggested that the M1 might have been stolen from a local farmer. After all, no one would have reported the loss of an illegal weapon.[3]

News that Gustave and Clovis had accused their father of the murders had been leaked to the press along with the statement that the identity of the murderer would be revealed within twenty-four hours, so the next morning Sébeille showed Gaston the headlines in the local papers announcing that he was the assassin.[4] Gaston flew into a terrible rage, launching a series of invectives, but was interrupted when Périès arrived and asked Sébeille to come with him and escort Gustave and

Clovis to the Grand' Terre. There they would find out where Gaston had kept the rifle.

They were met by a furious bunch of Dominici women, vociferously supported by Yvette's mother, Louise Barth. The most violent were Augusta Caillat and her daughter Marie-Claude. They had to be physically restrained by the police, but not before Augusta hit Francis Rico, a journalist from Nice, across the hand with an iron bar so hard that he was unable to work for a month. Rico sued Augusta Caillat for damages at the Digne court.[5] Augusta also threatened to kill Sébeille, saying, "At least I wouldn't go to prison for nothing!"[6] Her daughter waved a heavy stick and asked what they had given the brothers—"those traitors, those bastards"—to drink. Gustave did his best to avoid eye contact with the women, while Clovis ignored them, saying that they were all out of their minds. Yvette was in a frantic state, screaming that neither her father-in-law nor her husband was a criminal.

Ignoring the mounting chorus of imprecations, the police went about their business. Gustave and Clovis were led separately to the shed. Both indicated that the rifle was kept on the lower shelf on the right-hand side upon entering.

Yvette was ordered to come with the two brothers for questioning. She went to get her three children, and the party set off for Digne. Gustave, Clovis, and Yvette sat together in the police Citroën, thereby having ample opportunity to connive. On the way the police cavalcade stopped at Peyruis to pick up Clovis's wife, Rose. At Digne the two Dominici families were left free to have lunch, while the police tucked in at an adjacent table. Such an astonishingly lax procedure was typical of the entire investigation.

The interrogations began anew at 4:00 p.m. Périès questioned Yvette. Gustave's testimony to the contrary, she claimed to know nothing of the crime. When confronted with Gustave and Clovis initially, she had hurled abuse at her husband and brother-in-law for having denounced their father, but they both had said Gaston had confessed to having committed the crime. Gustave also had told her about the murder weapon and where it had been concealed. Although during his cross-examination the previous evening, Gustave had claimed to have told his wife everything, and he now apologized for having kept quiet. He said that he had done so because of the delicate state of her health due to her pregnancy. Yvette put on an impressive performance, first of indignation at the brothers' allegations against her father-in-law, then of surprise at their revelations, and finally of full acceptance of their version of events. Obviously her main concern was to make sure that her husband was kept above suspicion.

Meanwhile, Sébeille, assisted by Inspectors Cullioli, Ranchin, and Tardieu, questioned Gaston for four hours that afternoon. Getting nothing from him, they handed him over to Périès at 6:00 p.m. The examining magistrate merely ordered that he should remain in police custody and then went home. Sébeille and his three assistants went to dine in a local restaurant.

Gaston spent the night in the library of the law courts. First, he was guarded by Pierre Prudhomme, head of the National Police in Digne. Dominici remained silent, refusing to answer any questions. He merely shrugged his shoulders and rolled his eyes. Prudhomme then handed him over to two of his subordinates, Victor Guérino and Joseph Bocca, who were under the supervision of Sgt. Marius Sabatier.[7] The concierge brought him some food, but Gaston refused to eat.

Guérino chatted with him in their dialect. They had a common interest in hunting. Gaston grew increasingly sentimental, saying that he had cried throughout his wedding night and that he now had fourteen or fifteen grandchildren. Suddenly he burst into tears, muttering, "Ah, the little one, the little one!" The policeman asked him what was bothering him and suggested that it had all perhaps been an accident. Gaston nodded in agreement and blurted out, "Exactly! It was an accident. They attacked me. I killed all three of them." During the hour that remained of Guérino's watch, Gaston said that he had gone to look at the landslide and, as a hunter, had taken the rifle along with him "just in case." He claimed that Jack Drummond, taking him for a marauder, had attacked him, whereupon he had fired and "then the sparks began to fly."[8]

Guérino suggested that Gaston should repeat this confession to Sébeille, but he flatly refused, saying that the commissioner could go to hell. He'd had more than enough of "his shit." He did agree to talk to "the president," by whom he meant Commissioner Prudhomme, a man in whom he had every confidence. Gaston told Guérino that he could not write and that Prudhomme would be able to help him make a rough draft of a statement.

At this point Guérino was relieved by Joseph Bocca, who was accompanied by the concierge Simon Giraud (a retired gendarme) and Sergeant Sabatier. Guérino had Gaston repeat his willingness to make a full statement to Commissioner Prudhomme. He did so, but then he added that he was innocent and that he was merely taking the blame to save others. Sabatier went immediately to fetch Prudhomme from his home.

Bocca was now alone with Gaston, who rambled on about his dog and his farm. He blurted out that on their wedding night, his wife had admitted to being pregnant by another man and that she had said, "If you want us to be happy, you must be deaf, dumb, and blind." He now altered his story, saying that he had got up at four o'clock in the morning on August 5 to tend his goats. He returned to the Grand' Terre sometime between seven-thirty and eight o'clock. Yvette then told him that there had been a triple crime that night. He went on to say that the whole family was against him. Having first said that he knew that the carbine was not in the shed that night, he went on to claim that he had not seen it since he bought it from some Americans during the war. He had given it to Gustave, who had repaired it and then hid it. It was Gustave who had committed all three murders, but he would take the blame and save the honor of his grandchildren.[9]

The police were now confronted with a confusing series of confessions and accusations. Both Clovis and Gustave had accused their father. Gaston had confessed but then retracted it and accused Gustave. Although he explained his initial confession as an attempt to take the blame and save the family's honor, how would this confession save the family's honor?

Meanwhile, Sergeant Sabatier arrived at Commissioner Prudhomme's house and informed him of Gaston's confession. Prudhomme was not authorized to act on his own, so the two men went to see Sébeille, who was dining with his inspectors at a small restaurant Chez Julia. The commissioner, who was waiting for Prudhomme outside the restaurant, got into Prudhomme's car and drove to the law courts. Neither Sébeille nor Prudhomme saw fit to inform Périès, who alone could have given Prudhomme authority to take a sworn statement.

Prudhomme entered the library shortly before 8:30 p.m. Gaston immediately stated that although he was innocent, he had decided to confess to all three murders and save the Grand' Terre from misfortune. Quite how he imagined that he would achieve this aim by such means remains a mystery. He then asked Prudhomme to write a statement to this effect for him to sign. Prudhomme refused, whereupon Gaston became increasingly flustered, begging him for advice as to what to say. Prudhomme pointed out that he could not possibly invent a story on Gaston's behalf, but if he wished to make a confession, then Prudhomme would be prepared to write it down for him. Gaston, saying he was innocent, still asked Prudhomme to write that he was guilty so that he would be able to keep his farm. Again it is difficult to follow his logic.

During Gaston's trial Gustave testified that shortly before he and the policemen went to have dinner, one of the policemen, possibly Sébeille, had said to him that either he or his father was guilty. If it were Gustave, he would get the guillotine; if it were his father, he would be sent to a nursing home. Shortly before Christmas the Lurs postman, Francis Perrin, had told Paul Maillet that Gustave had confided in him that were he to be charged with the murders he would be executed, but his father would only receive a prison sentence. Maillet found this assumption extremely foolish. Perhaps Gaston also had been presented with this alternative and, in his confusion, imagined that he could take the rap while persisting in accusing his son of the murders.

Prudhomme grew increasingly impatient with Gaston, whom he accused of haggling. Getting nowhere, he suggested that Gaston might now want to have a word with Sébeille, who was waiting outside in the corridor. Surprisingly, given his intense hostility toward the commissioner, he agreed. Sabatier, Guérino, and Bocca left. Sébeille entered with Inspector Ranchin. Gaston asked Ranchin to leave, and Sébeille agreed. Prudhomme remained in the room. Gaston's attitude then changed completely. He was now relaxed and cooperative. The concierge again brought him some food, which he ate with a healthy appetite. He then dictated a statement, which Prudhomme typed. It reads as follows:

I am the author of the drama which took place during the night of 4/5 August 1952, in the course of which a family consisting of three English people—father, mother and a little girl—were killed. I am going to tell you how it all happened. At about eleven thirty on the evening of 4 August I left my house to have a look at what had happened to the landslide in one of my fields, which had been caused by excessive watering and which threatened to obstruct the railway line bordering it.

When I set out I changed my mind because when I brought my goats home that evening at about seven thirty I noticed those English people who had parked their car on the side of the road in order to camp there. I already knew these people by sight because I think it was the day before that I saw them camping below the watercourse, just past the curve in the road and near a path that leads to an olive grove. That day I had a conversation with the lady and the little girl. We talked about the weather. The girl listened, while the man was reading and did not speak to me. In the course of this conversation I learnt that they had come from Lurs or Ganagobie.

Getting back to Monday evening, 4 August, I ought to tell you that I went directly to the campsite by walking along my field along the side of the road. Before setting out I took a carbine in the hopes of killing a badger or some other beast. I took this carbine from one of the sheds. It was hidden between two planks, which are shelves on the right-hand side on entering the shed towards the rear. I think I took two or three cartridges, which were beside it.

I went as far as the mulberry tree, where I stayed watching for quite some time, perhaps about twenty minutes, while the lady undressed. She was wearing a short transparent chemise and a dark grey or blue dress. I went up to her. We exchanged a few words in a low voice, after which I touched her on several places on her body. She did not object. At this point the man, who was lying on a camp bed sort of behind the car, heard us and got up. He started to shout in his language. I did not understand and he lunged at me. We took hold of one another when I got my carbine, which I had left on the ground beside the woman's bed. The man, who was very tall, tried to disarm me by grabbing the carbine by the barrel. I lost my head at this juncture and I pulled the trigger. The bullet went through his hand, forcing him to let go. The man ran away across the road and I fired two or three shots at him. He must have been hit behind or at the side. The woman was screaming during this time. I think I only fired one shot. She fell on the spot. Then I noticed the little girl, who got out of the car by the rear doors and was running towards the Durance. I fired one round in her direction, but I did not hit her because she was still running. I saw her hurtling down the slope on the other side of the bridge and I ran after her to catch her. When I got beside her I saw that she was on her knees. I hit her once with the butt. I was completely crazy and did not know what I was doing. I descended directly towards the Durance in the direction that the girl's body was lying, where there is a gap that gives access to the river. I had blood on my hands. Having washed my hands, I took my weapon and threw it a few metres away to a spot where I knew the water was deep and which is wide open. I went along the path and got back to the farm having gone along the railway line. I sat down for a moment on my garden wall, and then I went back to bed. I got up at about four o'clock and took my goats to pasture on the Giropey side.

In answer to a question: I did not go back to the campsite that night, and I did not pick up any cartridges. I did not see Gustave when I left and afterwards I never said anything about what I had done that night. In addition, I never said anything to any member of my family.

In answer to a question: I have no idea whether Gustave went to the area afterward to see what had happened. I repeat once again that I am the perpetrator of this drama and that no one helped me. I sincerely regret what I did and I only fired at the man and the woman and hit the girl on the head with the rifle butt when I was utterly crazy. I completely lost control of myself when I saw the man leaping at me. I pulled the trigger out of fright. I stunned the girl so that she would not talk.[10]

There are many oddities in his statement. First, had his intent been to examine the landslide, he would not have walked along the side of the road to the campsite. Second, all other testimony indicated the shots were fired shortly after 1:00 a.m., so he obviously did not get up at 11:30 p.m. In a previous statement he also had said that he was awoken by a motorcycle at 11:45 p.m. Third, he could not have seen Anne undressing, because Gustave had testified that he had seen the Englishwoman and her daughter preparing to go to bed at about 8:45 p.m. Further, Lady Anne also did not possess clothes of that description. That Gaston said that he had left the carbine by her bedside at one point also suggests that she was already in bed. Fourth, since Jack Drummond was wearing shoes when he was found, he could not have been in bed at the time. Also, no bullet went through his hand. Fifth, Anne was hit by more than one round. Next, it was highly unlikely that Gaston had had much of a conversation with the Drummonds. The adults' French was very poor and his was barely understandable. Seventh, it would have been impossible for Elizabeth to open the rear door from inside the car. And finally, the sexual motive for the crime is simply not credible. Prudhomme, with a nudge and a wink, had suggested a prurient motive to Gaston, who had eagerly seized upon this opportunity to boast of his virility.

(During the trial Sébeille would be taken to task for failing to address the inconsistencies, incongruities, and anomalies in Gaston's confession.

He gave the lame reply that he was frightened that if he had pressed Gaston, then he would have retracted his statement.)

Gaston then asked the commissioner to bring him 80,000 francs ($230) in cash and 200,000 francs ($575) in share certificates, which were in two tin boxes at the farm. He also asked for some wine and to be allowed to have his dog with him in prison. Having let loose a series of imprecations against his wife, then he announced that he felt as if he would be able to have a good night's sleep.

Sébeille returned to the law courts at 9:30 a.m. on 15 November. Although Périès was already in his office, he went first to see Gaston, who appeared utterly exhausted. He stayed with him for three-quarters of an hour but astonishingly made no notes. All we know is that Gaston appeared distraught, burst into tears, and again confessed the crime.

At 10:15 a.m. the examining magistrate went to see Gaston rather than calling him to his office. Gaston was sitting in an armchair and gestured with his hand that Périès should sit beside him. Given that he was accused of an exceptionally brutal crime, it is remarkable that the police treated him extraordinarily gently throughout the proceedings. Gaston repeated that although he was not the murderer of the Drummond family, he was prepared to confirm the statement he had made the previous evening to save his grandchildren's honor. He went on to say that his son Gustave was the assassin, but as he was the oldest member of the family, it was his duty to sacrifice himself on everyone's behalf. After a frustrating quarter of an hour, Périès, having explained that he could make no use of such statements, left the room accompanied by the clerk of the court. Gaston shouted after them that if they did not note this down, "there would be a misfortune at the Grand' Terre." No explanation can be found for this strangely empty threat.

Sergeant Sabatier then told the crowd of journalists waiting in the courtyard in front of the law courts that Gaston Dominici had begun to confess the crime, but the version he gave was unsatisfactory. When pressed for details, he said that for the moment he had nothing to add.

Périès resumed his questioning at 11:15 a.m., intent on getting Gaston to drop the claim that he was sacrificing himself for the family's honor. He was sullen and resentful, moaning about his misfortune. Now he claimed that he could not remember at what time he had left the house on that fateful night. He went on to say that he had talked to Lady Drummond and her daughter just before nightfall and that he had been tending his goats at the area known as Saint-Pons when they approached him. He said that Anne spoke very poor French, but the little girl was quite fluent. They talked about the beauty of the landscape, while the husband sat some distance away, reading a book. Some time later, after he had returned to the farm, he noticed that the English people had established a campsite on the turnout at the edge of his property.

Gaston went on to say that he had left the house shortly after a motorcycle with a sidecar had stopped outside the Grand' Terre. He went to get the carbine, which was in the "garage" between two planks that formed shelves at the back of the building on the right-hand side. The magazine was on the carbine. Although he knew that it was fully loaded, he took a few extra rounds that were lying on the shelf nearby. He took the gun with him in the hope of seeing some badgers or rabbits. He had left the house with the intention of going to look at the landslide and then to do a little hunting. Contrary to this assertion, he said he approached the mulberry tree, near which the English were camping, by walking along his alfalfa field. The man was lying on a camp bed, which was up against the car. He appeared to be asleep. The woman was taking off her dress. He could not see the child but learned later that she was sleeping inside the car. He hid behind the mulberry tree and watched the woman undressing. She "had what it takes." He went on to say, "Suddenly I felt that I wanted to fuck her. I went up to her. I put down the weapon just before I got level with the front of the car. The lady was not scared when she saw me. Immediately I put my hand on her cunt. She did not react. I did not hesitate. I got out my dick. The woman lay down on the ground and I started to fuck her."[11]

Gaston said that they must have made a noise, because the husband got up shortly afterward and came up to them in anger. Gaston got up and went to get his gun. The man grabbed the gun by the barrel, which went off without him having pulled the trigger. He insisted that this first shot had been by accident. The bullet went through his adversary's hand, whereupon he grabbed Gaston by the throat. Fearing that the man was getting the better of him, because he was much stronger, Gaston fired another round at point-blank range. Jack then ran away, going around the rear of the vehicle. Gaston ran after him and fired another round while he was crossing the road. He fell down "for good" on the other side of the road.

The woman then started to scream. Gaston went back to her and fired a shot in her direction. He could not remember whether he fired at her once or twice. At this moment the little girl got out of the car by the rear door. She cried a bit but not much. She ran away in the direction of the bridge. Gaston followed her, firing one round, but it missed. He fired again. Again he missed. At this point he realized that the magazine was empty.[12] This he could not explain, because he thought it was full. He imagined that he must have lost some cartridges on the way. He also seems to have mislaid the two or three cartridges that he had put in his pocket when he had taken his carbine from the garage. Then he saw that the girl was crossing the bridge and hurtling down the slope toward the river. He asked himself how it was possible that he had been able to catch her. When he caught up with her, she was on her knees. She looked at him but said nothing. "I was plastered. I did not know what I was doing. I was mad. I maintain that the carbine broke with the first blow. The child collapsed immediately without even a moan."[13] He then went toward the Durance and threw his carbine into the river. He added that he had chosen a piece of high ground, a promontory about 22 yards from the place where he had hit the girl, from which to throw the rifle. Then he washed his bloodstained hands.

Gaston next retraced his steps. He thought that the little girl was dead because she did not move. He went to the campsite to see whether the parents were indeed dead. He covered up the woman's body with a rug that was lying on the ground beside the car. He then took a camp bed and covered the man's body. He did not rummage around in the car or in the stuff that was lying around all over the place.

Going back to the bridge over the railway, he turned right, without going to have another look at the little girl. He went along the railway line, crossed it, and returned to the farm by the path that led to the yard. He went back to bed at about 2:30 a.m. and got up again at 4:00 a.m. and left with his goats. He did not see Gustave when he went back to bed, nor when he left, but he did not go back to sleep and heard Gustave leaving the house on three occasions. He claimed not to have spoken to anyone about what had happened. He told neither Gustave nor Clovis what he had done.

When asked about the murder weapon, Gaston said that he kept it in the shed, on a shelf at the back on the right-hand side. He could not remember how the weapon came into his possession. All he knew was that they had owned it since some Americans had passed by. The early morning of 5 August was the first time that he had used the gun. He never made any repairs on the weapon, but he noticed that the barrel was attached to the handguard by means of a Duralumin collar.

His statement was read to him, and he signed it. He then said, "I hope that you understand. I have not got along with my wife for twenty years. I am too old to get divorced. I had here an opportunity to get out of this situation. I did not let it escape me."[14]

Again, a number of inconsistencies, contradictions, and obvious lies in this statement would seriously weaken the case against Gaston. In part they were due to Gaston's very poor French, which gave rise to a series of ambiguities and imprecisions—many of them deliberate—that the judicial police and the examining magistrate did not see fit to clarify. They claimed that they did not want to question him too much for fear that he might withdraw his confession. Faced with mounting pressure to secure a conviction, they preferred to go ahead with a weak case rather than prolong the investigation.

This statement about Gaston's meeting with the mother and child differs in several ways from his earlier version. Previously he had said that Elizabeth had remained silent and that he and the girl's mother had talked about the weather. He had earlier given the precise location of the encounter, but now he spoke of the general area. The only thing that was the same in both versions was that Sir Jack had been reading.

Gaston now claimed to have left the house just after the motorcycle with a sidecar had stopped at the farmhouse. He had previously stated that this was at 11:45 p.m. Were this true he must have been wandering around for an hour and a quarter before the shots were fired. The claim that he took the carbine along with him in the hope of doing some hunting is preposterous. No one would ever shoot rabbits with a .30 caliber gun. Furthermore, it was said that Gaston had not gone hunting since 1947 at the latest.[15]

One witness, Ode Arnaud, had spotted a motorcycle with a sidecar on the road to Manosque that night. He stated that the sidecar was on the left, suggesting that it might have been British. A man was driving; a woman was sitting in the sidecar. He was unable to see whether a child was also in the sidecar. Despite extensive investigations, no trace was found of this vehicle, but André Désirée, who ran a bicycle repair shop in Peyruis, stated that he had delivered a punctured motorcycle tire he had fixed to the Grand' Terre at eleven thirty the night before that of the murders. He had taken it on his scooter and had dropped the repaired tire off in the courtyard; so it may well be that the Dominicis had used this incident as the basis of their story of the strangers on a motorcycle. In any event Gaston only claimed to have seen a man, not the motorcycle. Gustave, however, could not have seen anything unless he had gotten up to investigate. (Further, in Gustave's defense the punctured tire on his motorcycle may explain why Yvette, although pregnant, had to ride her bicycle to Giropey to telephone the gendarmerie on 5 August 1952.)

The extremely crude language Gaston had used when describing his encounter with Lady Drummond was absolutely shocking at the time and still seems lubriciously prurient. No journalist dared print his statement verbatim, and nobody believed that a respectable English lady would willingly have sexual intercourse with a seventy-six-year-old peasant in the middle of the night while lying on gravel only a few feet away from her husband. Moreover, the autopsy revealed no sign of recent sexual activity, and Anne was fully clothed and wearing panties when her body was discovered.

Since Jack Drummond was wearing shoes, he almost certainly was not lying in bed fast asleep. The autopsy showed that he had an empty bladder, thus providing ample explanation for his shoes being unlaced. Gaston's statement that he woke up "shortly afterward" is typically vague. It is not at all clear precisely what act was completed immediately before Jack awoke, although it is implied that it was after the conclusion of this fantasy copulation.

Drummond had not been shot through the hand, although there was a gash across his palm. Had a bullet passed through his hand, he would not have been able to grab Gaston by the neck. Even if the gun had gone off accidentally, it must have been cocked with the safety catch released. No one ever questioned Gaston on this important point.

Gaston claimed to have fired one or two shots at Lady Drummond, but she was hit by three rounds. His testimony about the number of cartridges is also contradictory. An M1 magazine holds fifteen rounds. Gaston claimed it was full, yet after firing six or seven rounds it was empty. How was it also that all the rounds in his pocket had suddenly disappeared? In addition, there is the question of what he did during that period of well over an hour before he went back to bed. Last, again it would have been impossible for Elizabeth to have climbed out of the back of the Hillman as the rear door did not open from the inside.

Having obtained this signed confession, Périès wanted to reconstruct the crime that afternoon, but he was told that there was a crowd of about two thousand onlookers at the Grand' Terre. News of the confession had been broadcasted and it was a Sunday afternoon. He therefore realized that he would have to postpone the reenactment until the following day. In the meantime, he decided to confront Gaston with his sons Gustave and Clovis.

Clovis was led into the room, and his father's statement was read to him. He said that he stuck to his original statement. When Commissioner Sébeille had shown him the gun, he recognized it at once as the one that was kept in the shed at the Grand' Terre and that he had seen it two or three times. He had gone to the shed on 5 August and noticed that it was missing. He initially had taken this to mean that Gustave had committed the murders. He continued to believe so until sometime in the fall of 1952, while Gustave was in jail, and one evening after supper, when they were alone together in the kitchen, his father had said that he had shot the English. He added that on this occasion his father had "drunk more than usual." Given Gaston's reported phenomenal capacity for alcohol, it must have been a vast amount. Gaston did not deny this statement. He simply said that he could not remember the incident.

Clovis then repeated that his father had said, "I bumped off all three of them. If I had to do it again, I would do it."[16] Clovis had assumed that this reference to doing it "again" referred to his mother, with whom his father had just had yet another blazing row and who had gone to bed to escape his rage. Gaston muttered, "It's possible that I said that, but I can't remember."

Clovis then added one odd detail to his statement. He did not think that his father had initially taken the M1 with him that night but had returned to the farm to fetch it after a confrontation with the Drummonds. This version certainly made more sense. It suggested that Gaston wanted to chase the Drummonds away.

Gustave was then brought in to confront his father. He said that he had heard his father's footsteps at four o'clock in the morning and gotten up to ask him whether he had heard the shots. His father had replied in the affirmative, adding that he was responsible. At this point Gaston interjected, "Thank you very much, Master Gustave."[17] This snide remark set off a lengthy slanging match in dialect, after which Gustave continued his statement. He said that he had asked his father whether he had gone mad. Gaston replied that he had gotten up to see the landslide and to do a little hunting. He did not say how the quarrel with the Drummonds had started. He had simply said that after a discussion, the Englishman had approached him and that he had shot at him. Gustave then went to the spot where his father had said that the little girl was lying. He went next to the campsite, and when he went back to the farmhouse, he looked in the shed to see whether his father had used the American carbine. It was no longer there. That morning he did not notice whether there was a pair of his father's trousers hanging in the yard. Nor did he notice whether his father's trousers were bloodstained "at the time of these events."[18]

This is the first time that the question of the trousers hanging out to dry is mentioned in the written records. The matter was never pursued until the entire case was investigated anew. Gaston said that he did not have to wash his trousers, because they were not bloodstained. He added that he could not remember if he had told Gustave that it was he who had fired the shots. It is curious that Gaston readily admitted to having blood on his hands but fiercely denied that he had any on his trousers. The examining magistrate, appearing not to have noticed this anomaly, asked no further questions about the matter.

Gustave went on to say that he had spoken to no one about this incident until a few days after he had been released from prison. He said Clovis had confided to him, when they were working together in the Saint-Pons wood, that their father had fired the shots. Clovis, who had already told Sébeille about the Saint-Pons incident on 13 November, affirmed that this was indeed the case and that he had broached the subject. It seems hard to believe that the two brothers had not spoken to one another about the crime for over four months, even though Gustave was the prime suspect. Gustave then stated that his father had confessed to the crime at four o'clock in the morning of 5 August.

The brothers thus leveled serious accusations against their father, but they offered the examining magistrate no hard piece of evidence that could be used to bolster his case. Loath to probe any deeper for fear that the entire case would collapse, Périès decided to call it a day.

Gaston had thus confessed to the crime on several occasions: to his sons Gustave and Clovis, to the policemen Guérino and Bocca, to Commissioners Sébeille and Prudhomme, and to Examining Magistrate Périès.

On two occasions he had seized upon the suggestion of a motive. First, that it was an accident; second, a consequence of his thwarted sexual appetite. All of these confessions differed in several ways, but most were incongruously presented as a means of preserving the family's honor, particularly that of his grandchildren.

During the afternoon, Commissioner Harzic, the head of the Ninth Mobile Brigade in Marseille and Sébeille's superior, made a statement to the press. It contained a number of astonishing errors. First, he said that Gaston had confessed to the crime at seven o'clock in the morning, quoting him has having said, "Yes, I killed them. I acted alone." The initial confession had been in the early evening and was not in the form Harzic had claimed. He then went on to say that Gaston had left the house to hunt badgers that had been attacking his chickens, but there is no record of him ever having made such a claim. Harzic next stated that Gaston carried the gun by the sling, even though he must have known that it did not have one. He further said that Gustave had watched Anne while she was washing.

There followed a somewhat garbled version of the murders. According to Harzic, Gustave had been awoken by the shots and was waiting for his father in the farmyard when he returned. Gaston, it was claimed, had then confessed all. Clovis had come to the Grand' Terre in the morning and had been "let into the secret." Apparently it was Yvette who had persuaded her husband to tell Clovis and to make sure that he corroborated the story. None of this information can be found in the police records.[19]

With astonishing disregard for the principle of presumption of innocence, the local press outdid itself in denouncing Gaston Dominici. *Le Méridional*'s headline read, "Father Dominici Is the Drummonds' Assassin." *La Marseillaise* announced, "Gaston Dominici Is the Lurs Assassin." *Le Provençal* also confirmed that "Gaston Dominici is the Drummonds' assassin."

Given the inconsistencies between Gaston's various versions of the crime, Périès decided to go ahead with the reconstruction of the crime before pressing charges. He had a powerful motive for such a postponement. At that time under French law, a person had no right to engage a lawyer until charges were laid. Périès knew that the prominent lawyer Émile Pollak and his associate Pierre Charrier were hovering in the wings, eager to become involved in this sensational case. That both were active members of the Communist Party was a further reason to keep them off the case as long as possible. He certainly did not want them to be in any way involved in the reconstruction, and all subsequent attempts by the defense to reenact the drama were flatly refused.

During the night of 15–16 November, the gendarmes closed the road leading past the Grand' Terre. Journalists were permitted to witness the proceedings the morning of the sixteenth but were cordoned off by the gendarmerie on the other side of the road. The correspondent from *The Times* described this as "a conventional part of French police investigations, however strange to English eyes."[20] Somehow or other the Dominici family had been forewarned, because most of the family members, with the notable exception of Clovis, were ready and waiting in the farmhouse.

The prosecutors arrived with Gaston at nine o'clock. His appearance prompted shrieks of anguish from within the building, the chorus led by the redoubtable Augusta Caillat. The gendarmes' cordon was singularly ineffective. There was already a large crowd of curious onlookers, and as Gaston descended from the police car, many shouted out, "Death!"[21] He appeared to be unmoved by such hostility and waved cheerily to the press photographers.[22]

The proceedings began with a visit to the shed, where Gaston was asked to show where the carbine had been kept. Using his cane, he clearly pointed to the top shelf. Since the police photographer's flash did not function properly, he repeated this gesture three times. The transcript, however, clearly states that he had shown it was kept on the lower shelf, as his two sons had stated. Gustave and Clovis were then asked the same question. The photographs clearly show them pointing to the lower shelf. This discrepancy between the photographic evidence and the written testimony was to prove very embarrassing to the prosecution when the case was reopened. Yvette pointed out that if it had been kept on the lower shelf, everyone would have been able to see it. Faced with this awkward fact, Clovis would change his testimony and claim that it had been kept on the upper shelf.

Gaston then walked toward the scene of the crime. It is not at all clear from various accounts of these events quite what happened during the enactment. Did he carry the gun in his right hand and his cane in the left, or did he take the gun in his left hand and hold his hat in the right to cover his face, leaving his cane behind? Or did he walk with his cane in the right hand and his hat on his head, while Sébeille walked beside him carrying the weapon?

Precisely what then happened is also opened to conjecture. According to the transcript Gaston took charge of the proceedings, voluntarily and unhesitatingly reenacting the murder. Some of the journalists, who watched from across the road, confirm this version of events, but others insist that he was cajoled, questioned, and forced to change his story. One even claimed that he looked like a marionette, manipulated by the gendarmes.[23] Whatever the case, it seemed that Gaston more or less confirmed by his actions what he had said in the various confessions but with one important exception. In his confession to Périès, he had said that having fired the first shot, which wounded Jack in the hand, he had fired a second time virtually at point-blank range. Now he showed the second shot as having been fired at some distance and from behind as he had previously stated to Prudhomme. He only mimed having shot Anne once. Thus, during the reconstruction Gaston claimed to have fired only three shots, the number that Gustave and Yvette claimed to have heard, but it does not coincide with the coroners' evidence.

The vexing issues of the pool of blood by the sump and the piece of flesh on the Hillman's bumper were not addressed. Incredibly, no photographs had been taken of these valuable pieces of material evidence.

Using his cane to imitate the carbine, Gaston reloaded the gun after each imaginary shot, indicating that he did not know that the M1 was semiautomatic. He showed that he had fired from the shoulder, whereas the autopsy proved that the two shots on Jack had been fired from the hip.

A critical issue was to discover whether a man of Gaston's advanced age who always walked with a cane could have caught up with Elizabeth as she ran away. One of the inspectors played the role of Elizabeth, and Gaston ran after him at an incredible speed for a man of seventy-seven. It is also extraordinary that he put such an effort into this sprint, and it served further to strengthen Périès's conviction that he was guilty. But Gaston was a proud man, given to vaunting his strength, virility, and prowess. He was unable to resist the challenge. There was yet another motive. When he was halfway across the bridge, he scrambled up and onto the parapet, intent on throwing himself onto the railway lines. Here he showed considerably less agility, and Périès, who had been an enthusiastic rugby player in his youth, tackled him and thus frustrated his suicide attempt. The scene had an element of comedy in that Gaston and Périès both lost their hats in the chase. When they went back to get them, each took the other's and put them on. In their confusion it took them a while to notice their mistake and make the exchange.

Gaston was initially reluctant to reenact killing Elizabeth. Twice he refused. Then Sébeille's assistant, Inspector Girolami, knelt down in front of him while Gaston, brandishing his cane above his head, said: "Don't be afraid, I won't hit you!"[24] Gaston had always reacted violently whenever Elizabeth's name was mentioned, so this bizarre utterance was not untypical. Somewhat later when Sébeille told him that someone wanted to erect a monument at the spot where Elizabeth was killed, he said that even if they built a fence around it, the dogs would still shit on it.

Having mimed how he had killed Elizabeth, Gaston then went to the promontory where he had stood to throw the gun into the river. He went to the spot he had told Périès about the day before, not the one he had described in his confession to Commissioner Sébeille. He then pointed out the place where he had washed his hands, but he refused to walk down to the river. He now claimed that he went back to the campsite to cover the bodies before washing his hands, whereas in his statement to the commissioner he said that he had washed his hands first.

All those present were struck by the presence of Paul Maillet, who paced about inside the cordoned-off area, chain-smoking. With a beaming smile on his face, he kept repeating the phrase, "The old man wanted to get me, but I've got him!" This statement is strange, because nowhere in the records is there any mention of Gaston making an accusation against Paul Maillet. But that morning, when Gaston first noticed Maillet, he waved his cane at him and yelled, "Come here, punk! Fucking assassin! You held the carbine, eh, you bastard!"[25] The ambiguity of this statement is less obvious when translated into English. The implication is that Paul Maillet held the weapon in his possession rather than that he physically held it in his hands when the murders were committed. Neither the judge nor the gendarmes saw fit to investigate this accusation, and Gaston never repeated it. It can therefore be assumed that Gaston's outburst was simply directed at a man who had denounced his son and brought the Dominici family under suspicion. Similarly, Maillet's glee at Gaston's predicament was revenge for the shabby way in which he had treated his father.

The reconstruction of the crime having been completed, Examining Magistrate Périès and Commissioners Harzic, Sébeille, and Constant congratulated themselves in front of the journalists on a job well done. Such behavior, seemingly inappropriate in the extreme, was common practice in such cases at that time. What was very unusual was that Sébeille openly congratulated Paul Maillet with the words, "Well, Mr. Maillet, today you have witnessed your victory."[26] This remark is a clear indication not only of the degree of antagonism between Maillet and Gaston but also of the close relationship Maillet had with the commissioner.

The entire operation took a mere three-quarters of an hour. Such haste is possibly explained by the commissioners' fears that Gaston might withdraw his confession, although the journalists who witnessed the scene said that he was cool, calm, and collected throughout, apart from his outburst against Paul Maillet. Gaston was now bundled into a police van and formally charged with murder on the way back to Digne. Périès told him that he should now get a lawyer, to which he replied, "I don't want a lawyer—unless you are prepared to pay one for me." This was a strange remark given that Émile Pollak and Pierre Charrier had been at his family's side for the last fifteen months, ever since 6 August

1952. The following day Gaston had a defense team of four lawyers, but it is uncertain who selected them.[27] None were provided by the court. It also remains a mystery how the Dominicis managed to pay for Gaston's defense.

An angry crowd waited outside the prison in Digne for Gaston's return. As he was led back to his cell, there were cries of "death!" Lucien Grimaud in *La Marseillaise* abandoned his previous support for the Dominicis to give an absurdly bombastic expression of the widespread revulsion toward Gaston Dominici:

> Like one of the wild animals that he hunted down and slaughtered in the Lurs mountains, the old poacher, this ruffian from the banks of the Durance, has spat his venom, shown his fangs and once again spread evil. The confession of his atrocious crime aroused horror among those whose hopes for so many months were dashed by his threats and sarcasm. He sought to appear even more gruesome as he sank ever deeper into ignominy. As of yesterday the name of Gaston Dominici has joined those of the most odious in criminal history.[28]

Gaston was now an *inculpé*, which under French law meant a great deal more than simply the "accused." There was an assumption of guilt, such that henceforth he was referred to as "the assassin" in the press. Whereas the local press had already jumped the gun, the Parisian papers now joined in. *Le Figaro*, France's leading conservative newspaper, called him "the assassin, or more exactly the criminal, because it is not yet certain that premeditation was involved, in the case of old Gaston Dominici, an almost octogenarian horror."[29] It also called Gaston a "brute," a "savage," "an old bandit," "senile," a "vicious clodhopper," the "ogre of Lurs," a "megalomaniac," a "monstrous old man," "an old goat stinking of grease and *pastis*," "repulsively boastful," and "sadistic."[30] *Le Parisien Libéré* announced that the "Lurs Affair" had been solved, the "odious assassin" discovered.[31] Gaston Dominici was now painted as an "abominable brute"; a "sinister old man"; a "ferociously brutal, solitary and choleric poacher"; a "horrible and incomprehensible man out of a nightmare"; the "Lurs Killer"; the "tattooed killer"; a man "with his penis in one hand and a machinegun in the other"; and the "patriarch-assassin."[32]

The reaction to charges being laid against Gaston in the British press was quite different. British libel laws are severe. The accused is never described as guilty until judgment has been reached. The British press thus merely reports on the trial. Confessions made by the accused are never published.

Since this investigation was conducted in a foreign country, the British press had given it far greater coverage than would have been the case had it been done in Britain, but it never hinted that Gaston might have been the culprit. The differences between French and British law were often the cause of some confusion, particularly because the position of examining magistrate and the practice of having the accused reconstructing crimes do not exist in British law. The most that was said was an article in the *Daily Express* congratulating Commissioner Sébeille on the successful conclusion of a lengthy investigation.

The British press had been loud in its denunciations of French police methods over the last fifteen months, but now Sébeille proudly announced that he had silenced all such criticisms by the triumph of his "applied psychology" method. The British with their empirical bent remained unconvinced. The case rested on the denunciations of two of Gaston's sons, plus certain circumstantial evidence. Where, they asked, were the hard facts that could lead to a conviction? There were still a number of unanswered questions. Did Gaston act alone? Would he have needed an accomplice? Was he sacrificing himself for another? Was it really possible accurately to reconstruct the triple crime? What motive could be behind this appalling massacre?

With Gaston Dominici formally charged, Sébeille became a national hero. Although the case was now sub judice under French law, there were no restraints on the public reporting of the investigation, so Sébeille continued to talk openly to the press. Minister of the Interior Léon Martinaud-Deplat was presiding over a dinner in Marseille when he was given the news. Rising to his feet, he announced that Gaston had been charged and proposed that Sébeille should be promoted and awarded the

Légion d'honneur. Robert Hirsch, director general of national security, invited Harzic, Sébeille, Constant, and the rest of the Ninth Mobile Brigade of the judicial police in Marseille to dinner at the resplendent Parisian restaurant Pavillon Ledoyen. The heads of the judicial police, the gendarmerie, and the Office of Territorial Surveillance were in attendance. Praise was heaped upon Sébeille. The director of the judicial police asked for his autograph on the menu and told him to take a holiday. A promotion seemed imminent. Marcel Massot, a deputy from the Basses-Alpes, also called for a Légion d'honneur.

Sébeille received some five thousand congratulatory letters, with the post office offering to pay for any that were insufficiently stamped. A Swiss woman sent him 100,000 francs for his holiday expenses. In Lurs he was pampered, with the peasants offering him wine, the women kissing him. He was feted as the man who had delivered them from a nightmare. The *News Chronicle* seconded these remarks by describing Sébeille as a "43-year old crack detective."[33] The commissioner basked in this adulation, but he still had nagging doubts about the motive behind this brutal and senseless crime. It seemed to be a murder done in a moment of blind rage, but would this explanation stand up in court?

1. A disappointed Émile Pollak (*with cigarette*), who was Gaston Dominici's lawyer, and his wife leave the court on hearing the verdict.

2. Gaston Dominici during his trial for the murder of the Drummonds.

3. Gaston in court.

4. Gaston (*seated*) rests during the reconstruction of the crime.

5. Gaston with Father Lorenzi.

6. Gaston with his wife, Marie; his son Gustave; and Gustave's wife, Yvette, at the Grand' Terre.

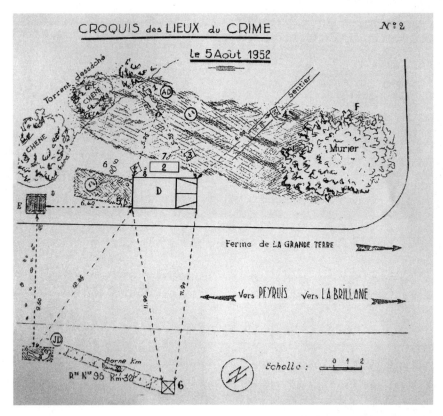

7. Gendarmerie sketch of the crime scene. *Key*: JD—body of Sir Jack Drummond covered by a camp bed; AD—body of Lady Drummond covered by a blanket; 1—cushion from a car seat; 2—camp bed; 3—suitcase; 4—cushion, under which a pair of sandals; 5—child's hat; 6—diverse objects; 7—half-empty bottle of Vichy water; 8—flashlight; D—Hillman registered NNK 686 with GB plate; E—sump; F—mulberry tree; G—electric pylon.

8. Gustave and Yvette Dominici.

9. The Grand' Terre, the Dominici farm.

10. Commissioner
Edmond Sébeille (*left*)
and Roger Périès, the
examining magistrate.

11. Émile Pollak visits Gaston in the notorious prison Les Baumettes in Marseille.

12. Commissioner Sébeille arrives at the scene of the crime (*black car in foreground*). Sir Jack's body was found on the left side of the road; the Drummonds' car, a Hillman Minx, is on the right.

13. The Drummonds: Sir Jack, his wife Anne, and their daughter, Elizabeth.

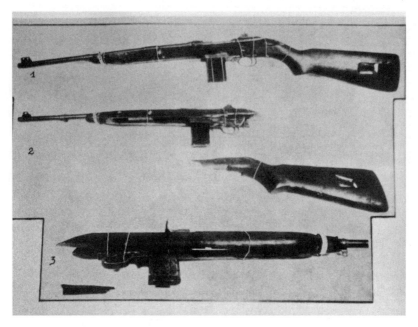

14. A photo of the murder weapon from the police file.

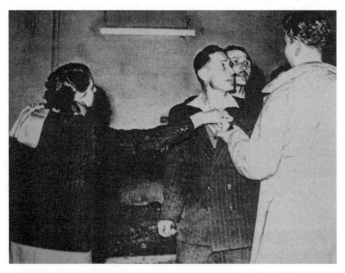

15. Yvette placates Gustave, who was angered by a journalist.

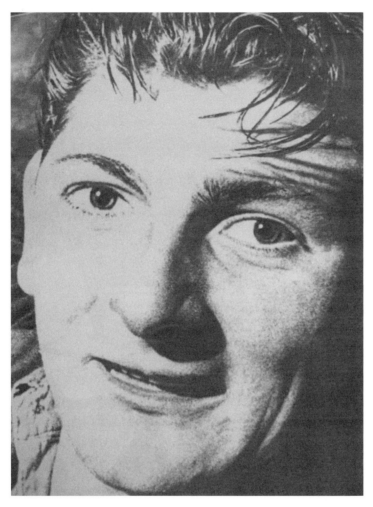

16. Roger "Zézé" Perrin, Gaston's grandson, whom he later accused of having a hand in the murders.

6 Two Lives

SIR JACK DRUMMOND

Jack Cecil Drummond was born in Leicester on 12 January 1891.[1] His father was a major in the Royal Artillery serving in India. Both parents died when he was very young, so he was brought up by his elderly aunt and her husband, Captain Spinks, a veteran of the Crimean War. Jack was sent to the John Roan School in Greenwich, a grammar school established in 1677; to the Strand School in London, which had originally been attached to King's College of the University of London; and to Tulse Hill in South London. His childhood appears to have been somewhat bleak. Mrs. Spinks was a strict nonconformist and insisted on dragging young Jack off to chapel at regular intervals. Captain Spinks was a keen gardener, and it is from him that Jack grew to love flowers and outdoor life.

He showed no particular aptitude at school, either in the classroom or on the playing fields. His enthusiasm for cricket far outran his skills. He just managed to squeak through the entrance examinations to East London College (now Queen Mary College), where he blossomed and graduated in 1912 with a first-class honors degree in chemistry. While an undergraduate he met Mabel Straw, a fellow student, whom he later married. She was soon widely known as a gracious and kindly woman and a charming hostess.

On graduation he worked as a research assistant at King's College, which led him gradually into the field of biochemistry. Having worked briefly on the staff of the Government Chemist, he moved to the Cancer Hospital Research Institute. Jack had joined the Special Reserve of Officers and held a commission in the East Surrey Regiment, but he was found unfit for active service in 1914 because of a heart condition. He therefore continued his work at the Cancer Hospital.

Professor W. D. Halliburton, head of the Department of Physiology at King's College, after whom the department is now named, was greatly impressed by Drummond's work and did much to further his career. Halliburton served on the Food (War) Committee of the Royal Society later in the war. Impressed by Drummond's work on nutrition in rats, he asked him to investigate the fat-soluble accessory food factors in butter and margarine. The work resulted in a joint paper published in 1917 that was later incorporated into the Food Committee's 1919 report.

Drummond became interested in vitamins and the practical application of nutritional knowledge resulting from this work, and such an approach remained his main concern throughout his professional career. He was part of the new discipline of biochemistry, which addressed exciting new ideas in the field of nutrition. In 1912 Frederick Hopkins, a professor of biochemistry at Cambridge, had referred to some recently discovered substances as "accessory factors of the diet."[2] They were referred to as "vitamines" (from *vital amines*), a term that the Polish biochemist Dr. Casimir Funk of the Cancer Hospital used for the first time in a paper that same year. Drummond in 1920 suggested dropping the *e* in "vitamins" on the grounds that the termination "in" implied a substance of unknown constitution.[3] Henceforth, "fat soluble A" became known as vitamin A and "water-soluble B" as vitamin B. Drummond's work on nutrition, particularly in the area of vitamin deficiencies and infant feeding, was widely admired and in 1918 was acknowledged with his being granted a doctorate of science. That same year he was appointed to succeed Funk, who had emigrated to the United States, as a physiological chemist at the Cancer Hospital.

In 1919 Drummond was appointed a lecturer in biochemistry at University College London, where in 1922 at the early age of thirty-one he was appointed to the newly created Chair of Biochemistry, a position funded by the Rockefeller Foundation. From 1920 to 1925 his research covered a staggeringly wide range of issues involving vitamins A and B and their practical application. Often accused of being more concerned with the broad sweep than with the tedious attention to detail, he darted from one problem to another with youthful enthusiasm, inspiring others to do the spade work while he reaped the benefits of their practical application. Although most of his work was concerned with some aspect of nutrition, he encouraged his graduate students to pursue their own interests and go their own way. As a result his department produced more professors than any other school of biochemistry. He was a gifted speaker, whose specialized lectures on nutrition were outstanding, given his ability to explain complex scientific ideas to lay audiences. Always interested in the practical application of science, he carried out a great deal of consulting work for industry, some felt to the detriment of his purely scientific work.

Many often said Drummond had an artistic temperament—he was a very talented amateur painter—and that his interests were too extensive for him to make any real contribution to science. He had boundless energy, playing as hard as he worked. He founded a dining club for informal gatherings between students and staff, played cricket with great enthusiasm, and was always willing to give informal talks to undergraduates.

By the 1930s there was widespread interest in nutrition, in part due to the problems arising from the Great Depression. In 1931 the Ministry of Health established a committee to examine general questions of nutrition, and in 1933 the British Medical Association followed suit. The latter's work resulted in the publication in 1936 of a report by John Boyd Orr titled *Food, Health and Income*, which came to the shocking conclusion that 50 percent of the population was seriously undernourished.[4]

Drummond became directly involved in the public health aspect of nutrition when he examined the findings of Dr. G. E. Friend, the medical officer at Christ's Hospital, that showed incidents of fractures among schoolboys rose when margarine replaced butter in the later stages of World War I and fell again when butter was restored in 1922. Drummond wrote in the preface to Dr. Friend's published report: "It is a fact at once surprising and humiliating that with thousands of years of human life and experience behind us we are actually engaged today in acquiring laboriously the knowledge necessary to enable us to feed and rear our children properly."[5] The Friend report was far from satisfactory because the research population was at a day school; thus, the boys spent most of the time at home, where there was no control over their diets. But the report's findings inspired Drummond to pursue his research into nutrition and public health.

The Rockefeller Foundation was most interested in Drummond's work. It awarded him a traveling fellowship for January to May 1936 to visit Holland, Germany, Czechoslovakia, Austria, Hungary, Switzerland, Poland, Russia, Finland, Sweden, Norway, and Denmark so he could examine problems of nutrition, particularly in the poorer sections of society. He was immensely impressed by the experiments in canteen feeding that he witnessed in eastern Europe and put the knowledge he gained on this tour to great effect when he began to advise the Ministry of Food in wartime Britain. Although he continued to do research into vitamins and general biochemical topics, he became increasingly interested in the historical aspects of nutrition, particularly with respect to the disastrous effects of the Industrial Revolution on public health.

Drummond became deeply involved in the subject in 1933 when he served on the British Medical Association's committee to examine the minimum weekly expenditure required for a healthy diet. His new interest resulted in the publication of *The Englishman's Food* (1939), which he coauthored with his longtime secretary Anne Wilbraham, whom he married the following year.[6] A fine piece of historical research, it collects under one cover a large amount of disparate material and presents it in a lively and readable style. The principal argument of their book is (in what now seems an astonishing claim) that despite our knowing all that was necessary about nutrition, the problem remains of how to give those whose health is adversely affected by faulty nutrition the essential knowledge and the appropriate food. This was an urgent problem among the poorest section of the community. Some of the science is now outmoded, some issues such as the contemporary concerns about cholesterol and trans fats are virtually ignored, and some of the historical statistics are questionable, but the book has survived remarkably well. Its relevance is scarcely diminished.[7] Drummond published a more specialized monograph, titled *Biochemical Studies of Nutritional Problems* (1934), in which he integrated biochemical research from his own and other laboratories with medical, social, and historical observations in a lively and readable manner.

Shortly after the outbreak of war Drummond was appointed chief adviser on food contamination to the Ministry of Food with the responsibility of examining the effects of poison gas on food. This work necessitated visits to the Porton Down Experimental Station to conduct experiments on decontamination and on standards of fitness for foods that had been exposed to poison gas. His findings were published by the Ministry of Food in 1940.[8]

Drummond was now somewhat in limbo. University College had moved to Wales, and he had been informed that his services would no longer be needed although he remained on the payroll. He was thus unable to do much scientific work, and his duties at the ministry had been fulfilled. In January 1940 the Parliamentary and Scientific Committee called upon his expertise to examine the question of wartime bread, a subject that had been suggested by his friend Dr. J. Vargas Eyre. The various ministries concerned were asked to send their scientific advisers, but the Ministry of Food had no such appointment. Drummond therefore addressed the committee in a private capacity. He made an urgent plea for whole-wheat bread and flour to be made readily available, particularly to the poor, and although he was certainly no vegetarian, he stressed that fresh vegetables and dairy produce were far more important than meat. The flour millers were soon up in arms against this proposal, arguing that the 25 percent taken from wheat for the production of white flour was an essential animal foodstuff. Drummond countered by pointing out that a smaller amount of wheat was needed to produce whole-wheat flour and that there were alternative forms of fodder.

On the same day that the committee met, on 31 January, Drummond submitted a memorandum to the Ministry of Food on wartime nutrition. His main suggestions were that bread should be of the highest possible nutritional value; that the consumption of potatoes, oatmeal, cheese, and green vegetables should be increased; and that expectant and nursing mothers, as well as children up to the age of fifteen, should be given at least a pint of milk per day. Margarine should be fortified by the addition of vitamins A and D. Meat shortages could be offset by increasing the consumption of cheese and fish.

The next day Drummond was officially appointed scientific adviser to the Ministry of Food. He had sufficient experience working in the laboratory, and his historical studies gave him the necessary background and perspective. His ability to communicate and to get on well with all sorts of people, combined with his energy, enthusiasm, and approachable manner, made him ideally suited to the post. He found himself in a somewhat tricky position, however: nutrition was the responsibility of the Ministry of Health, whereas the Ministry of Food was responsible for seeing that its recommendations were put into effect, and the Medical Research Council offered specialized advice. Drummond was thus in danger of not having a clear mandate. Furthermore, he was sharply critical of the medical profession for failing to take due account of the scientific basis of nutrition. But he had in Lord Horder—the king's physician and a pillar of the medical establishment—a powerful ally in that he was also a keen laboratory scientist with an interest in both nutrition and the social issues of health.

Drummond helped overcome a number of problems as a member of the Standing Interdepartmental Committee, established in 1941, where his easygoing charm and down-to-earth approach was greatly appreciated. The Ministry of Food was a relatively new institution, founded by Lloyd George's government in 1916, and did not carry much weight; but this changed when Neville Chamberlain appointed Lord Woolton minister in April 1940. He was a "nonparty" man of conservative leaning. His background was in the retail trade; his approach, practical. Realizing the importance of advertising and propaganda, he and his ministry soon became immensely popular. He even managed to sell the idea of a tedious concoction known as "Woolton Pie"—carrots, parsnips, potatoes, and turnips mixed with oatmeal and covered with a pastry or potato crust and served with brown gravy—to the hungry British public.

In 1940 the Lord Privy Seal Kingsley Wood, in his capacity as chairman of the War Cabinet's Committee on Food Policy, established a Scientific Food Policy Committee to determine guidelines on the minimal diet required to maintain national health during the war.[9] This involved addressing a host of problems, including the availability of supplies from both home and abroad, transportation, foreign exchange, and other complex economic issues. Dietary concerns—such as the nutritional value of various foodstuffs, supplies of fats and oil, minimal protein and vitamin requirements, and the use of dried milk and powdered eggs—all had to be addressed. Drummond played an important role in the committee, although it is not possible to say precisely what his contributions were to its deliberations.

His major involvement in the ongoing debate was to insist that reducing total food consumption would be a grave mistake and would necessarily lead to overall efficiency reductions, which had proved the case during the First World War. He was able to ensure that bread and potatoes remained off the ration plan throughout the war.[10] This was only possible because white bread was not produced until the war was over, only to be rationed in June 1946, and because the ministry grossly overestimated its requirements.

Drummond pointed out that before the war the nation's food supply was adequate for energy-rich foods but had been deficient in calcium, vitamin A, and vitamin B. It was estimated that in 1940–41 home production could cover one-third of energy requirements, two-thirds of the need for calcium, one-third of the necessary vitamin A, two-fifths of vitamin B1, and, thanks to increased potato production, all the vitamin C. He suggested increasing vitamin B1 by increasing the extraction rate of flour, or by fortifying white flour with the synthetic vitamin. He also called for increasing the importation of cheese, dried or condensed milk, pulses, canned fish, and the vitamin A and D concentrates needed to fortify margarine. The importation of fruits, other than oranges, should be reduced, because they used up valuable shipping space that could be used for essential foodstuffs that could not be produced at home. He singled out nuts in the shell and dates as being particularly uneconomical.

In September 1941 Drummond wrote a memorandum on the nutritional effects of two years of war. He pointed to an overall loss of weight in the winter of 1940–41 that could only be offset by an increase in home production. His insistence that people should grow as much food of their own as possible was the inspiration for an enormously successful "Dig for Victory" campaign, which encouraged people to turn their lawns and flower beds into vegetable gardens and to cultivate allotments. This campaign was supported by the pedagogically inclined cartoon figures Doctor Carrot and Potato Pete, who preached the nutritional value of vegetables that were in plentiful supply but were generally considered to be dreadfully bland.

Drummond's calculations were based on the generous requirement of twenty-nine hundred calories per person for a Spartan diet on a scale of "Spartan," "subsistence," "adequate," and "substantial," the last of which he defined as being higher than the prewar average. He overestimated the need for imports, for the British would have been adequately fed on supplies required for a Spartan diet; but if he erred on the side of generosity, he had his priorities right. He may have been lost in the details, but he had an intuitive grasp of the wider principles. He realized the importance of balanced meals in schools, in canteens, and in the hugely successful "British Restaurants," which were established by the Ministry of Food but run as nonprofit communal organizations by local authorities to provide excellent ration-free meals for the modest price of nine pence.[11] Levels were set for adding vitamins to margarine and orange juice, and a mound of useful information was distributed on the nutritional requirements under wartime conditions for all sections of society from babies to the aged. Drummond was particularly concerned with providing nutritional supplements such as cod liver oil, black current and rose hip syrup, and vitamin tablets to expectant and nursing mothers and their children. When milk was rationed, priorities were set that targeted vulnerable groups. He also chaired the People's League of Health, which produced a number of clearly written and practical pamphlets on nutrition that were widely distributed.

His greatest achievement, which won the Ministry of Food few friends, was the creation of the "national loaf," based on flour of 85 percent extraction, in the spring of 1942. This bread replaced the much-loved but vitamin-deficient white loaf of 70–75 percent extraction. In this effort he was ably assisted by Dr. T. Moran, the director of the Flour Millers' Research Association, who had been seconded to the ministry in June 1940. The headline of an obituary for Jack Drummond in the *Evening News* read, "He Gave Us the Wartime Loaf." It is doubtful whether many readers were particularly grateful.

The combined efforts of the various ministries and organizations resulted in a marked improvement in public health despite all the wartime shortages. This remarkable achievement was recognized by the American Public Health Association in 1947, when it awarded the Lasker Group Award to the Ministries of Food and Health for their outstanding efforts to improve the people's health. It was an effort in which Sir Jack played a key role. The citation pointed out that despite a host of adverse environmental factors, public health was not only maintained but also improved in many areas. Rates of infantile, neonatal, and maternal mortality and stillbirths reached the lowest levels ever. The incidence of anemia and dental cavities declined, the rate of growth of schoolchildren improved, tuberculosis was brought under control, and overall nutritional standards were higher than before the war. The Lasker Foundation's Award Committee singled out "four great leaders in this historic enterprise" for special praise: Lord Woolton, Sir Jack Drummond, Sir Wilson Jameson, and Sir John Boyd Orr.[12]

Drummond did a certain amount of traveling during the war. His most hazardous trip was to Malta in May 1942 to help solve the serious nutritional problems of the island, which was under siege and suffered continuous bombing.[13] He went to the United States on several occasions to supervise food supplies that were sent under the Lend-Lease Act. As a result Great Britain imported dried milk in 1941, and dried eggs came from California and Wisconsin in the following year. There was initially a problem of salmonella in dried eggs, but it was soon overcome. He was a delegate to the Hot Springs Conference in June 1943, which led to the formation of the United Nations Food and Agriculture Organization. Its chairman, the distinguished physiologist and professor André Mayer from the Collège de France, said in an address to the organization: "Monsieur Drummond, vous anglais, vous faites toujours des révolutions avec tant d'élégance!" (You English, your revolutions are always so elegant!)

After the D-Day landings, Drummond was appointed adviser on nutrition to the Supreme Headquarters Allied Expeditionary Force and to the Allied Post-War Requirements Bureau. He also chaired a special committee on nutrition established by the Council of British Societies for Relief Abroad that produced a manual for the use of relief workers.[14] In October and November 1944 he was responsible for food distribution in France and Belgium. In February 1945 he was appointed chairman of a special commission of doctors and scientists who were to address the needs of the malnourished and starving in Holland. In May, dressed in a Home Guard uniform and under a flag of truce, he was permitted to pass through the German lines. He was then appointed adviser on nutrition to the Allied Control Commissions for Germany and Austria and served in this capacity until 1946. His major contribution during this tour of duty was to devise special foods for former concentration camp inmates, who were so chronically undernourished that they were unable to digest normal solid foods.

Despite Drummond's heavy wartime schedule, he continued to lecture on nutritional subjects in his capacity as the Fullerian Professor of Physiology in the Royal Institution from 1941 to 1944. In 1944 he was appointed chairman of King Edward's Hospital Fund, and that work led to the publication of two important memoranda on hospital diet, a topic that had been sadly neglected. His life's work was acknowledged in 1944 with a knighthood and his election to the Royal Society. He was also awarded the U.S. Medal of Freedom with silver palms and in 1946 was elected an honorary member of the New York Academy of Sciences. The Dutch government made him a commander of the Order of Orange-Nassau, and the University of Paris awarded him an honorary doctorate. In 1945 he resigned his professorship at University College, London, and accepted the position of director of research at the Boots Pure Drug Company in Nottingham. Meanwhile, he was still seconded to the Ministry of Food to continue his work on the Control Commissions until 1946. Two years later he was elected to the board of Boots.

Some were surprised that Drummond left academia for industry, but he had always been more interested in the practical application of scientific ideas than in pure research. During his time at the Ministry of Food, he had shown exceptional ability as a team player and committeeman. He could grasp any given problem as a whole and stick to the principles rather than getting bogged down in petty details. Above all he enjoyed the wide range of opportunities open to him, in contrast to the restricted environment of the laboratory. In his new position at Boots, he saw an opportunity to bridge the gap between academic and industrial research. He could now fully use his ability to mix easily with all sorts of different people. As his close friend Professor G. F. Marrian from Edinburgh University said, an additional attraction was that he had been frustrated by lack of funds for research before the war, and Boots offered him generous support. A handsome annual salary of £4,000 ($16,000), which greatly exceeded the top of the academic scale, was doubtless an added attraction. Its Research Department had a staff of seventy scientists and was divided into six divisions: chemistry, pharmacology, bacteriology, biochemistry, horticultural and agriculture science, and veterinary science. Drummond paid particular attention to the expansion of the company's veterinary research department at Thurgarton, an estate with a thousand acres of farmland. The company also had two other experimental farms in Scotland.

While Drummond was a founding member and chairman of the Fine Chemicals Group of the Society of Chemical Industry, he abandoned his own research and ceased to publish any serious papers. This is also far from surprising. He was in no sense an outstandingly original scientist and made no further significant additions to scientific knowledge. He worked through others and had a direct influence on events. He was interested in the practical application of scientific research and was an effective popularizer and communicator of scientific ideas who furthered the careers of many who worked under him. His major achievement was that he seized the opportunity offered during exceptional wartime conditions to have a genuinely scientific approach to nutritional problems adopted on a national scale.

Drummond became greatly interested in the development of anti-biotics and the treatment of tropical diseases. His successor at Boots, Dr. Gordon Hobday, complained bitterly that he was too much of a philanthropist who paid immoderate attention to drugs for combating tropical diseases, where there was no money to be made. As Stanley Chapman sourly wrote in his biography of Jesse Boot, after Drummond's death, "the research programme veered over towards research projects with a more reassuring market potential. The emphasis shifted towards the search for drugs to alleviate what have been called 'diseases of civilisation'—rheumatism, peptic ulceration, cardio-vascular diseases and (very recently) mental disorders."[15] Boots, anxious not to be seen as unmoved by the brutal murder of this idealist who paid scant regard to the balance sheets, sent a contribution of £7,000 ($28,000) to a fund that established a professorship in his memory.

Under Drummond's stewardship, the major achievements of the Research Department in the early years included the discovery of Turke-san, an effective drug for the treatment of a disease in turkeys known as blackhead, and Cornox, a selective weed killer that was particularly effective against docks, thistles, and poppies. Cornox, originally known as 2,4-DP (Dichlorprop), was in fact a patent pinched from the German firm Schering AG in 1945. A German murderer had used this weed killer to considerable effect. Sir Jack also supervised the building of an expanded bacteriological and pharmacological research laboratory at the company's Beeston headquarters.[16] This expansion was greatly hindered by the building restrictions imposed by the government's austerity program.

Having moved to Nottingham, Drummond played an active part in public life, serving on the Regional Advisory Council for Further Education and the British Empire Cancer Campaign. As an enthusiastic first-nighter, he also was a director of the Nottingham Playhouse. He was a youthful, warm, and cheerful man who thoroughly enjoyed the good things in life. He had a love of good food and wine, and was an early member of André Simon's Wine and Food Society. He traveled widely and intelligently. Always anxious to please, he was easily approachable, although with his characteristic British reticence it was hard to develop any intimacy with him. He could be outspoken and even brusque; his humor was sometimes tinged with cynicism. The distinguished physiologist C. Lovatt Evans said that with his "steely inflexibility of purpose," Drummond "could be devastating towards incompetence and astringent to fools."[17] But he seldom displayed this side of his character and was widely popular, living his many-faceted life to the fullest.

He left an estate of £6,680 ($26,720). After the deduction of punitive death duties and the payment of outstanding debts, this left a mere £2,762 ($11,048).[18] These figures were published in *Le Parisien Libéré* and *Combat*.[19] The French police were anxious to know who the beneficiary of the will was. Sûreté Nationale wrote to the CID, saying that "the conditions of the succession is [*sic*] likely to put the investigation onto a new track." This proved to be an overly optimistic assessment. All the money went to Sir Jack's first wife, Mabel, because she had not remarried. The CID replied to Sûreté that Sir Jack's solicitors said that the will was perfectly normal and did not think "that the circumstances of the will opened up any new line of enquiry into the murder of Sir Jack Drummond and his family."[20]

GASTON DOMINICI

Gaston's mother, Clémence Rosalie Dominici, was the daughter of hardworking immigrants from Calabria, who owned an olive oil mill just outside Digne, the departmental capital of the Basses-Alpes.[21] She was a temperamental young woman who was barely able to speak French, communicating in a mixture of broken Italian and Provençal patois. After a series of scrapes and confrontations, she was thrown out of the house. She worked as a maid for a printer and bookbinder in the town. At the age of twenty she found herself pregnant and uncertain who was the father, although she claimed to be almost certain that it was her employer.

Having been unable to procure an abortion, Clémence's child was born at seven o'clock in the morning on 22 January 1877 in her small bedroom in la rue Montée-des-Prisons. The window looked out across the street at the bleak walls of the Saint-Charles prison. It was snowing lightly. Clémence decided to hand the child over to public assistance. The midwife, Mademoiselle Philippine Guichard, took the newborn child home and in the afternoon of the following day took the infant to the town hall, which was conveniently situated close by. The mayor's deputy was at a loss as what to do with a tiny, nameless, and fatherless child who had been rejected by his mother until Philippine suggested that she could try to persuade Clémence to change her mind.

Her efforts were successful. On 29 January, one week after the birth, Clémence Dominici went to the town hall and acknowledged her son, whom she named Gaston. It was an inauspicious beginning. Digne was a closed, intolerant society, a hive of petit-bourgeois respectability that was intolerant toward outsiders. It is a drab little town, hemmed in by grim mountains. The main street, the Cours Gassendi, is named after a local seventeenth-century priest, philosopher, and scientist who is best known for having given the aurora borealis its name. The thoroughfare lacks distinction and is as unmemorable as the lunar crater named after the genius. It comes as neither a shock nor a surprise that the prison occupies the commanding position in the town. Digne's other distinguished inhabitant was Alexandra David-Néel, explorer, occultist, anarchist, and Buddhist, who became a guru to the Beat Generation. She chose to settle in Digne because it reminded her of Lhasa, Tibet, which she had visited in 1924 when foreigners were forbidden entry. Digne's only delight is an abandoned, glorious Romanesque church slightly outside the town that is surrounded by masons' yards.

Digne's latest inhabitant was to become every bit as well known as Gassendi and David-Néel, but none could have foretold how or why. Here was a little bastard of Italian descent, who grew up to be resentful, aggressive, and emotionally deprived. Gaston was admitted to a monastic school but was soon expelled for cocking a snook at one of the brothers. His mother was soon pregnant again and lost whatever interest she ever had in her fatherless boy. Dressed in rags and seldom washed, he roamed the streets and the surrounding hillsides. When Clémence became pregnant for the third time, she decided to abandon him to the municipal authorities. His younger brother Léon soon followed him into their tender care. Clémence died in 1895, thirteen days after giving birth to her eighth illegitimate child.

On 15 November 1898 Gaston was called up for military service and was posted to the Seventh Cuirassiers in Lyon. By then he had received a rudimentary education that left him barely able to read and write. Since he never learned to speak French properly, he was reduced to speaking a local dialect. For the previous few years he had worked as an agricultural laborer for small farms near Digne. The army licked this undisciplined and rebellious Provençal into some sort of shape, and he finished his three years' service with a certificate of good conduct and with a torso covered with tattoos of naked women. He returned to civilian life in December 1901, a grown man who was answerable to no one and determined to go his own way. He was a handsome, well-built, hardworking lad who was fond of the girls and drank an average of three quarts of wine a day, with a few shots of marc to settle the digestion. He also had a quick temper and was ever ready to pick a fight.

He worked as a shepherd at the tiny hamlet of Entrevennes. Across the valley of the Asse lay the village of Brunet. With four cafés, a modest boardinghouse, and two dances every weekend, it was the liveliest spot in this remote part of Provence. Gaston would go there every weekend, but the other young men were careful to avoid this quarrelsome, hard-drinking primitive. They preferred to dance to a mechanical piano, while Gaston played cards with the older men in one of the cafés and downed vast quantities of the local rouge. One of these cafés was owned by a man named Maillet, who quite by chance was to follow Gaston as he moved and whose son was to play an important part in the Drummond murder drama.

Among the families living at Brunet was that of Germain. The father of two daughters, Marie and Rose, was a highly respected tenant farmer. He kept a close eye on the two young girls, who hardly left the house except to go to Mass every Sunday. Gaston, whom Monsieur Bec at Entrevennes had fired after tiring of his explosive nature, was now working as a shepherd at a nearby farm at Angelvin. He had been joined by a friend from Digne, soon to be known locally as "Little Sequin." The two went out on the prowl and soon spotted the Germain sisters. But they were now faced with an intractable problem. How could they get to know them? A casual flirtation was out of the question. Marriage was the only solution, and it was one that appealed to Gaston. His eye had fallen on Marie, quite a pretty little thing who was known to be hardworking and conscientious, and her father was not totally without means. Gaston, who had no intention of being a mere shepherd for the rest of his life, saw the match as an opportunity for social advancement.

Father Germain rejected his daughter's suitor out of hand. There could be no question of his little Marie marrying an Italian bastard without a bean, who was known in the village as a pugnacious outsider. Gaston pleaded but all in vain. It was suggested to him that if he saved up a little money he might have a better chance. To this end he began to steal sheep from his employer, but he was soon found out and once again shown the door. He was now without a job, and it was unthinkable that he would ever be able to marry Marie.

Then in August 1903 Germain suddenly announced that he would consent to the marriage. Gaston was so sure of himself that he attributed this remarkable change of attitude to his persistence rather than to any suspicious circumstances. On 3 October that year the mayor of Brunet joined together in marriage Gaston Dominici, a twenty-six-year old farm laborer, and Marie Germain, born in Les Mées on 28 July 1879. This bizarre union was witnessed by Marie's cousin Norbert and the village baker. The groom's witnesses were a local farm laborer and a retired policeman.

It did not take long for the truth to be revealed. On their wedding night Marie admitted that she was three months pregnant. A drunken Gaston flew into a towering rage and beat her mercilessly, then wept for hours in an orgy of self-pity. He never forgave her for this deception. For the fifty years they stayed together, he treated her with spiteful contempt and brutal hatred. His smoldering fury terrified not only Marie but also the Germains. They thought it prudent to employ Gaston for their common safety.

Marie's child, Ida-Agnès-Marie, was born on 19 April 1904.[22] On 25 June the following year she was joined by Clovis-Antoine-Justin. Augusta-Adrienne-Joséphine was born on 5 March 1907 and Gaston-Marie-Adrien on 25 February 1909. The simple shepherd was unable to provide for this rapidly expanding brood, which only kept going thanks to the generosity of the Germains. Gaston showed not the slightest gratitude to his parents-in-law. He continued to steal their lambs, using the money to rent a two-room apartment in the village. There he could maintain a semblance of independence and rule the roost as a caricature of a young patriarch.

Gaston's friend Seguin married Marie's sister Rose and soon grew to despise his brother-in-law. As a result, when the Germains died, there was a fierce dispute over the inheritance. Also at this time a farm at Ganagobie was available for lease from Benoît Estrangin, a nephew of one of the last monks, who had begun restoring the monastery. It was here in May 1910 that Gaston decided to try his luck as an independent farmer.

The plateau of Ganagobie, situated between the villages of Lurs and Peyruis, rises 2,132 feet above the Durance River. A Christian community was established here in the fourth century, but it soon vanished. Then in the tenth century the land came under the control of Cluny Abbey. The Benedictines remained there intermittently until the community was dissolved during the French Revolution. The beautiful Romanesque church was partly demolished and the stones used as building material. In 1891 a wealthy benefactor gave the land back to the Benedictines, and one or two monks lived there in seclusion. As a result of extreme anticlerical measures of Pierre Waldeck-Rousseau's government, and completed by that of Émile Combes, the Benedictines were expelled from France but returned in 1922 when a single monk lived among the ruins. The plateau was virtually inaccessible, and it was not until 1953 that work began to build an asphalt road up to the monastery.

The farmhouse was a wretched stone building with an outside staircase. The land was infertile and wooded, but at least it was full of wild boars and hares with which Gaston, who was soon to become an expert poacher, could feed his rapidly expanding family. It would clearly take a considerable time and an inordinate amount of hard work to make a living out of this deserted spot. But at last he was his own master, with his own herd of sheep and a burning ambition to show the world that this Calabrian outcast was indeed a somebody.

He might have hated his wife, but at least she offered relief for his exigent libido. Another daughter, Clotilde, was born on 17 June 1911, followed by Marcel on 6 April 1913, and Germaine on 30 April 1915. Gaston acted as midwife in all three cases. He had no choice. He did not have a telephone, and it would have taken several hours to reach a midwife or a doctor at Peyruis. He also practiced naturopathy, claiming to have cured his sciatica with rye infusions, and every morning he drank a concoction of rosemary mixed with white wine. This appeared to have been effective, for it was said that a doctor never visited the Dominicis. Gaston purchased a copy of *Le Grand Albert*, the work of the thirteenth-century Dominican Albert von Bollstädt. It was a compilation of magic spells and ancient remedies and represented for Gaston a canonical text.[23] Because he had such a large family he was exempted from military service during the First World War. This privilege was the subject of certain underhanded remarks on market day that, in turn, provoked Gaston to outbreaks of uncontrolled rage. He was a difficult man with violent likes and dislikes. He was a passionate republican, but he had an obsession for the emperor Napoleon. He flatly refused to sell his fruits and vegetables to Yvan Jaillans, an innkeeper and greengrocer in Peyruis, whom he considered to be a reactionary.

Although in no sense religious, Gaston was devoted to Joan of Arc, who was canonized in 1920. He presented a statue of the newly minted saint to the chapel at Ganagobie. When on death row in Marseille, he announced that he would never be guillotined. He would be burned like Saint Joan or crucified like Jesus Christ.

At his trial Mayor Estoublon of Lurs summed up Gaston's character succinctly, saying that he was a man who lived on society's margins. He was an uncommunicative, inward-looking, domestic tyrant who brooked no contradiction. He exploited his children and treated his unfortunate wife with undisguised contempt, referring to her as "the sardine" or "that old bitch." Tightfisted and mean spirited, he had a peasant's cunning and suspiciousness, but he worked extremely hard and even in very strained circumstances managed to feed his nine children. He was very hard on others but unsparing of himself as well.

An opportunity arose in 1915 when another tenant farm belonging to the priory, known as La Serre, became vacant. It was along the Durance valley in the direction of Peyruis at a spot known as Pont Bernard. Its soil was far richer than that of the rocky plateau of Ganagobie.

No work was available for the Dominici girls, apart from helping their mother with the housework and making cheese. Gaston tended his flock. Young Gaston and Clovis cultivated their patch of rich alluvial soil on the banks of the Durance. But there was soon nothing more to be gained from this property, and it was clearly time to move on. In 1917 Gaston tried to buy a farm from a Madame Blanc, but she was unable to do anything without the permission of her son. Gaston played many a mean trick upon the unfortunate woman in an attempt to make her change her mind but to no avail. The birth of yet another child, Gustave, in 1919 made it imperative to find some more fertile land.

The family was sealed off from the outside world until one by one the children left home to make their own lives. Meanwhile, they received an elementary education at a tiny school at Ganagobie run by Madame Muzy. She lived in Peyruis and picked up the children on her way. She left her bicycle at the Heyriès' house near La Serre, where Gustave and Aimé Dominici would be waiting along with the two Heyriès boys. At the school they were joined by Paul and Pierre Maillet, whose father, Auguste, had moved the family from Brunet and was now the tenant of the priory farm at Ganagobie. The children were a wild bunch with no interest at all in learning. They were filthy. Their hair was tousled, and they were dressed in such rags that whenever a tourist passed by the ashamed Madame Muzy hid them from sight. The most that could be said of their parents was that at least the children had something to eat. Madame Muzy passed La Serre every day for years, but come rain, come shine, the family never invited her to enter. When there was extra work to do, the children stayed home, and poor Madame Muzy sat sobbing in her empty classroom. She left Ganagobie with great relief, having failed to teach her charges anything. They then went to school in Lurs, where the rudiments of an education were drilled into them.

The Dominici children often slept on bales of straw rather than in their beds. They were roused very early and made to feed the animals. Gaston was unrelentingly strict with them, so they lived in a state of terrified obedience combined with a grudging sense of admiration and fear that was tempered by a growing resentment. All of this eventually served to make the family seriously dysfunctional. As his sons grew old enough to work, Gaston became increasingly idle, and now that he at last had his own vines, his intake of wine reached truly staggering proportions. He still skimped and saved, however, and in 1922 he was able to buy a farm close to La Serre for a derisory 10,000 francs ($820). This new property, with a ruined house and the land covered with undergrowth, was known as the Grand' Terre. Gaston gradually renovated the farmhouse and tilled the soil. The Dominicis eventually moved from La Serre in 1931.

Two incidents occurred during the Dominicis' time at La Serre that showed different aspects of Gaston's character, and both the prosecution and the defense used them during his trial. In 1923 he was involved in the arrest of a dangerous criminal. He was tending his flock when the man suddenly appeared. Gaston, who had already heard that there was an armed man on the run, had his gun at the ready. The bandit drew his revolver and fired. The bullet hit the barrel of Dominici's gun. When the revolver jammed, Dominici leaped upon his assailant. A fight ensued, but the gendarmes soon arrived and took the man into custody. Gaston was awarded a certificate acknowledging his bravery, and the local gendarmerie was always afforded a warm welcome at his farm.

The other incident was less creditable. Every year at Whitsun (Pentecost) there was a pilgrimage to the priory at Ganagobie to honor a vow made to Saint Roch when the plague struck Peyruis in 1720. After Mass the people held a picnic during which the wine flowed freely. On one such occasion Gaston picked a fight with his successor at the Ganagobie farm. Blows were exchanged. His opponent, Giraud, was flat on his back when Gaston suddenly seized an ax that was implanted in a chopping block. Giraud scrambled to his feet, rushed into the farmhouse, and bolted the door. Gaston hammered on the door and windows, yelled all manner of oaths and obscenities, and was clearly completely out of control. The crowd looked on in startled amazement. Father Lorenzi, the lone Dominican at Ganagobie, managed to calm him down. The festival continued, but Gaston's murderous rage was not forgotten.

In most instances Gaston's violence was domestic. He was an extremely heavy drinker, and it was widely known that when he began to babble or start humming, it was wise not to contradict or annoy him. Poor Marie, as noted previously, was a frequent butt of his drunken outbursts.

Situated on the banks of the Durance at the foot of the hill of Ganagobie, the Grand' Terre had once belonged to the baker at Lurs named Louis Arniaud. His family lived in the farmhouse until 1903. They left because they preferred the security of the village to living in extreme isolation, miles from anywhere. They sold the farm to Monsieur Conil from Peyruis, who tended it well for many long years until he decided to sell it to Father Lorenzi at Ganagobie for 9,000 francs ($735). Gaston offered an extra 1,000 francs ($82), and Conil accepted. The mild-mannered Father Lorenzi never complained about being outwitted.

It was a smallholding, consisting of a mere fifteen acres strung along the riverbank in a narrow strip. Only eight acres were eventually cultivated. With rich alluvial soil, it was some of the best land in the Basses-Alpes, but it was still only enough to scratch a bare living. Gaston grew wheat, potatoes, beetroot, grapes, olives, and fruit. He grazed his goats on the uncultivated land.

Gaston, now aged fifty-four, was at last the owner of his own farm after years of hard work and sacrifice. Although on the threshold of old age and despite a habit of now drinking at least a gallon of his own red wine every day, he was still healthy and strong. But he still faced a serious problem: his sons began to leave him. It was of no concern to him when one of his daughters left the family home. Women were superfluous. After all, the Sardine could do all the housework, and the rest were simply useless mouths to feed. They were obliged to serve the men at the table and to eat standing up. The men, however, were another matter. They could relieve him of the burden of work so that he could enjoy a well-deserved rest after years of toil.

Clovis was the first son to leave. He was the one who most resembled his father. He was strong, hardworking, stubborn, and quick tempered. Gaston hoped to leave the Grand' Terre to him. Clovis first left home in 1924 to do his military service in the light infantry. When on leave he worked hard on the farm. When it was over, his father accompanied him to the railway station at Peyruis. He was proud of his son in his colorful uniform, but when Clovis finished his military service, Gaston received a severe shock. Clovis announced he was leaving the farm. He had taken advantage of the fact that the national railway company, SNCF, had fired many men after a recent acrimonious strike and took a job there. Gaston was bitter and unable to understand why Clovis was so naive and immature as to want to work for others rather than being his own man; but all was not lost. There were still Marcel, Gustave, and Aimé to follow in his footsteps. Although Clovis lived only about four miles away at Peyruis, he decided to break away completely and did not go home for six years.

As the self-important owner of the Grand' Terre, Gaston became more open and hospitable, welcoming passersby to taste his wine, of which he was inordinately proud, and to sample his cheese. At Christmas he hosted a vast family reunion. A sheep was slaughtered and roasted on a spit in front of an open fire, and the wine flowed while Gaston sang songs and recounted tales from long ago. But Gaston had not suddenly been transformed into a benign patriarch. His newfound generosity was his form of boasting. He still exaggerated his achievements, held court at insufferable length, and was given to outbursts of meanness and uncontrollable fury.

The Maillets were frequent visitors to the Grand' Terre even though Gaston took great delight in deriding them. Maillet had once been the proud owner of a café in Brunet at a time when Gaston barely had enough money for a glass of wine. Now Maillet had taken over the farm at Ganagobie, where Gaston had lived before moving to La Serre, and was considerably poorer. The Maillets had fallen on hard times, with both the father and the eldest son having had severe bouts of brucellosis, a singularly debilitating disease. Auguste Maillet was already a trifle senile, or *fada*, as one says in Provençal. His two sons no longer worked on the farm. Paul, like Clovis Dominici, worked for the SNCF, and Pierre was an apprentice mechanic in Manosque. The family was just about able to keep their heads above water, while the Dominicis, by comparison, were marginally better off. Boasting that he had made enough money out of the Ganagobie farm to become a property owner, Gaston attributed the Maillets' straitened circumstances to indolence.

It was Paul Mallet, however, who persuaded his friend and workmate Clovis to visit his parents. Paul first had to convince Gaston to allow the prodigal son to return, and he was fortunate to find him in a begrudgingly generous mood. Gaston gave his testy consent. Clovis duly went on this difficult errand, accompanied by his wife, Rose—a levelheaded and punctilious woman—and their baby boy, Gilbert. The visit went well. Clovis and his family were welcomed back and were henceforth included in all the festivities. Gaston, although constantly complaining about his son, had a certain admiration for his singleness of purpose and determination to go his own way.

Gaston might have mellowed a little, but he had not changed into a human *santon*, or small "figurine," much beloved in Provence, in traditional dress and used to decorate elaborate nativity scenes. Indeed, he remained an appalling egoist, harbored a host of grudges, terrorized those around him, and could not control his temper. Marcel was the next son to leave the family home. On 13 April 1939 he married a widow who was fifteen years older and moved to a farm at Notre-Dame-des-Anges, a place of pilgrimage at the base of the hill on which the village of Lurs is perched. His brothers Gustave and Aimé tilled their father's soil, while Gaston simply tended his sheep. He gradually sold them off until he was left with a few goats, which are far less demanding animals.

Berthe, Gaston's half-sister, who was married to Cyrille Léotard, the postman at Lurs, was the person who was closest to him at this time. Their mother had died when she was very young, so she had spent her childhood in an orphanage. She worked as a maid from the age of sixteen and did not meet her brother until 1907. By a series of coincidences she ended up in Lurs, where every day she took the post to the railway station that was only 500 yards from the Grand' Terre. On the way she brought her brother the newspaper. More often than not Gaston was off working. Marie used to sit silently in the kitchen, refusing to acknowledge her sister-in-law. When he was at home he was often yelling at Gustave and Aimé, whom he regarded as incorrigibly idle. Frustrated at his attempts to get them to bend to his will, he would stomp off down into his cellar and drink heavily.

When Cyrille died, Berthe went to live in a tiny apartment in Forcalquier and gradually lost contact with the family. When her nephews and nieces got married, they did not bother to inform her, and the Grand' Terre was too far from Forcalquier for her to visit. Gaston sometimes went to the market at Forcalquier and would usually visit his sister, who would cook him a meal, but they were no longer particularly close. Berthe was careful to keep out of the public eye during the murder scandal. Of her five children, one died in childhood, and one was killed in July 1940 when the British destroyed the French fleet at Mers-el-Kébir. The three surviving children all found good jobs in Paris.

Gaston's half-brother Léon lived near Manosque. He had two sons, and the elder one, named after his father, was particularly close to his uncle Gaston. Young Léon, even though he seldom visited the Grand' Terre, managed to convince himself that his uncle Gaston was a kind of substitute father when Léon senior died, having fallen off a ladder when the boy was fourteen. He later used his questionable skills as a journalist to mount a campaign that proclaimed Gaston innocent of all charges, but his efforts were so riddled with contradictions and distortions that they were mostly dismissed as dismal efforts at self-promotion.

As Gaston grew older his alcohol intake increased to an average of 1.6 gallons per day. He took great pleasure in torturing his wife. He would eat alone, waited upon by his wretched wife or one of his daughters. If he did not like a particular dish, he would throw it at whoever had the misfortune to serve him. In 1939 Gustave was twenty years old and had passed the recruitment board. Aimé was seventeen. Neither were paid for the hard work they did on the Grand' Terre, but they picked up a few francs by doing odd jobs for their neighbors. They would spend their hard-earned money on the weekends in Lurs, where films were shown and dances were held in the Café Bonnet.

Gustave, like his father, liked to pick a fight. He found ample opportunity to test his skills during the dances, where the rivalries and jealousies of young men frequently exploded into unruly brawls. At one of these dances Gustave's roving eye fell upon a sixteen-year-old girl, Léone Roche. She responded to his advances, and they decided to get engaged. Her parents, who farmed nearby, had no objections. Gaston, knowing that the Roches had a bit of money, gave his consent. All looked well for the young couple, but Gustave had appendicitis and was whisked off for an operation in Forcalquier. While in the hospital he met a young woman from Marseille who made him forget Léone. Next there was the grocer's daughter from Brillane. His amorous adventures were rudely interrupted by call-up papers. He was posted to the Nineteenth Artillery Regiment, stationed in Draguignan, but the armistice was signed before he saw any action.

Now the old man looked after his goats and helped himself to wine, olive oil, and potatoes. Gustave was responsible for selling all the produce and for paying the taxes. He bitterly complained that he did all the work but received little recompense. Relations between father and son became increasingly strained. Gustave never had the strength of will to escape his father's domination and grew ever more bitter and resentful.

7 Gaston Dominici Awaits His Trial

On his return to Digne 16 November, Gaston was incarcerated in the Saint-Charles prison across the street from his birthplace. He was allowed to have as much of his wine as he wished, but his request to have his dog stay with him was denied. He offered his hand to the policeman who led him to his cell, but it was refused. In amazement he muttered: "Why refuse to shake hands? I am going to Elba!"[1] On the following day his legal team assembled, clearly indicating that it was already in place and ready to act. Unfortunately Émile Pollak was involved in a serious motor accident one week later that put him out of action for a while and left him less energetic than he might otherwise have been.

Back at the Grand' Terre the Dominici clan was divided into two factions. Clovis and his sister Germaine Perrin stood up for Zézé, while the rest of the family, under the histrionic leadership of Yvette, united against Clovis for his denunciation of Gaston and accused young Zézé of being a deceitful little liar. The weak-willed Gustave, shattered by his father's harsh accusations, submitted meekly to his wife's direction. He told any journalist willing to listen that one day the truth would come out, and everyone would be amazed.[2] He continued to repeat this remark until his death in 1996. His prophecy was never fulfilled.

Examining Magistrate Roger Périès took a few days' holiday on the Côte d'Azur before scrutinizing the dossier to decide whether the case should be forwarded to the court of appeal in Aix-en-Provence, where it would be examined by the prosecutor's office. A number of loose ends needed to be tied up. The precise charges had to be made clear, it had to be determined whether there were any accomplices to the crime, and the inconsistencies and contradictions in the confessions had to be clarified.

In short, his task was to go beyond the police investigation and complete a full judicial inquiry.

To this end Périès began by cross-examining Clovis once again on 24 November. He gave yet another slightly modified version of his father's confession. This time he said that he could not remember exactly why his parents had been quarreling, but both of them were in such a towering rage that he had said that if they did not stop at once he would not sleep in the house any more. Thereupon they had calmed down, and his mother stalked off to bed. Gaston continued to hurl imprecations at his wife and said, "I'm not scared of anyone. I've bumped off three of 'em. I'll bump off another if necessary."[3] Clovis had assumed that he meant the three English people and asked his father, "Is it you?" His father had replied, "Yes, but don't tell anyone."

Périès then asked why Clovis had lied about the carbine. He replied that he had initially tried to cover up as much as possible. He had told Gustave not to say anything either about having heard screams after the shots were fired or about having seen that the little girl was still alive. He had simply wanted to keep his brother out of trouble as initially he had believed that his brother Gustave was guilty, until his father confessed. Then his own obligation to keep silent was even harder, because when his brother was in prison, he had learned that his father was the murderer. He was naturally anxious to protect his family for as long as possible, but for how long?

Périès suspected that on 5 August 1952 Clovis might have helped Gustave rearrange the murder site from 7:00 and 7:15 a.m., between the time that Jean Ricard had walked by to catch the bus to Marseille and the arrival of the gendarmes. But Clovis had never been under suspicion, and not even his father in his wildest moments had ever accused him of the crime.

Périès next managed to glean some additional information from Gustave about the murder weapon. He said that he and Yvette had tidied up the shed in January 1951 shortly after his brother Aimé had married and left the Grand' Terre. At that time Gustave had not seen the carbine, but he spotted it sometime later and had noticed that it had been patched up. He had seen the two magazines but not any loose cartridges. He had never held it in his hands. He assumed that his father had previously kept it hidden in his bedroom, but true to form his mother, Marie, claimed that she had never seen it.[4] Clovis confirmed this story, saying that he had first seen the carbine sometime after Aimé had left home. He had taken a close look at it but, unlike his brother, had only seen one magazine. A slight problem with this account is that Joseph Chauve, the tinker from Marseille who testified that he had sold the Duralumin band used to bind the hand guard to the barrel, did not set up business in the area until 1952. Perhaps Gustave and Clovis had mistaken the date or maybe the repairs on the M1 had not yet been completed.

Paul Maillet also had further revelations to make. He had told a journalist from Paris, who had introduced himself as an official of the Ministry of Information, that on his release from prison Gustave had told him that he had "taken part in every phase of the drama." When questioned by Commissioner Edmond Sébeille, Maillet said that he had asked Gustave where he was when he heard the screams on the night of the shootings.[5] Gustave had then pointed in the direction of the alfalfa field. (Gustave, however, had said that he had not seen anything because the campsite was not visible from his bedroom window and that he had not left the house.) Maillet also stated that a truck driver named Gauthier had told him that the M1 belonged to Gustave. Gauthier refused to confirm this statement, saying that he was already ostracized for suggesting that he knew the provenance of the murder weapon. The commissioner did not seem to think that this piece of evidence was of any interest and did not bother to pursue it. If what Maillet had said was true, the question arises as to what Gustave was doing outside at the time of the murders. Did he just happen to go and look at the landslide at exactly the same time as the murders? Was his account of first having met his father around four o'clock in the morning a fabrication?

At Périès's request, Sébeille went to Brillane on 7 December and questioned Émile Escudier, the grocer to whom Paul Maillet had confided the previous year. He assured the commissioner that Maillet had told him that Gustave had seen that Elizabeth was still alive and that he had persuaded him to tell the police. He also confirmed that Maillet had said that he had important additional information that he did not wish to divulge at that moment.[6]

Neither Périès nor Sébeille bothered to question Paul Maillet again until ten days later, so he had plenty of time to think things over and mend bridges with Gustave. Périès decided to question Gustave first. He insisted that he had not heard his father get up until four o'clock in the morning. He said that he had heard the screams but that he had seen nothing because he had stayed in his bedroom. Gustave stuck to his story when confronted with Paul Maillet, vigorously denying that he had ever said that he was in the alfalfa field at the time of the shootings.[7] Maillet was nervously anxious and eager to leave because his wife was in labor. He told the waiting journalists that he was going to call his son Edmond—"like Sébeille."

Maillet having left, Gustave continued with his story. He now claimed that Gaston's dog, Mirza, had barked ceaselessly. This had kept him awake. In this new version of events, he said he had heard his father's footsteps in the yard at about two o'clock. He went downstairs and found him standing near the well, considerably agitated, and without his cane. Gaston had said, "I've thrown it away." Gustave imagined that he was referring to the carbine. Next Gustave went "in a state of panic" to have a look at Elizabeth. He noticed that she was still moving. He then went to the campsite but did not touch anything. When he got back to the farmhouse, his father had gone inside and the light was on in the kitchen. Gustave then went upstairs to tell Yvette what had happened. He did not go downstairs again until five o'clock. He insisted that he had not messed around among the Drummond's possessions and that he had not looked for the cartridges, but he had gone to the shed and noticed that the carbine and the two magazines were missing. He concluded his statement by saying that Clovis had often told him of his suspicions about Paul Maillet.

Périès then sent for Clovis, who acknowledged that he had initially suspected Paul Maillet because on the morning of 5 August he had arrived late for work. Clovis admitted to having recognized the carbine and had gone immediately to the shed, where he noticed that it was missing.

He had told Gustave, who then said that he knew it had already been removed. Until that moment the two brothers had maintained that they had first confided in one another at Christmastime in 1952.

The following day Périès made a surprise visit to the Grand' Terre and asked Yvette to give her account of what Gustave had done during the night of the murders. She took some time to collect her thoughts before answering. She began by saying that it was "all too hard" and that for the last year she had been extremely tense and on edge. She insisted that she had always told the truth. Then she said she had heard the screams when the shots were fired, but they had not been very distinct because the dogs were barking. They kept barking for a long time. At about 1:30 she had given the baby a bottle. When the dogs started barking again, Gustave got up. She could not remember whether Gustave had switched on the bedside light when he got up. She did not hear any footsteps outside or anyone talking, but when Gustave went back to bed some ten or fifteen minutes later, he said he had found his father in the yard. Gaston had appeared to be completely done in, as if he were drunk. Gustave, who was extremely agitated, told his wife that his father had admitted to having killed someone. Yvette was terribly shocked. Gustave said, "I ask myself why he went down there. Why did he do that?"

Neither was able to sleep again, although Yvette dozed off once or twice. She said that she heard her father-in-law going downstairs, but she could not say exactly when. It must have been before five o'clock because at that time she heard the goats' bells as he took his herd out to pasture.

Yvette stated categorically that Gustave had not told her that he had gone to the scene of the crime after he had spoken to his father. They got up at about five o'clock. Gustave went to tend his animals and then looked at the campsite. When he came back, he said that he had seen the little girl lying with a bloodstained face on the slope beyond the bridge. Yvette thought that he had not mentioned that the girl had moved until much later. She was unable to say how many times Gustave had returned to the scene of the crime.

She never told her mother-in-law what Gustave had said, and she always avoided talking about it with her father-in-law. She was not absolutely certain, but she thought Gustave had told her after she had returned from the market at Oraison on 5 August, the morning of the murders, that his father had used the American carbine. Although Gustave had said that the weapon was kept on a shelf in the shed, she had never seen it there. In response to a direct question, she said she could not remember when she had learned that Clovis knew who the murderer was. She added that her husband had not told her in detail what his father had told him in the yard, about an hour after the crime. He did not seem to know why his father had killed the English family.[8]

Yvette's testimony was devastating for Gaston Dominici. It was a coherent account that confirmed the denunciations of his two sons Gustave and Clovis. She soon denied, however, that she had ever made or signed this statement. When confronted with the duly signed document, she claimed that she had made it under duress, with Périès threatening to arrest Gustave as an accomplice if she did not do so. This assertion is quite contrary to Périès's nature and is absolutely out of the question. Furthermore, Yvette did not need a threat to realize that her husband was in a singularly precarious situation and that the slightest slip on her part could well land him in the most serious trouble. She had every reason to protect Gustave. She may not have had much affection for the man, but he was the father of her children and ran the farm. Were he to be charged with murder and probably guillotined, she would have been left fully dependent on her father-in-law.

Périès then showed Gustave his wife's signed statement. He said that it was perfectly correct and that he had gone back to bed between 2:30 and 2:45 a.m. He had not told Yvette that he had been to the scene of the crime, and he did not want to tell her that he had seen the child move.

Marie was briefly questioned. She only repeated that she had heard nothing, seen nothing, and knew nothing.

Both Périès and Yvette had gotten what they wanted. She had managed to protect her husband while Périès had obtained valuable testimony that strengthened his case against Gaston Dominici. The examining magistrate was hesitant to pursue questioning Gustave, because that could well mean suspending the preparation of the case for trial. The res judicata before the magistrate's court was final, so any new elements could only be introduced by reopening the case against Gaston. The public in France and Britain, fueled by the popular press in both countries, demanded that the case be solved after such a painfully lengthy investigation; thus, prolonging the case was the last thing that either Périès or Sébeille wanted.

At this point the public prosecutor in Digne waxed poetic about the context in which the crime had taken place. He portentously announced to the press:

> Here we have poultry thieves, fights among drunks, poachers whom we consider to be monsters and who are treated without reason or pity. It is the country that demands that. A sun-scorched land, meagre pastures, lavender water distilleries where the alchemist's fire burns. This is not rich soil, where everything grows easily, but a hard country: avaricious, charred and arid. Everything that grows in our poor communes has a particular taste and power: our thin red wine, our stunted wheat and our rare, short hay. Everything burns, everything is strongly scented and everything exudes passion: men, animals, and plants. It is under this sky, the purest in France, during these crystalline nights teeming with stars, across which travels an enormous moon, that the most primitive instincts demand satisfaction.[9]

In Jean Giono's novel *The Hussar on the Roof* (1955), set in Basses-Alpes, Pauline says, "We have fallen among monsters!" Angelo replies, "No, we have fallen among something worse than that—decent people who have ceased to fear the gendarmes." Here was another Provence, far removed from the quaint tourists' idyll: dark, violent, passionate, and brutal, with charmingly stereotypical characters transformed into vicious psychopaths, pathological liars, and mean-spirited bumpkins. The horrors that lay behind the picturesque facade titillated Parisian newspaper readers and reaffirmed their vision of Provence as a primitive backwater that hardly could be considered part of civilized France.

Périès could not resist questioning Gustave again after Christmas.[10] He altered his story once again. This time he admitted that he had gone to the campsite around 2:00 a.m., but he denied having met his father in the yard. Consequently, there was no question of Gaston's having admitted committing the triple murder to his son that night. He repeated that the carbine was kept in the shed and that there were two magazines. Gustave now tried to pretend that it was Clovis who had first denounced their father, but after further grilling he had to admit that he had been pressured by the family to say so.

On 30 December Gaston was taken to the law courts, where he was confronted by his sons Gustave and Clovis. A crowd of journalists were waiting for him. He appeared to be relaxed and cheerful. He now told Périès that he had first got up at 4:00 a.m. to take his goats out to pasture and had returned at about 8:00 a.m. It was then that Yvette told him of "the drama." Faustin Roure, who had returned to the Grand' Terre at the same time, had witnessed this exchange between Gaston and his daughter-in-law.[11] Gaston now claimed that the police had made him confess, saying if Gustave took the rap he would have his head sliced off, whereas he as an old man would merely get a prison sentence. He claimed to have been so exhausted that he had confessed rather than face the ordeal of further questioning the next day. He declared he had been so ridiculed during the reconstitution of the crime that he had tried to kill himself. When asked about his sons' accusations, he muttered: "Let 'em come!"

Gustave was the first to confront his father. With his denunciation having been read out aloud, he was asked whether it was true. After a long silence, he emphatically denied it. Then, addressing his father, he said, "He only had to tell the truth." Quite what he meant by this remains a mystery. The truth would be his undoing if he were guilty. If his father were innocent, where was this "truth" that could absolve him?

Gaston's lawyers asked that Gustave be questioned once more about what he had done during that fatal night. Périès refused without giving any reason for his demurral.

Pollak then asked Gustave why he had denounced his father. He replied that he had been forced to do so by the police. Asked why he had now retracted his statement, he gave yet another of his enigmatic replies: "Because there are some witnesses who bear me out." Neither the examining magistrate nor Gaston's lawyers pursued this point. Gaston beamed with delight at his son's retraction, but his mood changed abruptly when Clovis was brought into the room.

Clovis stuck to his story of a drunken Gaston's row with Marie and his confession that he had "bumped off" the Drummonds. He had no answer when asked whether Gaston had told him what had led him to shoot the Drummonds. When he was reminded that he had given a different answer on previous occasions, he admitted that he had been told that Sir Jack had tried to wrench the gun from Gaston and that it had gone off by mistake. Asked about his father's remark that he had killed three people and would kill a fourth if need be, Clovis said that he assumed that his mother, Marie, was the next one on the list.

Gaston went into a towering rage and denounced his son as a "fucking bastard," a Judas, a bandit, a base liar, and a "Bazaine," adding that "if there had been a weapon at the Grand' Terre, it was you who brought it!"[12] Clovis, who was all too familiar with such treatment by his father, muttered, "You've made us suffer far too long!" The defense lawyers took this as evidence that revenge for past injustices was Clovis's motive for concocting an accusation against his father. Clovis was now sent home, while Gustave and his father remained at the law courts although kept apart. Having been given something to eat, Gaston was taken back to prison. He appeared to be in good cheer, remarking to one of the warders, "Young man, I'll be back on my farm in the spring!" It is difficult to see quite what were the grounds for such optimism.

In the afternoon Gustave was questioned by Sébeille, but no record was kept—a fact that the defense team took as evidence of intimidation. Périès took over at six o'clock, and Gustave collapsed, claiming that he had been incapable of denouncing his father face to face. He asked that he not have to go through such an ordeal ever again. Périès, imagining that Gustave was in a cooperative mood, tried to get him to admit that he was outside at the time of the crime and that he had seen his father. Gustave flatly denied that he had been in the alfalfa field during the shootings. Getting nowhere and possibly attempting to mollify him, Périès offered Gustave a taxi to take him home.

Despite having reverted to his original denunciation of his father and repeating it on numerous occasions, Gustave proclaimed his father's innocence on every possible subsequent occasion. On 19 January he posted a letter, written on 10 January, to his father, who had been moved to Les Baumettes prison in Marseille for psychiatric evaluation:

Dear Dad,

please excuse me, but I am suffering terribly. I think of you more than ever and I promise you to be strong and to tell the truth, even in the face of threats. The truth must come to light.

Périès pointed out on 4 February that Gustave hereby admitted that he had previously not told the truth and that he had been subjected to unspecified threats. Did they come from within the family, or were they from the police?[13]

Gustave replied that the purpose of the letter was to tell his father how sorry he was that he had falsely accused him. He now told Périès that he knew absolutely nothing about the circumstances of the crime. Also, he claimed that his father had never told him that he had murdered the Drummond family. He stated categorically that he had seen the carbine for the very first time on 6 August 1952, when Commissioner Sébeille showed it to him.

He now gave yet another version of the night of 4–5 August 1952. He had gone to bed at eleven o'clock but had woken up half an hour later when a motorcycle stopped at the farmhouse. Then he fell asleep again, only to be woken by several shots. He heard screams in the distance, and the dogs began to bark. He realized that the shots did not come from a hunter but were from either a revolver or an army weapon. He and Yvette speculated as to what might have happened, and he was unable to get back to sleep. He heard nothing inside the house until his father got up at four o'clock, but he had heard a couple of cars pass by the farm about a quarter of an hour after the shooting. There were others, but much later.

Gustave said he got up at about five o'clock, drank a cup of coffee, gave the horse some fodder, and then went to look at the landslide. He had not been able to decide on which side of the Grand' Terre the shots had been fired. Was it toward Peyruis or in the direction of the Lurs railway station? Then he thought perhaps the English family had been attacked. To settle his curiosity, he went to the campsite but did not see anything unusual. There was a bit of a mess around the car, but that was all. It was only after he had crossed the bridge across the railway that he saw the little girl. Her arm moved. He then went back to have another look at the campsite. Just as he reached the main road, a motorcycle passed. Then he decided to go back to the farmhouse, walking along the side of the road. At that moment Olivier appeared, and he flagged him down.

Disregarding the fact that Gustave could not have seen Elizabeth's body without walking deliberately across the path and peering down the slope toward the river, Périès asked him to elaborate on the accusations he had made in his letter dated 10 January to his father about the threats the police had made to him. He reassured Périès that the examining magistrate had always treated him correctly and that he was merely complaining about the way the police had treated him on 12 and 13 November 1953, during the reconstruction of the crime scene and his father's arrest. He had only told the same story to Périès that the police had extracted from him by extreme measures. Gustave had failed to share that detail because he was frightened of being sent to prison were he to contradict himself. He ended on a pitiable note by telling Périès that he had always treated him "like a brother."

Gustave thus retracted all his previous statements doubtless for fear of his father, as well as due to intense pressure from his wife and the Dominici clan. He had reverted to his original story. His strategy, whether conscious or not, was to introduce some fresh piece of evidence that might lead to further confusion. During this session he had suggested that a revolver might have been fired that night and that two cars had passed by shortly after the shootings. This was something that he had previously specifically denied. Such tactics were frustrating both for the police and Gaston's defense team. As Pollak said despairingly, "Amidst this hodgepodge of lies, contradictions, retractions and telling silences concocted by the clan, which accumulated during the months of enquiry, there were precious few grains of truth."[14]

With Gustave having retracted his accusations against his father, Périès decided to go ahead and confront him that same day with Clovis, who doggedly stuck to his story. Périès began this tense session by telling Clovis that his brother, contrary to his previous statements, now claimed to know absolutely nothing about the crime perpetrated against the Drummond family. He now insisted that his father had never admitted to the murders and that he had never known about the existence of an American carbine at the Grand' Terre.

Clovis replied that part of the Dominici family was taking Gustave for a ride. Having himself received a death threat from his brother Gaston, Clovis was hardly surprised that Gustave had changed his tune. He repeated his statement that when he had told him that the carbine was no longer in the shed, Gustave had said that he had already noticed that it was missing. Clovis had then asked him whether he had used it to commit the crime. Gustave replied that he had not.

Questioned on this point, Gustave confirmed what his brother had said, whereupon Périès pointed out that only moments earlier he had denied knowing about the carbine before 6 August 1952. Gustave was trapped. He had to admit that he had seen the weapon in the shed, as he had shown to the police on 16 November, but asserted that he had only seen it once, shortly after his brother Aimé married and left the family home.[15] Then Périès reminded Gustave that in a previous statement he had said that he had first seen the weapon in early 1952 but that Aimé was married in December 1950. Gustave was unable to explain this discrepancy. In reply to another question he said that he had no doubt that Clovis suspected him of the murders. Clovis interjected that when he had asked him whether he was involved in the shootings, Gustave had replied that their father had acted alone and had confessed to Gustave in the early morning of 5 August as he was setting out to take his goats to pasture. Clovis claimed that he had not taken any notice of this, because he could not imagine that the old man could possibly have committed such a terrible crime. However, at heart he still believed that Gustave was guilty. His suspicions did not dissipate until his father told him that he indeed had shot all three of the Drummonds.

Gustave now felt obliged to retract the statements he had made earlier to the effect that his father had never spoken to him of his guilt. He stated that he should have told Clovis that his father had admitted to the crime "that very day." It was not until the conversation at Saint-Pons, shortly after he was released from prison, that he had heard that their father had made a similar admission to Clovis. When Périès asked why he had lied earlier that day, Gustave simply shrugged his shoulders.

Périès was an exceptionally self-effacing and tolerant man, but he was rapidly losing patience with Gustave and decided to talk to him alone. After Clovis left the room, Périès gave Gustave an unaccustomedly harsh dressing down: "Your behaviour in this affair has been absolutely unacceptable. Even if the contradictions and denials might possibly be considered admissible before 15 November last, they certainly are not now that your father has admitted that he murdered the Drummond family."[16] He pointed out that on 13 November Gustave had stated that his father had admitted to the crime, but at first he had denied having ever seen the carbine. He had said the opposite the next day and then retracted once again by stating that he had only seen the gun once or twice shortly before 5 August 1952. On 5 December 1953 he had claimed that his father had confessed to the crime at four o'clock in the morning of 5 August 1953. After a confrontation with Paul Maillet on 17 December, he had changed his story, saying that his father's confession was made at two o'clock in the morning. This point he confirmed on 28 December, only to retract it two days later when confronted by his father. Later that same day he had taken it all back once more, claiming that he was frightened of accusing his father to his face. Today he had started by saying he knew nothing of the circumstances surrounding the crime and that his father had never confessed to him. As soon as

Clovis entered the room, however, he went back to the original version of his story.

Gustave replied that since his father's arrest his family had continuously harassed him. His brothers, sisters, and sisters-in-law simply refused to believe that his father could have possibly committed such a crime, and they took him to task for having denounced him to the police. He had repeatedly told them that his father had confessed to him at two o'clock in the morning of 5 August 1952, about an hour after the shootings. They simply did not believe him. Gustave said that he was desperate and did not know what to do. He had written to his father only to cheer him up. Gaston was, after all, his father. He had worked all his life for the family. For this reason Gustave was incapable of repeating what his father had said that morning in his presence.

Périès decided to get back to the question of the carbine. He pointed out that when questioned at the law courts in Digne on 15 November 1953, Gustave had stated that it had been at the Grand' Terre ever since some American troops passed by during the war. Gustave claimed that this was simply speculation on his part since he was away from home at the time on a mission with the Francs-Tireurs et Partisans Français. He repeated that he had only seen it once, and that was shortly after Aimé's marriage in December 1950, when they cleaned the shed after his departure from the Grand' Terre. No other member of the Dominici clan, apart from Clovis, had known of its existence. Gustave had never dared ask his father about the weapon for fear of getting yet another brutal tongue-lashing. Clovis had said that there was one magazine, but he had seen two. When Périès asked Gustave which of his family members had dictated the letter he had written to his father, he adamantly replied that it was all on his own initiative. Exhausted after this long and frustrating encounter, Périès let Gustave go home.

Lucien Tardieu questioned Aimé Dominici. Although he remembered having seen the Americans visit the farm, he stated he had never seen the weapon.

Gustave was again cross-examined on 23 February. Périès suggested that Gustave had told his family that he had only denounced his father after he had heard that Clovis had already done so.[17] Gustave eagerly took up this suggestion, saying that he had first heard of his father's guilt from Clovis. Périès pointed out that shortly after Gaston's arrest, Gustave had testified that Gaston had confessed to him at two o'clock in the morning of 5 August 1952 and that he had told the entire family about it. Gustave, repeating what he had said less than three weeks previously, replied that a few days after his release from prison in November 1952, he had told his family what his father had said. No one believed him. His father claimed that he was innocent, and Gustave's sisters all told him to stop accusing him. Gustave claimed to have asked himself whether his father could have possibly committed such a terrible crime and whether Gaston's confession was perhaps all a vivid fantasy induced by his drunken state. Gustave's testimony on this point, as in many other instances, varied widely. Sometimes his father was represented as calm and collected, at other times he was highly nervous and agitated, and now he was drunk. Périès asked why Gustave continued to accuse Gaston although he repeatedly insisted on his innocence. He did not reply directly; instead, he referred to the carbine, which all the rest of the Dominici clan claimed never to have seen. In yet another version of the story, he now maintained that when he had seen it in the shed some three to six months before the crime, he had asked himself how it could have got there but that he never asked anyone about it.

With Gaston in prison, the Grand' Terre was run by Yvette's father, François Barth. Quite why this was necessary is not immediately apparent. On the one hand, Gustave was admittedly something of a caricature figure—a feebleminded, mendacious, and pigheaded peasant with a blank expression and an oafish smile who was completely under the influence of a strong-willed and attractive wife. On the other hand, as the Grand' Terre was a very small farm, there was not much to do during the winter months. Barth was every bit the authoritarian Gaston was. He was not only a militant communist with connections throughout the area but also a man of integrity and a competent administrator. It was said that the party faithful frequently held meetings at the farm, but nothing is known of what transpired.[18]

Clovis had written to Barth at the end of January, asking him to do what he could to persuade Gustave not to withdraw his denunciation of his father. He should blame "the old scoundrel" for all "the wrongs he has made us suffer." It is indeed surprising that Clovis should have written such a letter to Barth, who was one of the most outspoken champions of Gaston's innocence. When Périès questioned him on this score on 4 February, Clovis replied that he feared that Yvette and his sisters, by asserting that Gaston was innocent, were pointing the finger at Gustave whether they realized it or not. Clovis insisted that Gustave would be absolutely incapable of committing such a crime, and he wanted to warn Barth that he was putting his son-in-law in serious danger.[19] Périès reminded Clovis that Gustave had spoken to him of his father's guilt a couple of days after the murders, and Clovis made the astonishing reply that he had forgotten "that detail." Périès was scandalized by this inappropriate remark, which Clovis tried to explain away by saying that at that time he had imagined that Gustave had committed the crime. The examining magistrate did not ask why that although he had once suspected his brother, he now thought Gustave was temperamentally incapable of perpetrating such a violent crime.

Clovis said that he had written the letter to Barth at his wife's prompting but that he was entirely responsible for its contents. He had signed it and taken it to the post office. Périès did not ask why he had written to Barth rather than going to talk to him. After all he was Yvette's father, lived only a few miles away, and was a fellow member of the Communist Party.

Gaston's daughter Clotilde Araman was the next person Périès questioned.[20] She staunchly upheld her father's innocence. She had written a letter to Gaston dated 25 November that ended with this enigmatic phrase: "You have already arrested an assassin and are definitely about to arrest a second, but unfortunately for you that would bring you too many laurels." Périès asked her what she meant by this. She replied that it was a reference to the role Gaston had played in arresting the bandit, Luigi Gualdi, in 1923.[21] Périès then asked her whether Gaston was in a position to secure the arrest of the Drummonds' murderer. She replied,

"If he had been able to do so." She went on to say that her sister Germaine Perrin and her brother Clovis were plotting against their father out of sheer spite.

Making little sense of Clotilde's perplexing answers, Périès decided to ask Gaston about the letter he had written in response to his daughter. He began by asking what he meant when he wrote: "Misfortunes always come from the same direction." Gaston leaned forward and, almost whispering, replied, "I've been thinking. I have the impression that my grandson Roger [Zézé] Perrin might be the assassin. He's a con artist."[22]

Périès, who was unable to get Gaston to say anything further on the subject, decided to question Zézé Perrin.[23] He was no more able to make sense of young Perrin's web of lies, contradictions, and trickery than had Sébeille and the police beforehand. However, no one felt that Zézé's almost pathological inability to tell the truth was due to his involvement in the crime.

During his earlier questioning of Clovis regarding his letter to Barth, Périès had told him that his father had said that the carbine belonged to him and that he had perhaps lent it to Zézé Perrin.[24] Clovis denied this categorically, and Périès never returned to this line of questioning.

On 9 February, at the request of Gaston Dominici's defense team, Périès had ordered an examination of all the weapons that the Dominici family possessed to compare the oil used in them with that in the M1. Clovis's and the Perrins' weapons were requisitioned along with those at the Grand' Terre. Maillet's guns were not deemed to be of interest. The report from the police laboratory delivered on 9 March showed that there was no similarity between the oils used in the M1 and Roger Perrin's two 16-gauge shotguns, but two of Clovis's three weapons had traces of a similar type.

Armed with this information, Périès went to visit Clovis, who said that he only used olive oil of his own making to lubricate his guns. According to Périès's notes, Clovis had used oil from the 1953 harvest on his guns, but there was none left. Périès took a sample of the 1954 oil with him. (Clearly there is a mistake here in the record. Olive oil is pressed in the autumn, but these tests were made in February or March.) The experts had difficulty in analyzing the oil in the Rock-Ola, because it had been in the water for several hours. It was therefore not possible to say with absolute certainty whether it was identical with what Clovis used. The prosecution did not pursue the matter, possibly because it might well have weakened their case against Gaston. But the defense team also did not see fit to refer to this piece of evidence. Clovis had not been at the Grand' Terre the night of the murders and was never a suspect.

Périès visited Gaston in his cell at Les Baumettes on 21 April for a final interrogation. He found Gaston calm and collected. He was confident that he would be acquitted and that he would soon return to the Grand' Terre in glory, just as his hero Napoleon had returned from Elba. He understandably brushed aside the examining magistrate's reference to an incident in 1897 when he had hit a neighbor viciously over the head, leaving him bedridden for days, and another fight he had had with neighbors in 1925.

The dossier was formally closed on 27 April 1954 and sent to the chamber of indictment at the court of appeal in Aix-en-Provence, which was to decide whether the case should go to trial in an assize court before a jury.

Three jurists from the court of appeal presided over a hearing in private at which both the prosecution and the defense presented their arguments. Émile Pollak, who led the defense team, realized he had little chance of securing a dismissal at this stage. He felt his only hope was to convince a jury of his client's innocence. Nevertheless, he made a desperate attempt to get the case dismissed on procedural grounds. In his submission to the court, he argued that the law of 8 December 1897 required that a suspect be indicted as soon as the charges against him were sufficient. Once indicted the accused had the right to have an attorney present when being questioned. Gaston Dominici should therefore have been indicted before the reconstruction of the crime on 16 November so that he would then have benefited from legal advice during the reenactment of the crime.

At the court of appeal Gaston's case was handled by the specialist lawyer André Mayer, who argued along lines suggested by Pollak. He insisted that since the reconstruction added nothing new, the indictment should have been made against Gaston beforehand. He also pointed out that when Gaston was interrogated for the last time, no one mentioned to him that the dossier had been given to his lawyers. In addition, there was no evidence that the clerk of the court had formally notified the defense team of the writ of committal. The appeal judge, Maurice Patin, was a distinguished expert in penal law known for his passionate defense of civil liberties. He conceded these last two points but insisted that Périès's delay in indicting Gaston was due to caution rather than a deliberate attempt to deny the suspect of his rights.

The court ruled that Périès was guilty of a minor infraction of the 1897 law and therefore set aside Gaston's final confession and the writ of committal. These two instruments were sent to the court in Grenoble for revision. The net result of this action was a further postponement of the trial. This reversion to a higher court gave Gaston a brief respite from prison. He traveled to the Dauphiné capital at public expense. It was a welcome change of scenery.[25] Shortly after his return to prison in Digne, he was informed that his trial had been set for 17 November 1954.

8 The Trial Opens

Gaston appeared in court on Wednesday, 17 November 1954, at 9:15 a.m. with a red-and-blue scarf around his neck, his hair closely cropped, and his mustache carefully trimmed. In daily life his baggy velvet trousers fell on his hips, revealing a flannel waistband, a blue shirt, and a leather belt. He usually wore a woolen vest under a loose jacket. Now he was dressed in his best suit, a blue cotton shirt with a new tie, and a herringbone overcoat. His flat hat was planted squarely on his head. He projected a reassuring air of the naive simplicity typical of a French peasant, patriarch, and grandfather of sixteen grandchildren. He was, in short, the clichéd image of a santon, an *image d'Épinal*, or a figure like Mr. Seguin from Alphonse Daudet's *Lettres de mon moulin*.[1] Jean Giono, the chronicler of Provençal life, who was present at the trial, said of Gaston: "I know a thousand Dominicis. They are interchangeable."[2]

Giono and the playwright Armand Salacrou were given places of honor to observe the trial. Other distinguished guests included the prefect of the Basses-Alpes; the typographer Maximilien Vox, who had begun to convert Lurs into one of the most desirable villages in Provence; and Madame Pélabon, wife of Prime Minister Pierre Mendès-France's cabinet secretary, who was said to be the prime minister's designated observer at the trial. The famous writers François Mauriac, André Maurois, and Simenon were expected to attend the trial, but they failed to appear. A hundred journalists from all over the world were present.

The court of appeal in Aix had courteously contacted the British Consulate General in Marseille to ask whether it should reserve a seat at the trial for a member of the staff. The Foreign Office felt that it would be inconvenient for the consul to spare a member of his staff for several days, was concerned that it would involve unnecessary expenses, and argued that it might well look as if it had no faith in the French legal system were a member of the consular service to attend.[3]

Gaston's entrance was greeted with a barrage of flashbulbs as photographers fought to get a shot of the accused. The resulting pandemonium prompted the presiding judge to order all photographers to leave the room. This was met with shrieks of protest. Initially five minutes had been allotted for photographs, after which the use of flash was to be forbidden. The presiding judge, Marcel Bousquet, who had arrived from Nice the previous day, then called a halt after thirty seconds. It took some time for the press to calm down.

From the outset it was the dossier, rather than Gaston, that was on trial. Public Prosecutor Louis Sabatier from the Digne bench and Advocate General Calixte Rozan from Aix-en-Provence, vigorously assisted by Judge Bousquet, set out to defend the dossier and to disguise its many holes and deficiencies, while Émile Pollak, Pierre Charrier, and Léon Charles-Alfred were determined to expose its lacunae and weaknesses. At stake was Gaston's head.

The selection of the seven jurors took some time. The defense objected strenuously to the choice of a woman, arguing that the case involved the brutal killing of a ten-year-old girl and that a woman could not possibly be objective in such a matter. The objection was sustained.

The clerk of the court then read out the charges. He began with a description of the accused as a man who was "authoritarian, a drinker and secretive."[4] Gaston protested, then sat back with a sigh of resignation. The clerk reminded the court of the chronology of events. On 5 August 1952 the Drummonds had been murdered. In November 1952 Gustave had been convicted for failing to render assistance to Elizabeth. That month Clovis had heard his father admit to the murders. In November 1953 Gustave had accused his father of the murders and then retracted his statement. Clovis stuck to his original version. When the clerk suggested that Gaston might have seen Lady Drummond undressing, the old man smiled salaciously and stroked his mustache. Only Elizabeth's murder was considered to have been premeditated.

Next came the naming of witnesses. At first it seemed that Yvette, Gustave, and Clovis had vanished, but they were soon found. They explained that the crowd was so dense that they had been unable to enter the courtroom. Aristide Panayotou was present, cutting as strange a figure as ever. Since he had led the police down the garden path, many found it surprising that he was there at all. Zézé Perrin, the pathological liar, was present, with the defense lawyers anxious to have a crack at him. The entire Dominici clan, with the exception of the traitor Clovis, was lined up for the defense.

The presiding judge then called for an intermission. The photographers rushed toward the box. Gaston thumbed his nose at them and hid his head. His lawyers came to talk to him.

The court resumed at 10:30 a.m. Pollak rose to his feet, bitterly complaining that vital evidence had been withheld from the defense. The Hillman had been returned to England, so it was not possible to examine it. He had not seen the camp beds. He expressed his outrage that he had not been permitted to witness the reconstruction of the crime on 16 November 1953.[5] The advocate general suggested that a similar model Hillman be made available, but Pollak insisted that it had to be the Drummonds' own car. The advocate general then suggested that the British consul in Marseille be asked whether it would be possible for the Hillman to be returned to France. The court adjourned to deliberate until 11:05 a.m. It was then announced that the station wagon could not be sent back. The next day Katherine Elliot from Weston-super-Mare, who had bought the car for £650 ($1,820) and put it in her wax museum in Blackpool, charging morbid holidaymakers one-shilling admission, offered to send the vehicle to Digne; but the suggestion was refused.

The presiding judge then launched into a biographical sketch of the accused. He reported that the mayor of Lurs had said that Gaston lived "on the margins of society" and hardly ever went to the village. Gaston testily replied that he had work to do. Bousquet said that Gaston was "easily roused and impulsive." Gaston countered that he did not like to be mocked. He was then reminded that he had hit a man with a cudgel, causing serious injury. Gaston shrugged his shoulders and said that the incident had happened fifty-six years ago, and anyway the other person had hit him first. He was then accused of being too severe with his children, to which he replied that he had never hit them, and anyway "if a father is not severe with his children, what's going to happen, eh, Mister President?" The judge then suggested that Gaston was unduly hard on his son Gustave. Gaston noted that he got everything that he wanted. His son took all the farm produce and never gave him a cent for it, even though his father had made the farm what it was. Anyway, Gustave was a bone-idle liar.

The accused initially appeared to be remarkably relaxed and self-confident. His arms were crossed as he leaned back with his head resting on the wood paneling. Constantly chewing on lumps of sugar, he stared fixedly at the presiding judge with the air not of someone who was on trial for a triple murder but of a worthy peasant about to receive a medal for a lifetime of hard and honorable work. But he soon began to tire under the presiding judge's relentless grilling.[6]

It is doubtful whether there was ever a judge so inordinately fond of the sound of his own voice as Bousquet was. He would interrupt witnesses to make laborious analyses of what he imagined the witness was trying to say, often to no apparent purpose and frequently in a misleading manner. He fired a seemingly endless series of questions at Gaston, most of which he had great difficulty in understanding. Words such as "prolixity" and "susceptible" did not exist in his vocabulary. When Madame Muzy, the Ganagobie schoolteacher who had taught his children, described him as "crafty," "authoritarian," "hard," and "severe," he took all four as compliments. The problem of language soon became central.

There were many instances when the court was unable to understand the exact meaning of local slang. Zézé Perrin, for example, said that he had lied to the police because he was afraid "d'être marroné." A Parisian would understand that he was afraid of being beaten up. For Jean Giono, however, it meant "get dressed down," "have a strip torn off him," or "get yelled at." In prison jargon, it meant "get nabbed by the police."[7] In these cases, the witnesses were never asked precisely what they meant.

From the outset, the presiding judge adopted a blatantly accusatory tone, which most of the journalists present found shocking. British journalists, who had no reason to be sympathetic to Gaston Dominici, found it outrageous that a French judge should treat the accused in a manner sadly reminiscent of Prosecutor General Andrei Vyshinsky in the Moscow show trials or Roland Freisler, president of the Nazi People's Court. They assumed that this behavior, although regrettable, was normal practice in a French court. French journalists, however, were equally appalled by this court's blatant lack of objectivity.[8]

The proceedings were conducted in an atmosphere of mutual incomprehension. Not only did Gaston Dominici speak a Provençal dialect and had great difficulty in understanding standard French, there was also the extreme clash between the mentality of the peasant world and that of the urban jurists. The gulf between *urbs* and *rus*—the urban and the rustic—could barely be spanned. Technical legal language and hermetic procedures mystified most of the journalists present as well. They were utterly incomprehensible to those whose vocabulary was largely restricted to rural colloquialisms. Even in a conversation conducted at a common intellectual level, a large part of that which is communicated is nonverbal. Socially conditioned gestures, inflections, and facial expressions have also to be understood. In the theatrical setting of a law court, such factors are of even greater significance.[9] Gaston frequently overacted, failed to notice the traps that were set for him, and shrugged off a number of accusations in the absolute certainty that he would be acquitted. In a few instances his peasant cunning enabled him to score a point against the president and the prosecution, but most of the time it was impossible to determine whether his reactions were due to sheer incomprehension, or to certain assurances he had been given, or to a determination to assert his innocence. French law has no provision for a milder sentence should the accused enter a guilty plea, so the police could have given him precious little in the way of assurances.

Heavily indebted to Jean Giono's account of the trial, the literary theorist and semiologist Roland Barthes was to argue that since the material evidence was uncertain and often contradictory, the court attempted a reconstruction of Gaston Dominici's mentality in terms of a universal psychology "descending from the charming empyrean of bourgeois novels and essentialist psychology." The trial, in short, was a literary construct. A further problem resulted from the myth of the transparency and universality of language, as evidenced when Gaston and Judge Bousquet frequently talked in different languages and at cross-purposes.[10]

This form of psychology is "adjectival" in that the accused is treated as an object with certain attributes such as selfishness, irascibility, lecherousness, or cunning magisterially attributed to it. *Le Monde* described the prosecutor as an "extraordinary story-teller" of "dazzling wit." Edmond Sébeille waxed eloquent in his summary of the case: "Never have I met such a dissembling liar, such a wary gambler, such a shifty narrator, such a wily trickster, such a lusty septuagenarian, such a self-assured despot, such a devious schemer, such a cunning hypocrite. . . . Gaston Dominici is an astonishing quick-change artist playing with human souls, and animal thoughts. . . . This false patriarch of the Grand' Terre has not just a few facets, he has a hundred!"

Justice, for Barthes, here took on the mask of realist literature, with the accused robbed of his language and transformed into a literary construct. He thus saw the trial as a confrontation between the highly educated readers of *Le Figaro* and a primitive peasant, between the cultured and the uncouth. It was a blatant example of hegemonic power and class justice. This was an elegant expression of a widely held view.

After a two-hour pause for lunch the court resumed at 3:00 p.m., and Gaston was questioned about his life. Toward evening he began to tire, to the point of becoming a sad, pathetic old man, desperately proclaiming his innocence. The accused stated that he had heard three or four shots at 1:10 a.m. on 5 August 1952. He imagined that they had been fired by poachers on the other side of the Durance. He got up at 3:30 a.m. but saw nothing. Having taken his goats to pasture, he returned to the farmhouse at 7:30 a.m., and Yvette told him that a crime had been committed.

Bousquet then questioned him at length about the various versions he had given of events that morning. Gaston repeatedly answered by saying, "I've done no harm to anybody!" He then said that he was standing by Elizabeth's body when someone found a piece of wood under her head. That person handed it to him, and he gave it to the police. His previous story was that he was the one who had discovered the splinter of wood from the carbine's butt and handed it over to the police. When challenged on this point, he said, "Perhaps I've made a mistake. I was out of my mind. I can't remember." In fact, it was a gravedigger from Forcalquier, sent to bring the bodies to the morgue, who had made the discovery. Asked about Clovis's reaction when he saw the carbine, he said, "If Sébeille had done a decent job, he would have gone after Clovis. I don't want to pay for another."

The judge then asked Gaston about the statements he had made to Victor Guérino in the law courts in Digne. The judge reminded Gaston that he had said, "It's Gustave who did it, but I'm going to confess to the crime in order to save the honor of the family." He then admitted that he was the guilty party. Gaston said he had been interrogated from five in the afternoon until eight in the evening the following day. A policeman had approached him, his mouth agape, yelling that he was an assassin. Gaston told the court, "I had only had a glass of water and was feeling a bit gaga. Mister President, what would you have done in my place?" The courtroom burst out in laughter. Bousquet called for order, testily remarking that this was no laughing matter. When asked about what he had said to his son when they were confronted in front of Examining Magistrate Roger Périès, Gaston said that he could not remember.

He was utterly exhausted and simply let things roll over him. To most questions he wearily repeated that he was innocent.

The judge then addressed the question of the reconstruction of the crime on 16 November 1953. Gaston said, "What they did to me that day showed them up to be a bunch of cowards!" Bousquet brusquely called him to order. Gaston told the court that during the reenactment of the crime, he had been "crazy" and that the investigators had a fine old time making a mockery of him. The judge reminded Gaston that on nine separate occasions he had confessed to the triple crime. Gaston flatly denied it. Bousquet then said that he had confessed to save the honor of his grandchildren. Gaston grunted, "Don't go over all that again!" Bousquet's final question was about the carbine. Gaston replied, "I have never seen it. I haven't killed anyone, and my conscience is clear."

The court resumed the next day, Thursday, 18 November, at 9:15 a.m. Gaston appeared to be well rested. The presiding judge opened the proceedings by stating, "Among your statements you have accused your sons Gustave and then Clovis. On another occasion you let it be known that your grandson Roger (Zézé) Perrin might also be guilty. So I am now asking you bluntly whether you have a solid suspicion, a precise fact, or a clear accusation. You must make a categorical statement to the court and not simply cast suspicions."

Bousquet was thus trying to get Gaston to accuse Gustave, Clovis, and Zézé Perrin, but Gaston hit back: "I have one simple thing to say. I do not accuse either Gustave or Clovis. I have sometimes said what I thought of Roger (Zézé) Perrin, because he's a ne'er-do-well. But it was only a suspicion." Gaston then accused the judge of speaking as though he thought he was guilty. He continued to insist that he was innocent. Bousquet turned to the jurymen and asked them whether they had any questions. They remained silent. A series of questions were asked about his acting as a midwife for his wife on three occasions and for one of his daughters on another, the implication being that this was singularly primitive and brutal behavior. Gaston muttered, "They were alone in the house. Should I have left them to die in agony?"

Gaston's principal defense lawyer, Pollak, cut a strange figure with his olive skin, his mane of grey hair, his muffled voice, and his childish pout. He obviously had not done his homework, but he compensated for his lack of detailed knowledge with his neat turns of phrase and his commanding presence. He made elaborate gestures with his hands, which were embellished with incredibly long nails. Renowned in the courts for his verbosity, he was known as "The Word." He tried to defend his client by saying that although violence had not been used against him, the sheer length of his interrogation was such that an old man's wits were liable to become dulled.

Pollak then attempted to cast doubt on the medical evidence, but it made very little impression. First, he pointed out that the autopsy showed that Lady Drummond had been hit by three bullets, whereas Gaston had testified that he had fired only once. Similarly, the autopsy revealed that Elizabeth had received three or four blows to the head, whereas during the reconstruction of the crime, Gaston had indicated having hit her only once. He made much of the two statements Gaston was reported to have made about Anne's death. One was "the woman did not suffer"; the other, "the woman can't have suffered." Then he took up the issue that the footprints at the murder site had not been duly examined. He mocked the notion that had Dominici been the murderer, he would not have disposed of the carbine by throwing it into the river only a few yards from his home. Then he asked why the mason who claimed to have seen Gaston buying a carbine from some American soldiers had not been produced as a witness. Rozan glibly replied that it would have served no purpose, because the man was a hopeless drunk.

Pollak then addressed the question of Gaston's confessions and the circumstances in which they were made. There followed a lengthy discussion of the precise meaning of the statements Gaston had made to Guérino, with Pollak insinuating that it had been Pierre Prudhomme who had suggested the sexual motive as having triggered the murders.

The presiding judge now announced that he had received an interesting letter from Madame Duron, who lived in the Rue des Grands-Augustins in Paris. She had discovered an American gabardine raincoat in the abandoned railway station at Lurs where Clovis worked. It had stains on it that might have been blood. He thought that the lady was on her way to Digne and would appear in court as soon as she arrived. The defense team did not seem particularly interested in this witness.

Subsequent investigations revealed that a British-made blue gabardine raincoat had been found by a "private agent"—that is, a psychic specializing in the examination of electromagnetic radiations—by the name of Reine Ribot, who had spent some time at the murder site in the early stages of the investigation.[11] A cutting with the stain and the label was sent to Scotland Yard for analysis. The raincoat was manufactured in Chorley but was not exported to France. The stain, which the French police with their belief in "applied psychology" had not even bothered to analyze, proved to be red oxide from house paint. None of the Drummonds' neighbors recognized the raincoat. Although Sir Jack was known as an enthusiastic do-it-yourself man, the most recent paint job, on a greenhouse, had used a paint containing white lead. Besides, the work had been done by men from Boots, much to the management's surprise and annoyance. Further, it is unlikely that Sir Jack, known to be a dapper dresser, would have taken a heavy, paint-stained raincoat with him during the dog days of August in Provence. It was later discovered that a railwayman by the name of Squillari had been living with his family in the abandoned railway station's bunkhouse. He was a Frenchman who had lived in England, hence the provenance of the raincoat, which he had left behind when he moved out shortly after the crime.[12]

The next witness was Dr. Merlan, a psychologist who had examined Gaston Dominici at Les Baumettes prison. He stated that Gaston was a strong man who was physically and psychologically normal. He had shown no signs of being sexually obsessed and was in all respects perfectly normal, apart from slight traces of amnesia. The good doctor did not think it abnormal that "he liked to joke about women." When Pollak asked him whether Gaston was "sensually obsessed," the doctor replied that he was not. As were many Frenchmen, he was merely *égrillard* (dirty minded). Gaston thanked the doctor profusely as he left the witness stand. Dr. Merlan's assessment was seconded by that of Dr. Henri Alliez, who added without a hint of irony that Gaston was "mildly alcoholic."

When Bousquet said that a number of Gaston's acquaintances had said that he was "somewhat lacking in gallantry towards women," the old peasant reacted violently. He muttered, "I had my own wife!" When the presiding judge asked him whether that was enough, Gaston replied, "You can bet your life on it!" Sébeille was convinced that he was excessively prurient. Once, when an airplane flew overhead, he had said, "Those fellows up there have all the luck. They can see the couples making out in the bushes!"

Dr. Henri Dragon, who had been the first to examine the bodies, was the next medical witness. The seventy-year-old, speaking in an affected manner, said that he had first examined Elizabeth. She had suffered two terrible blows in the face. Her nostrils were bloody. Her bare feet showed no signs of any abrasions. He then examined Lady Drummond's body. One bullet had pierced her heart, which would have proved mortal. A second had gone through her lung. Sir Jack had received a bullet through the liver. The parents' bodies were already stiff but not that of the daughter, from which he surmised that Elizabeth had died two or three hour later. Questioned on the state of Elizabeth's feet, the doctor said that she might have run barefoot, or she might have been carried. The police testified that they had tested another ten-year-old, who ran barefoot on the same route. Her feet had shown no signs of abrasions. The doctor further stated that with such massive blows to the head Elizabeth would have died instantly.

Questioned about how long Elizabeth Drummond might have lived having received such terrible blows to the head, Dr. Paul Jouve—a specialist in cranial injuries who readily admitted that he had not examined the body—confidently stated that she could have survived for several hours. He cited two cases to support this view. One involved a child who had fallen from a second-floor window, resulting in a serious fracture of the skull. The child survived for eight hours. Another was that of a young man on a motor scooter who had driven into a reinforced concrete post, and his skull was fractured in two places. He had been in a coma for several hours. This testimony directly contradicted that of Dr. Dragon. An inconclusive argument ensued as to whether Elizabeth had tried to run away or she had been killed as she was lying down and then carried to the slope down to the river.

The court was then adjourned until 3:00 p.m.

The afternoon's proceedings began with the testimony of Dr. Paul Nalin, one of the two doctors who had conducted the autopsies. He disagreed with his colleague Dr. Dragon on several issues. He argued that the difference in the degree of rigidity between the parents and the child was not a result of the times at which they were killed but because of their difference in ages. There was considerable discussion of the pool of blood near the cesspit. How big was it? Had Jack died there? Could he have crossed the road on his own after having lost so much blood? No definite conclusions were reached.

Professor Guy Marrian was the next witness questioned. He spoke in English with a teacher from the high school in Digne acting as an interpreter. Speaking in a low and dignified voice, he insisted that at no time had his close friend ever worked for the secret service and that the entire notion of the murders involving espionage or clandestine operations was utterly absurd. Later in the trial Commissioner Fernand Constant stated that Roger Autheville, the former Communist Party boss in the Basses-Alpes and captain in the Francs-Tireurs et Partisans Français, had assured him that the prevalent idea that Sir Jack had anything to do with the local Maquis was pure fantasy.

Guy Marrian also stated that the Drummonds had expressed their intention of camping out that night. With distinct disgust he told of how Gaston Dominici had shown him the places where his dear friends had died: he had done so with the detachment of a museum guide and clearly expected a tip, by holding out his right hand and rubbing the thumb and index finger together. Gaston was outraged at this insinuation and growled that peasants in the Basses-Alpes never asked for a reward when passing on information. At this point someone in the courtroom yelled out, "Bravo!"

Mrs. Phyllis Marrian confirmed her husband's version of Gaston's behavior, thus provoking another outburst from Gaston. He accused her of lying in such outrageous terms that Pollak ordered him to be silent.

Professor André Ollivier then testified about the carbine and the weapons found in the possession of Paul Maillet. He stated that all the cartridges and bullets found at the scene of the crime had been fired by the Rock-Ola. He had discovered a certain similarity between the oil used on the carbine and the guns belonging to Clovis. Paul Maillet had used a totally different type of oil on his weapons. Pollak was able to get the professor to admit that although the oil used on the Rock-Ola and on Clovis's guns was similar, it bore no resemblance to that used on the guns at the Grand' Terre.

There followed a lengthy technical discussion of the distance at which the shots had been fired. The result was inconclusive, with Ollivier arguing that with the techniques then available it was impossible to establish precisely the exact degree of closeness. The principal issue here revolved around the wound on Sir Jack's hand. The doctors all agreed that it certainly was not a bullet wound.

Several minor witnesses then followed. Marceau Blanc, a truck driver from Gap, had passed the scene of the crime at 4:30 a.m. He reported the rear doors of the Hillman had been open, and a camp bed was in front of the vehicle. Joseph Moynier, a chauffeur from Laragne, drove past half an hour later. The car's rear doors were then shut, and the camp bed was no longer in front of the Hillman.

The final witness on the second day was Roger Roche, a farmer who lived at Dabise, a village situated on the opposite bank of the Durance and a little farther than a mile from the Grand' Terre. He had heard five shots at 1:15 a.m. When asked whether they were fired in a burst or shot by shot, he replied shot by shot. He clearly stated that he had looked in the direction of the shots for a quarter of an hour. He saw no vehicles pass along the *route nationale* N96 that went past the Grand' Terre.

The first two days of the trial had failed to shine much light on the case. There was a massive police file against Gaston Dominici, but no tangible evidence had been presented. It was therefore hoped that when Gustave, Clovis, and Zézé were questioned the case against Gaston would be more compelling.

The third day of the trial began with other witnesses who had driven past the Grand' Terre on the night of 4–5 August 1952. An eagerly awaited witness that Friday morning was a distinct disappointment. Aristide Panayotou claimed to have been at the scene of the crime at about 1:10

a.m. He had stopped about 80 yards from the crime scene, not as he had previously claimed to relieve himself, but because his lights had failed. He heard some screams and a number of shots, but he was unable to say how many. He saw a man staggering across the road. That man was followed by a "gentleman" who was about forty years old and had prominent cheekbones. He was carrying some unidentifiable object in his left hand. The judge asked him why he had not informed the police, but Panayotou did not reply. Then the judge pointed out a number of inconsistencies and contradictions in Panayotou's testimony. He claimed that there had been two bursts of fire, while all other witnesses spoke of single shots. He had not heard any dogs barking, whereas others had. Panayotou was such an unreliable witness, his testimony so full of contradictions and nonsense, that the court soon grew impatient. Pollak asked why he had not been charged for giving the police such a patently absurd story. The advocate general, Rozan, gave the rather lame explanation that the court had decided to give Panayotou a final chance to tell the truth in the assize court. Sabatier apologized for having wasted the court's time while still seconding Rozan's reasoning.

It was with some relief when Jean-Marie Olivier, a rather more serious witness, took the stand. He stated that he had been stopped at 5:50 a.m. by Gustave, who had asked him to inform the police. He had seen Marie and Yvette standing by the garden wall. He reaffirmed his statement that Gustave had emerged from behind the Hillman. Prior to the trial, he had insisted that Gustave had not stopped him; rather, he had stopped of his own accord because of the disarray around the Hillman.

Faustin Roure was the next witness. Gustave had visited him on the evening of 4 August to tell him about the landslide. Roure got up early the next day to examine the damage, taking a red flag with him in case he had to stop the train. He had found Clovis standing by Elizabeth's body, the sight of which had shocked him deeply. He then followed Clovis toward the house. It was then that he saw a camp bed that was parallel to the Hillman. At the farmhouse Yvette told Roure that she had heard shots during the night. Clovis asked Gustave whether he had informed the police. He said that he had, but that it would take some time before they arrived. At that point Gaston returned to the farmhouse. He said something had happened during the night and asked what it was. Yvette said that there had been a killing, and Gaston asked where. She said at the end of the field. He then left to take a look.

Roure was thus witness to a nice little charade, with Gaston pretending to know nothing of the murders and to be surprised at being put into the picture by his daughter-in-law. On 6 August Gaston had told Sébeille that it was Gustave who had first told him of the murders. Why had they felt it necessary to change the story?

For the defense Charrier pointed out that the witness had failed to mention that he had stopped at La Serre on his way back, where he had seen Zézé Perrin. The defense lawyer asked why he had only mentioned Elizabeth and not the other two bodies. Roure replied that he had not seen the others; one was covered with a blanket, the other by a camp bed. Charrier solemnly declared that it contradicted the testimony of Madame Roure on what her husband had told her. Her statement was then read out loud. It was identical to what her husband had just said, leading the courtroom to burst out in loud guffaws. No reference was made to Roure's statement in March 1953 that he could not remember if he had visited La Serre that morning and his categorical denial of having told Zézé Perrin about the murders.[13]

The presiding judge called for order. Gaston was then asked what he thought of Roure's testimony. He replied that he had not seen Roure when he returned to the Grand' Terre that morning. Roure was somewhat surprised at this statement but remarked that it was true that they had not spoken to one another.

Jean Ricard, the traveling salesman who had been camping at Ganagobie, was the next witness. He had arrived on the scene shortly after Roure had. He stated that Anne's legs were uncovered below the knee, whereas Roure had said that her body was completely covered. The body was still parallel to the Hillman.

Captain Albert then stated that when he arrived, the body had been moved so it was at an angle to the car. He imagined that it was because someone had been looking for spent cartridges.

The fourth day of the trial began that Saturday with the cross-examination of Zézé Perrin. He created an exceptionally bad impression. His face was distorted by a rictus that resembled a hideous parody of a grin. His legs shook, his fingers drummed on the bar of the witness stand. To one journalist he looked like a cornered fox, ready to bite.[14]

It was suggested that Zézé had spent the night of 4–5 August at the Grand' Terre and that his perpetual lying was designed to disguise this fact. First, he claimed that he had worked all day long at La Serre. The judge reminded him that he had also worked for Mr. Delcitte, who had a field across the road. Zézé admitted that was indeed the case. He then said that he got home at about 7:00 p.m. and had supper with his mother. Gustave drove past on his motorcycle while they were eating, but he did not enter the house, as Zézé had previously testified. When asked why he had lied about this, he remained silent but was visibly nervous. The presiding judge then asked him why he had told the gendarmes that he had gone to Peyruis to get bread the next day. It was a false alibi because the shopkeeper in question, Mr. Puissant, had died three years previously. Zézé again remained silent when confronted with this lie. In response to another question, he said that he had borrowed a bicycle belonging to Clovis's son, Gilbert, to go to the fete in Digne. He had then used it to go the Grand' Terre on the morning of 5 August, but the gendarmes had stated that the only bicycle at the site was one that belonged to Gustave.

Zézé admitted that Yvette had told him that the English had come to get water, but he added that she had asked him not to tell the police. Pollak, in his attempt to show that Zézé had been at the Grand' Terre the night of the murders, made much of his statement that Sir Jack had been wearing blue pajamas when his body had been covered with a camp bed. This suggested that Zézé had seen Jack before he was killed, but a police photograph was produced that showed the pajamas were visible under the camp bed.

For the civil suit, attorney Claude Delorme asked about Gaston's statement that his grandson was a ne'er-do-well. Gaston looked perplexed. Zézé turned crimson. Gaston then blurted out, "It's possible that he's the murderer. I don't know, but he could be. Honestly why would Clovis accuse me? He's my son and I've always got on well with him." The judge then asked, "Why would he accuse you? Is it because Roger (Zézé) is guilty?" Gaston replied, "To save someone else. As for me, I've never even killed a grasshopper at home. All the same, Mister President, have you ever seen anything like that, a son who accuses his father? It's incredible!" He went on to say that it could very well have been Zézé Perrin, because he often went off poaching with Gustave during the night. "He's a layabout, a poacher, always cooking up something shady with Gustave, fishing when it's forbidden, catching rabbits and thrushes with snares." Bousquet then asked him whether he thought that Gustave was guilty. Gaston replied, "I wouldn't say no. Both of them were always out hustling."

At this point Delorme raised the question of the canvas bucket, asking that the Marrians be brought back to the witness stand. Mr. Marrian said that he had not personally seen the object in question, but his wife had. She confirmed this point.

Zézé's mother, Gaston's daughter Germaine, was a thin-faced woman of thirty-eight. She created quite a stir when she took the stand. Well dressed, with some impressive jewelry and a fresh permanent wave, she did not conform to the typical image of a peasant's wife. She said that she had spent the night of 4–5 August with her husband at the Cassine, a farm to which the family was about to move. When she got back to La Serre, she found a note from Zézé saying that there had been an "accident" at the Grand' Terre. The previous evening she had had supper with Zézé. Gustave had driven past on his motorcycle and had honked the horn as usual, but he did not enter the house. She went on to say that Yvette had told her that the English had come to get water. When asked whether Zézé had spent the night at the Grand' Terre, she said that he no longer went there because she had had a row with her father and was not on speaking terms with him. She had been very angry with her father for the previous two years. The judge interjected that she had previously stated that Gustave had entered the house and had taken Zézé with him to spend the night at the Grand' Terre. Germaine denied this.

Charrier repeated Bousquet's questions by saying that she had told Sébeille that Zézé and Gustave got on well together and that Gustave had stopped at La Serre to take Zézé with him to the Grand' Terre. Germaine continued to insist that this was not true. When asked why she had broken with her father, she said that he had accused her of being a slut. Thereupon, Gaston launched into a denunciation of his daughter's morals but added that her husband was the one who had told him that she was sleeping around. At this point the court adjourned for lunch until three o'clock.

The principal witness that Saturday afternoon was Paul Maillet. A voluble and vulgar braggart, he addressed the court as if it were a meeting of the Lurs Communist Party cell. He repeated how Gustave had said to him, "If you had heard the screams! It was horrible!" When he asked where Gustave had been at the time, Gustave replied that he had been in the alfalfa field. Pollak objected, saying that Paul Maillet had hidden this important revelation for months. Maillet replied that it was because he thought that Gustave had been involved in the crime. At this remark, Gaston lost his temper and shouted, "Maillet used to be a friend! Now he is accusing me. He's been plotting with Clovis for the last eighteen months to get me charged. He's a liar!" Pollak also accused Maillet of being a liar in terms that revealed the contempt of a party militant for one who had been excommunicated.

At this point Bousquet turned to the question of why there had been no discussion of the supposed meeting of Communist Party members at the Grand' Terre on the evening of 4 August 1952, as so much had been written about it in the papers. The answer was quite simple: there had been no mention of it in the dossier. This oversight proved once again that the dossier had some serious omissions. Was this meeting just a journalistic fabrication, a result of village tittle-tattle, and a collective hallucination; or had there been a concerted effort to hide a compromising truth?

Commissioner Constant was then questioned about Gustave's contra-dictory statements. He replied that he had never believed a word Gustave said. His story was simply unbelievable. Constant denied that he had met with a "wall of silence" in the community of Lurs. On the contrary, people had been cooperative and helpful. The one exception was at the

Grand' Terre, where he had often thought that Gaston was about to attack him. Asked about the meeting on the eve of the murders, he said that he had been unable to get any precise information. There followed a brief but inconclusive cross-examination of Inspector Tardieu before the court adjourned for a day's rest on Sunday.

The trial resumed on Monday, 22 November. The principal witness that day was to be Commissioner Sébeille. Before he could take the stand, Pollak, who was increasingly frustrated by the persistent lying of the Dominici clan, requested that Zézé Perrin be placed under oath. With a dramatic flourish he pronounced, "May the thunderbolts of the law strike all liars!" The advocate general professed to be in full agreement. He argued that all the Dominicis, not merely Zézé, should be placed under oath because the whole lot of them were liars. Lawyers for the civil case also supported this move. Bousquet then asked whether Gaston was agreeable. With a broad smile, he said that he would be delighted.

The court then adjourned to discuss the proposal. They returned quickly, and Bousquet announced that the defense team's request had been denied. The Dominicis would not be placed under oath. There was a murmur of disapproval in the courtroom. Pollak muttered, "That's all right! The witnesses now know that they can lie without running any risk." Bousquet ordered him to show due respect and spare such comments on a court decision.

The defense's motive for requesting that the Dominicis be placed under oath was obvious. If they could be trapped into committing perjury, there would be good grounds for an appeal or a retrial. This was precisely what that court wanted to avoid. The point in law was contestable. Paragraph 322 of the code of criminal procedure stated that the parents and relations of the accused were not to be placed under oath, but the code also states that the court could permit it, provided that the prosecution and the defense did not object. In this case the prosecution did not want to see fifteen months of investigation rendered worthless because of almost inevitable perjury by the congenitally mendacious Dominici clan.

Most of the rest of the day was devoted to hearing Sébeille's deposition. He gave a careful and detailed account of his investigation, explaining how he had come to the conviction that the murderer came from the Grand' Terre and leading up to Gaston's confession when he had blurted out: "I'm going to do you a favor, kid. I killed the English. It was a romantic misdeed."[15]

There was a cry of horror in the courtroom when Sébeille related his questioning of Gustave about his discovery of Elizabeth's body. First, there was incredulity when he said that Gustave had thought that her parents had murdered her, then indignation when he claimed that he had thought that they had run away. This reaction turned to anger when Gaston reportedly said that he had gone to the Hillman to keep a watchful eye on the Drummonds' property.

Bousquet asked the commissioner why he had not questioned Clovis after he had obviously fallen apart when he was shown the murder weapon. Sébeille's answer was hardly convincing. The scene had happened on the main road. He was surrounded by journalists. He had questioned Clovis for two hours later in the day but to no avail. He then went on the counterattack by complaining that Professor Ollivier had taken several months before delivering his report on the murder weapon. As for Panayotou, he was a storyteller, "to put it mildly."

Gaston listened to Sébeille's testimony with lively interest. He leaned forward with his elbows on the box, his chin resting on his hands, a wry smile on his lips.

Pollak interrupted Sébeille on several occasions, protesting that the judge was prejudiced against the accused. Bousquet condescendingly announced that even in the most difficult of cases, his impartiality had never been called into question. Gaston then caused quite a stir when he claimed that he had only made his confession because his coffee had been drugged. Pollak engaged in some swift damage control by assuring the court that he was convinced that his client's coffee had not been drugged but that in his confusion he might have imagined that it had been. The commissioner indignantly replied that his conscience was clear.

The court was then adjourned.

9   The Verdict

Marcel Bousquet's plan for the trial's next day was to concentrate on the events of 14 November 1953, the day that Gaston Dominici confessed to the murders. Victor Guérino was the first witness to be heard on Tuesday, 23 November. He gave a sober account of events that led to Gaston's making a confession. He stated that they had conversed in a friendly atmosphere, exchanging stories, for which Gaston had used the word "parabolas." Gaston had rambled on about good times and bad: his snaring seven hares in one day, his military service, his years toiling at Ganagobie, his marriage, his discovery on his wedding night that his wife was carrying another man's child, and his saving for years to buy the Grand' Terre. Then suddenly he had blurted out: "Yes, they attacked me. They thought I was a prowler."[1] He next told Guérino that he wanted to see "the President." The policeman assumed that by this he meant Commissioner Pierre Prudhomme.

Shortly afterward Gaston told Guérino's colleague Joseph Bocca that he was sacrificing himself for the sake of his family. In his deposition, Guérino said, Gaston had repeatedly muttered, "Oh, the little girl!"[2] Léon Charles-Alfred for the defense pointed out that these words did not appear in the transcript. Émile Pollak added that it was unacceptable to have considerable differences between the statements made before the trial and the testimony made in court, especially from the same witnesses.

Gaston claimed that he could not remember a thing because he was in such a confused state after hours of interrogation, but Bocca confirmed his colleague's account. Gaston had claimed he would shoulder the blame to save his grandchildren's honor, because he did not mind going to prison if he could take his dog with him. He loved that animal more than all the rest of the family. Bocca went on to say that Gaston had told him the following: Gustave bought the carbine at the time of the liberation, that it was he who did the deed, that Yvette had told him that three people had been killed, and that he got up two or three times during the night. "Now they are all putting the blame on me!"

Commissioner Prudhomme was then called to the stand. He said that he could not remember word for word what had passed between him and Gaston, but it had been more of a conversation than a cross-examination. He had asked the old farmer whether the Englishwoman had anything to do with it, whereupon "the patriarch launched into a very compromising account of what happened."

Pollak and Pierre Charrier tried to show that Prudhomme's statement contradicted those of Bocca and Guérino on several points. Pollak stressed that Prudhomme had not even mentioned the mulberry tree, even though the newspapers had talked about it for months on end. He also asked at what time Edmond Sébeille had joined Prudhomme at the law courts, because Gaston had made his formal statements to these two men alone. Gaston claimed that he could only remember talking about the carbine, whereupon the advocate general remarked that his amnesia was remarkably selective. Staff Sgt. Marius Sabatier testified next that on 14 November 1953 Gaston had said that he had run after the little girl and had hit her over the head with a rifle butt.

Gaston's wife, Marie, was the final witness that morning. "The Sardine" was a tiny, thin old woman, her face deeply lined. She said, "I don't know anything. I didn't hear any shots that night or any screams. I just heard the dog barking. At about six o'clock Gaston told me that there was a little girl dead by the bridge. That's all." Bousquet asked her, "Weren't you upset? You have grandchildren; you are a mother and a grandmother. You didn't think of going to help the little girl?" She replied, "Good heavens no! I didn't think of it!" She maintained she had not seen the English people the previous evening; in fact, she had seen nothing, heard nothing, and knew nothing. When asked about her married life, she answered that she had never lacked anything, that she missed her husband since he "went away," and that she rejected out of hand any suggestion that he might have been involved in the crime. Gaston was visibly moved by this demonstration of loyalty. He asked her, "Is it true that you saw my trousers covered with blood?" She replied, "Your trousers? They were dry. And clean. As usual."

Yvette was the first witness called that afternoon. Smartly dressed in a blue suit and a green and red pullover, with a gold heart on a chain round her neck, she was carefully made up and her hair was freshly permed. She made a gesture of acknowledgment to her father-in-law as she took the stand. Before she had a chance to speak, Pollak interrupted the session and insisted that she be put under oath. The presiding judge adjourned the court for longer than an hour to discuss the matter with his assistants, but again they denied the request.

Yvette then gave her version of events during the night of 4–5 August. She and her husband had gone to bed at ten o'clock but were awoken at eleven thirty by the dogs' barking. They heard Gaston talking to three strangers, asking them where they were going and what they were doing. The strangers left, and she and Gustave went back to sleep, only to be awoken again at one o'clock by gunshots. Gaston got up at four thirty; Gustave, half an hour later. The courtroom was deeply shocked when she recounted her actions that morning: how she had failed to even look at a little girl whom she knew was still alive; how she had taken her baby and gone to Oraison to buy some medicine; how she had had a leisurely lunch with her parents, the Barths; and how they had all gone back to the Grand' Terre "to have a look at the bodies."

She withdrew all her previous statements to the effect that she had heard cries in the night; that her husband had got up to "have a look"; that he had seen her father-in-law "looking distraught" while walking up and down in the courtyard; that she had ever said, "Gustave didn't tell me why my father-in-law had killed the English"; and that Clovis was the one who had told them that Gaston had committed the crime. Now she knew nothing, remembered nothing, and denied everything. She previously had maintained throughout that she had never seen the MI, but she now claimed to have heard two cars immediately after the shootings. She insisted that "the English" had not come to the farmhouse to ask for water. She said that Zézé Perrin had confused them with three Swiss people who had come to the house with a canvas bucket three days before. This claim did not explain how Zézé knew that Elizabeth could speak French and her mother could not. Yvette's was such an impressive piece of stonewalling that the public prosecutor, Calixte Rozan, said in his summing up, "What a kid!"[3]

Getting nowhere with this obdurate witness, Bousquet called Clovis to the stand. Short and stocky, he bore a close facial resemblance to his father. He wore a pair of velvet trousers, a jersey, and a gray jacket. Spruce and clean-shaven, he appeared to be calm. Unlike the rest of the clan, he gave answers that were clear and unequivocal. He began by stating categorically that his son had not lent Zézé his bicycle until two weeks after the crime, on 18 August. Zézé had said that he had given the bicycle back on 18 August, thus sowing further confusion, but it did not alter the fact that only Gustave's bicycle was at the Grand' Terre on the day of the murders. Clovis also said that he had first seen the carbine when he went into the shed to look for some string, but he did not specify the date.

On 5 August 1952 Gustave had told him that he had heard shots in the night and that he had found the body of a little girl. She had groaned a little but was dead by the time he approached her. Clovis had asked him whether he had alerted the gendarmes, and Gustave had replied that he had. Clovis then went to look at her and returned to the Grand' Terre with Faustin Roure, who had checked the landslide. It was then that he had seen the bodies of the parents. One was under a blanket; the other, covered by a camp bed.

Two days later Sébeille had shown him the murder weapon. He recognized it and had felt weak in the knees. Bousquet asked him how he had reacted. He said he knew that the weapon had come from the Grand' Terre, so he asked Gustave about it. He told him that their father was the one who had fired the shots. At first Clovis had refused to believe it. He knew that his father was quick tempered, but he could not believe that Gaston was capable of committing such a terrible crime.

Clovis then repeated his story that when Gustave was in jail, his parents had asked him to sleep overnight at the Grand' Terre.[4] One evening, when

Gaston was in a terrible rage, he had blurted out in patois, "I've killed three. I could easily kill another."[5] Clovis still found this hard to believe, but when Gustave was released from prison he said that at four o'clock in the morning of 5 August 1952, while he was taking out the goats to pasture, their father had told him everything. The presiding judge asked Clovis why he accused his father of murder. He replied that it was because of what Gustave had told him. Asked whether he was certain, he stated that he always stuck to his word, even though it was a terrible thing for a son to have to accuse his father. Clovis was now obviously under great strain and had difficulty in maintaining his composure.

Asked about a letter that he had written at his wife's entreaty to Gustave's father-in-law, François Barth, and called upon him to encourage Gustave to "tell the whole truth," Clovis said he had done it so Gustave would clear himself of all suspicion. Bousquet asked him whether, once his father had confessed to the crime, he still suspected his brother. He replied that he did not know what to think and then, after a brief pause, said that he had never suspected Gustave.

Zézé was the first to appear on the witness stand at Wednesday's session, the seventh day of the trial. Captain Albert, head of the Forcalquier gendarmerie, said that Zézé's testimony on 5 August 1952 had been a fabric of lies and that his alibi for the previous night had been proven false. Pollak agreed with Albert that Zézé had lied, but he pointed out that it was important to find out why he had done so. Zézé was questioned throughout the morning, but the net result was extremely meager. When asked why he had lied he simply shrugged his shoulders, saying that he did not know. Bousquet asked him whether he had spent the night of 4–5 August 1952 at the Grand' Terre. He artfully replied that he had not slept there since he was eight years old. He was sixteen in 1952. This agreed with Gaston's answers to this question. On 4 August Zézé had helped his mother water the beans in the family's new farm. He had returned that evening to the farmhouse at La Serre, from which they were moving soon, and had eaten supper. He spent the night alone there, his mother having left to rejoin her husband at the new farm. Contrary to his previous statement that Gustave had stopped off at La Serre on his way back from seeing Faustin Roure at Peyruis the evening of 4 August, Zézé now stated that he had simply seen him ride past on his motorcycle. Bousquet asked him why he had lied. Zézé again said that he did not know.

When Gaston was asked what he thought of his grandson's testimony, he replied that he was a little crook who went poaching with Gustave. Although almost all the peasants in the area were dedicated poachers, to describe someone as a "poacher" was an extreme insult. He then rambled on, asking why Clovis was accusing him of the murders when he had thought it was probably Gustave who had committed the crime. He then returned to his denunciation of Gustave and Zézé. After some hesitation he said, "Both of them are poachers." Clearly Gaston was suggesting that Gustave and Zézé were out poaching on the night of 4–5 August and were thus implicated in the crime.

As Zézé had testified that his aunt Yvette had said that Anne and Elizabeth had come to the Grand' Terre to ask for water, the Marrians were called back and asked whether they knew if the Drummonds had a canvas bucket with them. Neither of the Marrians could answer this question. Mrs. Marrian had previously testified that she had seen a canvas bucket, but she was unable to say with any confidence whether they had taken it with them.

Germaine Perrin—Zézé's mother and Gaston's daughter—readily admitted that there were problems between the Perrins and the Dominicis, but she was unable to offer any useful evidence in the case at hand. Pollak cried out in desperation, "We refuse to give up when faced with the lies of the Perrin family!" Paul Maillet was equally reticent in answering the questions fired at him, provoking Pollak into histrionic outbursts of frustrated rage.

Gustave was called to the witness stand when the court resumed at three o'clock that afternoon. He did not create a good impression. Although a handsome, well-built man, he had a weak mouth and a mirthless smile and spoke with a thin, high-pitched voice. He soon became enmeshed in a series of lies and falsehoods to the point of appearing almost feebleminded. He began by blurting out, "I've been lying all the time. My father is innocent!" He then launched into a garbled account of events since the evening of 4 August 1952. In answer to the judge's question why he had continually changed his story, he said that the police had told him that they had to "finish this business." He said, "They accused me of all manner of things, and they beat me. They simply wanted to make me lie. Now I say that my father is innocent, just like all the other family members do. We don't know anything about this business." He accused Clovis of having thought up the idea of denouncing their father, whereupon Gaston leaped to his feet yelling, "That's not true! You were the first to accuse me!"

Gustave cut a pathetic figure. Obviously terrified of his wife, his father, and his brother Clovis, he became entangled in a web of lies and contradictions. His pathetic efforts to defend his father only served to make the case against him stronger, and the poorly prepared defense team did nothing to help. Judge Bousquet, unable to restrain his contempt for the witness, denounced him in no uncertain terms:

> You are a coward, a creature without the slightest trace of guts. You were the first to accuse your father, to make him into a suspect accused of murder. Now you claim that the police beat you up in order to get out of you what you now claim to be a pack of lies. You claim that you were forced into lying. Thus you were prepared to lie and accuse your father of murder and you continue to lie. You are a coward and your behavior is unconscionable.

Gustave appeared to be unmoved by this outburst. Dressed in his Sunday best, he stood there impassively, a look of utter stupidity on his face, moving nervously from one foot to another. Judge Bousquet, Advocate General Rozan, Deputy Public Prosecutor Louis Sabatier, and the attorney Claude Delorme got nothing out of him but an uneasy smile, a blank stare, and endless assertions that the entire Dominici clan was innocent. The defense team of Pollak, Charrier, and Charles-Alfred were left equally frustrated. The more Gustave lied the more the conviction grew that he knew a great deal about the crime. Gustave, the key witness whose testimony had led to Gaston's arrest, now retracted everything and thus placed the entire case against Gaston in serious question.

The judge reminded Gustave that he had said upon finding Elizabeth's body that he had not gone to see her parents because he thought they had murdered their own daughter. At this point there were murmurs in court. He then asked how Gustave could possibly have thought such a thing. Gustave replied, "It happens all the time!" At that there were howls of protest. Bousquet asked him if he really thought that it was a common occurrence for parents to kill their children. At this Gustave replied that he had not realized that they were her parents. Having been caught in this obvious absurdity, he blandly stated that everything he had ever said was a lie. Five minutes later, to general astonishment, he announced that he had never told a lie. Shortly afterward he retracted this obvious falsehood.

Clovis was recalled to the witness stand to answer more questions about the Rock-Ola. When questioned about the similarity between the oil used in it and his own weapons, Clovis confidently asserted that the carbine had never been in his possession. He further claimed that he had never gone poaching. He said that the carbine was kept at the Grand' Terre, but he did not know who owned it. It took the court more than an hour to understand that Clovis recognized the weapon, but that did not necessarily imply that he knew to whom it belonged. He then said he did not believe his father had taken the gun with him when he first went outside. After all, why should he take a gun that he had never used with him to walk a couple of hundred yards along the railway line? This implied that Gaston had deliberately gone to collect it with intent to use it against the Drummonds.

When Pollak asked Clovis why he had never mentioned the carbine when he had accused his father in front of the magistrates, he answered that he did not want it to be known that it had come from the farm. Pollak then demanded to know why Clovis had not revealed the ownership of the carbine when it had first been shown to him. Clovis remained silent. A long discussion ensued, during which the defense pointed out certain minor inconsistencies in Clovis's testimony regarding the murder weapon.

Gaston was then asked what he had to say. He stood up, pointed at his son, and with his voice trembling with rage, claimed that Clovis was bearing false witness. He yelled, "I'll tell you the pure and simple truth. I'm a loyal Frenchman. And you [pointing at Clovis] lie every time you breathe. I'm going to refresh your memory. First of all on Christmas Day you came to eat at the Grand' Terre. You now say that you couldn't eat anything because of your worries and that you couldn't eat a thing. That was not the real reason. You were not hungry because you'd partied all night in Peyruis. You were completely plastered and puked all the way. Bastard!" Clovis, equally furious, swore that he was telling the truth. Gaston said that he was a liar and ought to be ashamed of himself. His final remark was to yell, "I have a clean conscience, but your brother and you—" As things were now getting out of hand, the judge prudently adjourned the court for lunch.

When the court resumed in the afternoon Clovis's wife, Rose, stated that her husband had been very secretive about the whole affair. She had been very annoyed at his reticence, and in an argument on this score, Clovis had said that he hoped that his father would either hand himself over or write a confession and then kill himself. She then said that the story that Clovis had got blind drunk that Christmas Eve was a complete fabrication but confirmed that he had vomited on the way back from the Grand' Terre on 25 December. Finally, she spoke of the letter he had written to Yvette's father, in which he implored him to make sure that Gustave and his wife told the truth. The rumor was that Gustave was guilty, but Rose believed he was absolutely innocent and wanted him to clear his name.

There not being enough time that day to question Gustave once more, the court agreed that some minor witnesses suggested by the defense might be heard. Various passersby during the night of 4–5 August 1952 were questioned. Nothing of any value transpired.

The eighth day of the trial began with yet another confrontation with Gustave. He was soon entangled in a series of demonstrable lies. Sabatier for the prosecution announced that he did not want to go over all the witness's lies again. It was up to the jury to decide which parts of his testimony were true and which were false. Charles-Alfred for the defense announced that his team refused to question Gustave, saying that it was beneath the men's dignity to question a man like that. The courtroom was getting restless as the situation was once again clearly out of hand.

Bousquet called an adjournment, after which he consented to the defense team's request to go outside and look at a Hillman, similar to the one owned by the Drummonds, ostensibly to see how Sir Jack might have wounded his hand on the rear bumper. The red gowns of the judge and prosecution and the black gowns of the defense team fluttered around the car as they wandered around in the mud for an hour. It proved to be a totally pointless exercise that cast no light on the case. The court resumed deliberations at 11:35 a.m.

Judge Bousquet called Roger Périès to the witness stand to hear his version of Gustave's interrogation. It was a most unusual move to call the examining magistrate in a case as a witness. Examining Magistrate Périès was placed under oath. His statement went as follows:

I learned that Gustave wanted to speak to me. I received him. He told me that he had been mistreated, but had not been beaten. I asked him whether he had any bruises. He was unable to show me any. If he had done so I would have called for a doctor to examine him. Anyway, the magistrates did not leave the law courts during the three days of interrogation between 12 and 15 November. If there had been any ill treatment, we would not necessarily have heard any screams, but we would certainly have noticed something.

Gustave replied that he had told Périès that he had been punched in the stomach. Périès flatly denied that there was any evidence to support such an accusation.

French court procedure required at this point that the accused be given the right to question Périès in his capacity as prosecuting magistrate. Bousquet refused to make such a ruling, thus provoking an indignant outburst from the attorney Scapel, who was acting as representative of the Marseille bar to make sure that due procedure was observed.[6] He demanded that the hearing should be suspended. He invoked the imprescriptible rights of the defense, and with loud support from Gaston's defense team, he insisted that the proceedings be suspended.

Bousquet, who was visibly irritated, brusquely refused this request and continued to question Gustave amid constant interruptions from the defense lawyers. He concentrated on Gustave's different accounts of what had happened on the night of 4–5 August 1952. Gustave blurted out that he had heard screams that night. When reminded that he had previously insisted that he had heard nothing, he replied that he had "thought" he had heard them. Gustave was gradually worn down until he finally blurted out, "I've been lying all the time! It's entirely false! My father is innocent. They made me lie." Bousquet was scarcely able to control himself and yelled at Gustave, "This is monstrous! You were lying when you accused your father. This is more than a lack of courage; it is more than cowardice. It is unspeakable!"

At this point Gaston stood up and with a trembling voice said, "Gustave, I pardon you, but tell the truth. In what of a state have you placed your family? Look at me now, sitting in the dock. It's shameful. He [Gustave] has disowned his mother, who gave him her breast. He has disowned his brothers, with whom he led a joyful life. He disowned his father. Ah well, a son! They treat me like a sheep in the fold. You have committed a mortal sin in accusing your own father."

On hearing this emotionally charged statement, the courtroom for once fell silent. Gustave muttered that he had never accused his father of anything.

Gaston then blurted out, "When you were in the alfalfa field with another, after having heard the screams, you knew where the weapon was and where it came from. It didn't come from us. But it didn't come from far away!" Gustave muttered, "I didn't go into the alfalfa field that night, not with anybody."

Bousquet let father and son continue this bizarre exchange as if it were of little concern to him. He then asked Gustave how many shots he had heard. He replied there were five or six. When the judge pointed out that the previous day Gustave had said that he had thought he only had heard some screams, Gustave murmured something about having thought so.

The courtroom became increasingly restless as Gustave replied to further questions with denials, silence, or "I don't know." Gaston again stood up.

> GASTON (loudly): I want to say to Gustave: you know the truth. Think of the entire family. Think of the honor of all my grandchildren. Tell the truth!
>
> GUSTAVE: I'm thinking of that. I don't know a thing
>
> GASTON: So, you prefer to let your father stay in prison. Your father, who never harmed anybody.
>
> GUSTAVE: It's all Clovis's fault!
>
> GASTON: You were the first to accuse me. I've said that I pardon you, but tell the truth.

Gustave remained silent.

Bousquet, rather than following up on this interesting lead, in a tone of utter contempt, ordered him to return to his seat and adjourned the court. Deputy Director of the National Police Charles Chenevier, who later led an inquiry into the case, wrote that Bousquet had lost an opportunity to reveal the truth and sabotaged the entire trial when he ordered the adjournment. Chenevier later wrote: "Law faculties now take this case as an example of what not to do when presiding over a criminal trial."[7] Gustave's "truth" was never revealed.

Clovis's brother-in-law, Jacky Barth, was called briefly to the stand. He was asked why he had not reported to the police that Gustave had told him on the morning of 5 August 1952 that Elizabeth had groaned when first he saw her. He replied that he had not even thought of it.

Augusta Caillat, Gaston's oldest daughter was the next to testify. A corpulent woman, she appeared to be confused and highly strung. Speaking with a pronounced stammer, she proclaimed her father innocent. She was forced to confront Clovis, whom she wrongfully accused of having denounced his father before Gustave had. She then demanded to know why he had accused their father. He replied that it was because Gaston had told him that he had killed the Drummonds. Even though she had not been present when Gaston confessed to Clovis, Augusta insisted that her father had said that "they," not "I," had killed three people and would kill another, meaning Paul Maillet. This revelation caused a prolonged stir in the courtroom.

A further argument ensued over what precisely Gaston had said and continued over the question of whether the carbine had been kept at the Grand' Terre. At this point Gaston interjected, "That carbine was never at the Grand' Terre. The false witness who stands before us [referring to Clovis] knows very well where it comes from. We talked about it. My son-in-law Roger Perrin [Zézé's father] said, 'If I had had the carbine I would have killed the wild boar!' You have in front of you the most discreditable witness."[8] To which Augusta added, "And the most cowardly." Clovis simply shrugged his shoulders. The effect of this outburst was somewhat weakened when Gaston claimed that it was Clovis who had mended the carbine with a metal band. Clovis laughed off this claim, for it showed that the weapon had indeed been at the Grand' Terre and that Gaston was well aware of its existence.

Augusta's husband, Clément Caillat, was the next witness. He dutifully claimed that Clovis had told him that he had never seen the carbine at the Grand' Terre and that he suspected Paul Maillet.

Two further witnesses were brought to the stand—Paul Deloitte and Germaine Perrin's lover, Jean Galizzi. Both men testified that Zézé Perrin had asked them to give him an alibi, begging them to tell the gendarmes that he had come to fetch milk at 6:00 a.m. on 5 August 1952. On 29 January 1953 Zézé told the police that 6:30 a.m. he went to the Garcins' farm, where his mother and father were tenants, to collect milk. Then Faustin Roure had arrived to buy a bottle of wine at La Serre and had told him of the murders at the Grand' Terre. On 17 March Zézé admitted to a Sergeant Romanet that he had lied and that his mother had bought the milk. Then he promptly changed his story, claiming to have gone to Peyruis at 6:00 a.m. to fetch bread and milk. The dairyman told him that the milk had been picked up by Jean Galizzi and taken to the Garcins' farm. Zézé promptly went to the farm, picked up the milk, and returned home to La Serre. Then Roure had appeared at 7:00 a.m. to ask if they had any milk. The dairyman's wife, however, had no recollection of a visit from Zézé Perrin on 5 August and added that her husband had died in November 1951. Roure stated that he often went to La Serre to pick up some wine, but he could not remember doing so on the morning of 5 August. A few days later Galizzi told Romanet that Zézé's story was a pack of lies.

Gustave and Clovis were then confronted with one another. Both adopted a truculent manner and stuck to their recent versions of events. Bousquet asked Gustave whether he had accused his father. He replied that he had but that it was all a pack of lies. At this point Gaston said that it was Gustave who had repaired the carbine and went on muttering something meaningless.

This unseemly family squabble, which the judge seemed incapable of controlling, reached fresh depths with the testimony of Gaston's son-in-law, Angelin Araman. Having given a brief and pointless testimony, he turned to Bousquet and said, "Mister President, I want to clear the courtroom!" Bousquet asked him what on earth he was talking about. Angelin replied that there was someone in the courtroom whom he did not like and who had stolen a metal cart. Bousquet asked him whom he meant. Angelin replied that it was Paul Maillet. When asked what harm he had done, Angelin replied, "None." In desperation Bousquet asked what this had to do with the Dominici case, to which Araman responded, "Nothing whatsoever!"

Amid much laughter at this bizarre interlude, Angelin's wife, Gaston's formidable daughter Clotilde Araman, was called to the stand. She was in an ugly mood. She stated that she had never seen the carbine at the Grand' Terre, adding that she suspected that it belonged to Paul Maillet. When asked why, she replied that Clovis had thought the same. Clovis flatly denied that he had ever suspected Paul Maillet. Gustave, when questioned on this point, said that he too suspected Paul Maillet. Gustave punched Clovis on the shoulder and, eyeball to eyeball, shouted: "You've lied too! I want the truth to come out today." Fearing that they would soon come to blows, the judge called for order.

Gaston demanded to know why Clovis treated him as an assassin. Clovis replied that he was simply repeating what Gaston had told him. Gustave yelled at his brother, "Yes, and can you remember what you said to me? 'It's that old bastard who killed them!'" Gaston then said that the carbine belonged to Clovis, but he denied this, saying that it was kept at the Grand' Terre.

Things were once again getting out of hand, but there was a slight lull in the storm when a fresh witness, Aimé Dominici, was cross-examined. He also said that he had never seen the carbine at the Grand' Terre. This was confirmed by young Gaston Dominici's wife, Marie, who asserted that there was no reason to doubt her father-in-law's innocence. She further claimed Clovis had said that "it would be better if it were the old man, rather than a young innocent." An outraged Clovis denied having ever said such a thing. In a feeble voice Gaston repeated that he was not guilty and that he did not want to take someone else's place. When Marie was asked what she thought of Gustave, she replied, "He's a weakling."

Gaston's nephew, Léon Dominici—his half-brother Leon's son—was the next witness to be called. He was a good-looking man, well spoken, intelligent, and polite. He was the only one of the entire Dominici clan who made a favorable impression. He said that he had never seen his uncle lift a hand against his children. He also thought that Gustave was a feeble creature, lacking any strength of character, whereas Clovis had backbone. Once, when Léon was eleven years old, he had amused himself while at the Grand' Terre by throwing stones at the porcelain insulation units on the electric pylons. Gaston had caught him in the act and had simply said, "Pack your bags and fuck off!"[9] He was at least able to cast a little light on the bizarre business concerning Paul Maillet and the metal cart. Maillet had sold it to Léon's cousin Bonino for 1,000 francs ($3). One day some employees of the electric company reclaimed it, saying that it had been stolen from them some time ago. Bonino went to Paul Maillet and asked for his money back. Maillet replied that it was pretty stupid of him to get caught. The story did not reflect well on Paul Maillet's honesty, but it contributed nothing to Gaston's defense. Léon tried to put Clovis on the spot by saying that although Gustave was spineless, he had not reacted when shown the murder weapon; whereas the tough Clovis had fallen apart.

The court now heard attorney Delorme speak for the civil party.[10] He had some experience in such matters, having won a symbolic 1 franc in damages in the court at Aix-en-Provence in a case against the seventy-three-year-old Georges "Dr. Sarret" Sarrenjani, who was accused of murdering three people and dissolving their bodies in sulfuric acid. Delorme began by saying that there was a fourth victim in this case, Lady Drummond's mother, Mrs. Wilbraham, who had suffered a stroke on hearing of the murders. He gave a moving account of Sir Jack's career and his family life with Anne and Elizabeth. He expressed his deep repulsion at the way in which Gaston had insulted his victims with his obscene and mendacious account of his exchange with Lady Drummond on the night of the crime. "It was not enough for Gaston Dominici to assassinate Lady Drummond, he also wanted also to dishonor her!" At this a number of women in the courtroom shouted, "Bravo!" He praised all those involved in the case and closed with a periphrastic flourish: "In order for the immense stain on our country to be removed, and to give back to the population the peace of mind to which they are entitled, justice must be done by punishing this terrible crime that you are called upon to judge."

Friday's session ended with Deputy Public Prosecutor Sabatier giving a passionate defense of the dossier. He began by stating categorically, "I am convinced that Gaston Dominici is entirely culpable, totally culpable and solely culpable." He gave a brief account of the course of the investigation, stressing Gustave's lies, the contradictions in the statements made by Yvette, and the fact that Gaston had made a voluntary confession, which he could have easily retracted when Périès questioned him. Sabatier discounted Dr. Dragon's testimony about Elizabeth's condition on the grounds that there was enough grass along the path for her feet not to have suffered any abrasions and because expert testimony had shown that rigor mortis begins much later in a child. He cleared Zézé Perrin of any suspicion, because had he been guilty he would not have testified that the Drummonds had come to the Grand' Terre to get water and would not have said that Gustave got up much earlier than usual on the morning of 5 August. He gave a violent temper as the motive for the murders: "You have before you a brutal and savage crime, committed by a violent man in a fit of rage. In my opinion it was the act of a single man. If there were a second person involved that would involve complicity—that is to say, a coolheaded action. I do not believe this. Just look at Gaston Dominici's character. He is proud. He says himself: 'I'm afraid of no one.' This crime is a reflection of his personality: anger possibly combined with alcohol."

As Gaston left the courtroom, there were many cries of "*à mort* (death)!"[11]

On Saturday morning, 27 November, the tenth and final day of the trial, Advocate General Calixte Rozan, who had lost his voice the day before due to influenza, had to use a microphone during his summary of the case for the prosecution to be intelligible. A technical fault resulted in his speech being heard over loudspeakers by the crowd outside the courtroom. It would be difficult to imagine a prosecutor who looked more prosecutorial. With small, beady eyes; a long, pointed nose; and bitterly ironical mouth, he was the very image of an inquisitor. Speaking in the flowery tones and rich cadences of an actor from the Comédie-Française, he dismissed out of hand a series of fantastic versions of the crime, the most persistent of which was that secret services were involved. He could do so with utter confidence, for he had seen a letter written by Patrick Reilly, the British minister in Paris, that had been given to attorney Delorme that testified that Sir Jack had never been engaged as an intelligence agent.[12] Rozan also was convinced that Zézé Perrin had not been at the Grand' Terre the night of the murders and that Gustave was innocent. He argued that Zézé's lies were designed to hide the fact that he had got out of bed late, which would have angered his father. Then Rozan played another dubious trump: Zézé would never have dared leave the farm during that night, because the horse stabled at La Serre, worth 100,000 francs ($300), might have strangled itself with its halter. Further, Gustave would have been exhausted, having spent the entire day threshing, and would not have wanted to wander around in the middle of the night poaching.

Rozan spoke to the "jurymen from the Basses-Alpes," men "with their feet on the ground," while constantly repeating that he came from the same region. His thumbnail sketches of the witnesses were remarkably succinct. Panayotou was "a piece of shit." Yvette "owed nothing to Jacques Fath and to Elizabeth Arden, but owed everything to our sun and our sky. . . . She's pretty but she's only a little '*garce*' and you, gentlemen of the jury from the Basses-Alpes, you know what that means."[13] Gustave was "a pathetic creature. . . . In this part of the world when one says he is nothing at all one has said everything." He quoted Michel de Montaigne and Alphonse Daudet, heavily underlining that the jurymen had probably never heard of them. He then paid tribute to Gaston Dominici's sterling qualities as a hardworking farmer. Gaston was clearly delighted at such praise.

Having voiced his appreciation of Sébeille's patient and exhaustive investigation, Rozan then launched into a lengthy description of the crime. It was embellished with many a rhetorical flourish. Turning toward the accused he declaimed, "You washed your hands in the Durance. As a result the people in Marseille drank some of little Elizabeth's blood." His description of Elizabeth's childish face bathed in moonlight, her little eyes full of an indescribable horror, her little hands imploring for mercy brought tears to many eyes. After two hours of flowery eloquence, he concluded by pleading with the jury to answer yes to all the seven questions they were going to have to answer "in the name of little Elizabeth, who is our little girl." In a parting shot he pleaded with the jury, "You should have no pity for this man, who had no pity for a ten-year-old child!" It was a magnificent show and a superb theatrical performance but was woefully lacking in substance.

For the defense, attorney Léon Charles-Alfred used a tone of biting irony to praise Rozan's exquisite rhetoric. He painted a glowing portrait of the stalwart patriarch and expressed his profound indignation at the methods used to extract his confession, but he offered little apart from a feeble attempt to present Gaston as an innocent old man who had confessed to the crime to save his grandchildren's honor.

Pierre Charrier, the Marseille Communist Party's lawyer, spoke next for the defense. He described the advocate general as a man who was overwhelmed by the task of defending a questionable dossier. He claimed that Rozan did not have a single decisive fact on which an objective judgment could be based.

The defense ended with Émile Pollak's plea. He argued that the case had been judged in advance and that it was based entirely on a confession. In a British or American court, where lawyers all have at least a fleeting acquaintance with Jeremy Bentham's "Rationale of Judicial Evidence," the weakness of such a case would have been self-evident; however, Pollak had to remind the court that a confession is worthless without material evidence. Sébeille's much vaunted psychological approach had ignored a great deal that might have bolstered his case. Furthermore, knowing exactly under what conditions Gaston's confession had been obtained was essential. Here Pollak became enmeshed in his own grandiloquence, even comparing Gaston's ordeal in the law courts to that of Christ on the cross. Indeed, he worked himself up into such a state that the court had to be adjourned for him to be able to change into a fresh shirt.

Pollak then dwelled at length on the lies and inconsistencies in the testimonies of Gustave, Clovis, and Zézé, a group that he described as "that disturbing trio." He reminded the jury of the Richauds' terrible murder at Valensole, for which two teenagers had been convicted. Who could say that Zézé Perrin, aged sixteen at the time of the murders, was incapable of committing such a crime? Pollak next claimed that Clovis was full of hatred for his father and that he was the owner of the murder weapon. He painted the reconstruction of the crime as "a pathetic movie." Pollak then solemnly announced that whereas Clovis was motivated by hatred, Gustave was motivated by fear. Turning toward him, he said,

"Gustave! If you are guilty, or if you know something, come here and speak out. We at least have no fear of the truth. Gustave! I go down on bended knee and beg you!" Gustave remained silent.

Pollak described Gaston as the victim of his two sons, whom he described as "wild beasts" and as "monsters who want to disembowel their father." He then turned to the jury:

> Are you going to be satisfied with this scapegoat? Are you going to find this innocent man guilty? Are you going to accept liars' words? Are you going to shed the blood of a decent man? Do not be cowards! Only count on yourselves. Do not bank on the prince's clemency. There is no legal provision for saving the old man from the scaffold. Accept your responsibility. It is not crimes that remain unpunished that wring the hearts of governments and the people, but the condemnation of the innocent.

He warned the jury of the terrible consequences of judicial error, mentioning the infamous cases of Jean Calas and Alfred Dreyfus.

The jury appeared to be unmoved by this florid peroration. At a quarter past twelve, Bousquet announced that the proceedings were over, whereupon he left the courtroom followed by his associate judges and the seven jurors in single file. Gaston's final words as they left the room were: "I'm here in place of another. I've already spent a year in prison. I'm honest and loyal. I'm innocent." This plea also made no impact on the stone-faced jury as the men left for the conference room to reach a verdict.

At two-thirty that afternoon, the bells rang, calling the court to reassemble. The presiding judge—who with his huge round head, thin lips, bulging eyes, and plastered-back hair, bore a marked resemblance to the prominent resistance leader and founder of the Mouvement Républicain Populaire (Popular Republican Movement), Georges Bidault—turned to the jury. In a low Provençal voice without a trace of solemnity, he asked the jury to announce its answers to seven questions: Was the accused guilty of the murder Sir Jack Drummond? Was he guilty of the murder of Lady Anne Drummond? Did he murder Elizabeth? Was Elizabeth's murder premeditated? He asked three further questions as to whether each murder happened at the same time as the other two. The jury answered yes on all seven counts.

The presiding judge then read out passages from paragraphs 302 and 304 of the criminal code and 351 and 367 of the code of criminal procedure in a monotonous tone. Then, raising his voice somewhat, he announced, "The court and the jury condemn Gaston Dominici to death!"

At first Gaston appeared to be unmoved. He sat quietly chewing a lump of sugar. Then as he left the box, he began to murmur some incomprehensible phrases. Then he exclaimed, "Must I pay for others? Ah! Those bastards . . ." It was unclear whether he was referring to the members of the jury or his own family.

Minutes later Bousquet called the court back into session so he could read the verdict of the civil case brought by Anne's mother, Mrs. Wilbraham, and in which the jury was not involved. She was awarded the symbolic one franc in damages.

Gaston was then asked whether he had anything to say. He launched into an antiphony of "I'm honest and loyal" and the like until he was interrupted by Charrier, who said that the invitation to speak on his own behalf was merely a formality and that he should say nothing. Immediately Gaston muttered, "Ah, so it's a formality. I don't understand anything, nothing at all!" Catching sight of Clovis, he spat out, "You filthy bastard!" After ten grueling days the trial was finally over, but was the Dominici affair now closed?

Gaston's nephew Léon, a strongly built man with a commanding presence, was standing in the corridor outside the courtroom when he heard the verdict. Overcome with emotion he rushed outside to where Gaston's grandson Marcel Dominici was waiting anxiously in the courtyard. Together they walked in silence through the wind and rain to a little hotel where the "clan of the faithful"—Yvette Perrin, Gustave Dominici, and Augusta Caillat—were eating sandwiches. On hearing the news, Yvette fell sobbing into her husband's arms. Augusta ran out of the room to hide in their car, quietly sobbing. Marcel, then drove them all to the Grand' Terre, where old Marie had a wood fire burning. They stayed until six o'clock, and then Marcel drove Augusta home.

Clovis, who had left the courtroom alone with tears in his eyes, entertained some journalists in his modest home in Peyruis. He told them he was convinced that his father had acted alone but confessed that he had not thought that Gaston would receive a death sentence.

Commissioner Charles Gillard, a senior policeman from Paris who was present at the trial as an observer, told the press, "The verdict and the condemnation to death cannot be considered satisfactory. A disagreeable impression remains of lies and of the impossibility of knowing whether one is more guilty than another."[14] The commissioner, who would play a prominent role in a later inquiry into the case, thus demonstrated that he was already predisposed to believe that Gaston Dominici had not acted alone.

With the trial over, the "Lurs Affair" became known as the "Dominici Affair." A trial that had been expected to last for four days had stretched to ten. The outcome came as no surprise. The newspapers had already created the picture of a vicious old man, a homicidal patriarch, and a drunken brute. This impression was reinforced by the representation in court of his curriculum vitae. Much here hinged on interpretative nuance. Was he miserly or economical? Was he healthily libidinous or sexually obsessed? Was he harshly authoritarian or merely strict with his children? Much was made of how he had aided in the birth of several of his children, implying a bestial indifference to his unfortunate wife; but the reports did not mention that this practice was common since there were no midwives in the region at that time and the doctor lived miles away. The Dominicis had neither a telephone nor a car, and at that time the road was unpaved. Even the fact that he had been involved in a fight fifty years earlier weighed heavily against him.

The Gaston Dominici who appeared in court seemed to bear little resemblance to the sadistic brute of the public imagination. Here was a simple old man in his Sunday best, full of native cunning, frequently smiling, slyly winking, joking with the warders, being sarcastic, and innocently believing that he would be able to speak his mind, would be heard, and would be believed. He played many roles—archetypical peasant, clan chieftain, simple goatherd, politician, and demagogue—but he never once looked as though he were a man charged with an appalling crime on trial for his life. Under constant attack from the presiding judge, Gaston frequently lost his temper, so he increasingly appeared as a violent, intractable, arrogant, authoritarian, and proud man who believed in nothing, who cared for nobody, and who was governed by feverish egotism.

The communist press, once the ardent defenders of the Dominicis but now determined to disassociate themselves from a man who was universally reviled, had no doubt that Gaston was guilty. *Le Dauphiné Libéré* gave twelve reasons for his guilt:

1. He had told Edmond Sébeille that Lady Drummond had died "without suffering."
2. He had claimed to have found a splinter of wood from the butt of the carbine under Elizabeth's head at nine o'clock in the morning of 5 August, when a gravedigger had found it at three o'clock that afternoon.
3. He had gone without the slightest hesitation to the shed where the carbine had been kept.
4. He had positioned himself during the reconstruction of the crime at the exact spot where the ejected cartridges had been found.
5. He knew that a bullet had wounded Elizabeth.
6. Without knowing the contents of the autopsy report, he knew that Sir Jack had been shot in the back.
7. He alone knew that the first shot had caused the wound on Sir Jack's hand.
8. He knew exactly where Inspector Henri Ranchin had found the barrel of the carbine and the spot where he had washed his hands in the Durance and maintained that he "didn't have to wash his trousers as there was no blood on them."

9. He admitted that, just like the murderer, he did not know how to shoot the carbine.

10. He had given details of the aluminum band used to repair the carbine, even before it was known that it was from a bicycle license plate.

11. He had told Pierre Prudhomme that Lady Drummond was wearing a dress with a leaf pattern.

12. He had claimed that Gustave was in the alfalfa field at two o'clock in the morning, but on another occasion he had said that at that time he was talking to him in the courtyard. After his confession, he had also told Sébeille exactly where the bodies had been before they were moved.

All this information was in addition to his own confessions, made without intimidation, violence, or drugs, plus the denunciations of his two sons. Quite apart from the dubious assertions in several of these points, particularly numbers 5–8 and 11, that the communist press insisted so vehemently on Gaston's guilt was grist to the conspiracy theorists' mill. Further, it was taken as further evidence of the Soviet Union's complicity in the murders.[15]

The French had serious misgivings, for the trial had been conducted according to a dubious procedure introduced by the Vichy regime that had not been repealed. In 1941 the "jury of peers," analogous to the British jury system, was abolished and replaced by a seven-man jury, accompanied by three judges: the presiding judge—in this case Marcel Bousquet—and two assistants (*assesseurs*), Roger Combas and André Debeaurain. The verdict was by simple majority vote. Thus, since the three judges were almost certain to vote guilty, only the votes of three jurymen were needed for the accused to be condemned to death. The judges, experts in the law, would not find it difficult to persuade most jurymen of their point of view.[16]

Gaston's arrest had taken a load off France's conscience, but now it became troubled again. The general agreement was that although the court was biased against the accused, with the presiding judge desperately trying to defend a less than satisfactory dossier, Gaston was guilty of the murders of Sir Jack and Lady Drummond; but there was considerable doubt about whether he alone had killed Elizabeth. A Gallup poll showed that 45 percent of the French thought that Gaston was solely guilty; 25 percent thought that Gustave had had a hand in the murders; 10 percent already believed in some form of conspiracy involving the British secret service, the Maquis, or the Soviet Union; and the remainder had no opinion. It was not long before doubt was cast on the verdict, not least because the spectacular trials of Marie Besnard, who was accused of being a serial arsenic poisoner, happened at the same time. She was in the end acquitted. Would Gaston also be eventually exonerated? What truth was hidden behind the body of lies created by the dreadful Dominici clan?

The British press was delighted at the conviction. The "Lion of Lurs" was now "a cold, cunning and pitiless old man of 77," from "a tight-lipped hostile and fearful peasant community unable or unwilling to help (the police)."[17] But the papers had little time to analyze the trial, for on 30 November the nation celebrated Winston Churchill's eightieth birthday. In France the question of German rearmament was at the top of the agenda, a fresh controversy having been stirred up by Churchill's sensational announcement that in 1945 he had ordered Gen. Bernard Montgomery not to disarm the Germans because they might soon be needed for use against the Russians.[18] The French press also had its pre-occupations: French rule in Indochina had come to an end, the polar air route to North America was opened, Vyshinsky had died, and Colonel Nasser had replaced Gen. Muhammad Neguib, beginning a new and threatening era for the colonial powers in the Middle East.

The Dominici trial had been an extraordinary show. White-gloved Republican Guards presented arms each time the court rose. Pretty young law students from Aix-en-Provence adorned the front row seats. Photographers clambered all over the place to get good shots, resolutely ignoring the presiding judge's ruling against the use of flash. Women screamed and fainted. Lawyers shouted. Witnesses gesticulated. The public booed. Most of the Dominici clan lied, even over such trivial points that it seemed as if they did it for fun. Gustave received a chorus of boos when he said that he was not lying when he said that he had lied. Clovis left the courtroom smiling. Gustave looked grim. Zézé, the *Daily Mirror's* "rosy-cheeked butcher's boy," whistled a merry tune and took a ride on a carousel at the fair. Most of the Dominicis went to the cinema. All this took place in the dingy little town of Digne-les-Bains, where it rained for seventeen straight days.

Once the initial excitement was over, a period of reflection and unease began. The French press, uninhibited about the way the case was reported because the concept of contempt of court did not apply, was unsparing in its criticism of the trial and particularly of the performance by Judge Bousquet. Although frequently hard hitting, the coverage overall was evenhanded. There was no attempt even on the part of the communist press to revive the absurd stories about Sir Jack Drummond's being a secret agent who had parachuted into France to work with the Maquis, nor was there the slightest attempt to discredit him in any way. With the exception of *L'Aurore*, the French press was uncertain whether Gaston had committed the crime, and even that paper thought that he might not have acted alone. The press pointed out there was no convincing motive for the crime, and the medical evidence about the time of Elizabeth's death did not seem to fit very well with the prosecution's version of events. It pointed out the police had gone to exaggerated lengths to obtain a confession, and it widely criticized the president's refusal to place the Dominicis under oath. Furthermore, the press expressed much concern about the comparatively recent changes in court procedure, as a result of which the president of the court and his two assistants sat with the seven jurymen during their retirement. The practice of summing up in open court, as in the British system, had been abandoned in 1881 on the grounds that it usually amounted to little more than yet another speech for the prosecution. Critics of these changes argued that formerly the summing up was in the presence of the counsel for the defense, whereas under the then current system the presiding judge's influence was likely to be even more unfavorable to the accused because he consulted privately with the jurors. The widespread feeling was that condemning the old man was the best way of getting rid of an embarrassing case. Anyway, at his advanced age he would not be executed, so no great harm would be done.

There was widespread criticism of the police's policy of conducting an open investigation with daily press conferences so that professional confidentiality gave way to a sensationalist journalism, turning the case into a detective story that inevitably inflamed public opinion. The police also ignored material evidence and concentrated solely on getting a confession, which on its own was insufficient proof of guilt. Many commentators in France argued that had the case been tried in an English court, where the accused was treated with a far greater degree of impartiality, Gaston Dominici would never have been convicted.

In Britain the Dominici trial soon came under attack as a blatant example of the inadequacies and injustices of French criminal law. Outspoken criticism came from surprising sources. The *Times* pulled no punches in an editorial:

> France, like Britain, is a member of an alliance of countries bound together not only by bonds of interest but also by a community of ideals. Those who set store on the good example of the western alliance cannot help feeling disturbed at recent trends by which French justice—turning back on the reforms, however imperfect, of the Revolution—seems to be reverting to practices of an earlier regime: the confessions under pressure, the toleration of police methods which the law reproves, the prolonged detention of suspects before trial, the admission of irrelevant evidence, and the licence allowed to the Press, to witnesses, and even to magistrates to besmirch reputations and constantly to ignore the essential presumption of innocence.[19]

The writer boldly suggested that at least the conviction was not a foregone conclusion. But in 1949 a longshoreman named Jean Deshays was accused of murdering an old man and of the attempted murder of his wife. He was condemned to twenty years' imprisonment, but after four years the true culprit was found. Deshays was released. Marguerite Marty, condemned for murdering her rival in a ménage à trois in 1953, was declared innocent. The Dominici case was also subject to a form of revision with a fresh inquiry against an "Unknown" (or "X"). Procedures, methods, and practices may be bad, it was argued, but the aims of a fresh inquiry were laudable. This distinguished current practice from the forms of partisan justice after the liberation. Public outrage at the police's dubious and often ruthless methods was bound to lead to reform.

A number of British newspapers, particularly the *Daily Telegraph*, the *Daily Mirror*, and the *News Chronicle*, were prone to sensationalism. They suggested sinister political motives were behind the murders and that Sir Jack had been involved in clandestine operations during the war, but at least they were restrained by British libel laws and the concern not to be found in contempt of court.[20]

The Dominici trial set off a healthy debate in France on reforming the criminal justice system. Attorney Reliquet, chairman of the Federal Union of French Magistrates, wrote an open letter to President René Coty protesting the press and radio attacks on the magistracy in connection with recent trials. Magistrates were, he claimed, themselves the victims of "an archaic judicial organization" and were well aware of "grave imperfections" in a system of criminal justice that was "already technically ill-adapted to the requirements of modern life." Vicious attacks of this sort merely hindered the vital process of considered reform. Who, he asked, would want to become a judge or magistrate in such an atmosphere? People in such responsible positions needed "the esteem and confidence of fellow citizens." The conservative daily newspaper *Le Figaro*, which was outspoken in its criticisms of the criminal justice system and thereby became the principal target of Reliquet's ire, defended itself by saying that "strict observance of the letter of the law would be sufficient to eliminate many of the abuses which have been brought to light in recent trials" while lamenting that "judicial habits and usage have deteriorated in France to a serious degree."[21]

10 The Chenevier Inquiry

On 28 November, a few hours after he was condemned to death by the guillotine, Gaston Dominici took pencil and paper and scribbled a note addressed to his daughter Clotilde Araman. It read:

Dear All,

I am writing these few lines to give you my news, which could be a great deal less awful and better than they are, and less cruel. I am always thinking of you all and that you have not abandoned me in my suffering and my distress. The grief that I endure at the moment is due to an evil person, who has dragged me into the greatest and most cruel form of dishonor that a man could endure. All sorts of lies, I do not dare blame him, I thought he would give himself up to tell the truth to the magistrates, but he has not done so at all. I thought he would say it, but Maître Pollak has not been able to make him do so. OK, so I will tell Maître Charles-Alfred tomorrow, because I cannot stand such dishonor.

Dear Clotilde, I think you might want to go and get my two goats, a white and the light brown one. Leave the longhaired ones. I am telling you this, because you deserve it. Go and get them as soon as possible. I have written to your sister Augusta at the same time as to you. I asked her to go and get your mother as soon as possible and take her down with you. I have told your sister and Clément [her brother-in-law] everything they should take.

Share my pictures [by which he meant his military records and certificates of agricultural merit and of civil courage] and do your best, because the bailiffs will come soon, because the farm will be sold to pay all my costs in the civil case. You might like to write to me, because you cannot come and see me. I have asked to sign an appeal. On Saturday I got a letter from Belgium asking me for the story of my life. They will give me seven million.

Signed: DOMINICI Gaston[1]

The letter caused something of a sensation when it was published on 4 December. It was widely assumed that Léon Charles-Alfred would soon reveal the full truth. It was also read to mean that Gaston had resigned himself to spending the rest of his life in prison, and that in itself was a confession of guilt. Some felt that he no longer hoped to clear his name but that he would identify an accomplice, who was believed to be Gustave. In the bars in the region, people spoke of Gustave's role in the Resistance. He was openly accused of murder and robbery. Even the Dominici clan were now distancing themselves from him. After his mother left the Grand' Terre, none of the family came to visit him. At the market in Forcalquier, Yvette's father, François Barth, announced to all and sundry that the Dominicis were a bunch of bandits, and they all deserved to hang.

The day after the sentence was delivered Gaston had signed an appeal in the prison warden's office in Digne in the presence of his lawyer, Charles-Alfred, and a representative of the Digne court, Madame Gabrielle Guieu. On leaving the prison Charles-Alfred told the assembled journalists that he felt that the case had reached a turning point. Gaston regretted that his family had not had the courage to speak up in court, but he still hoped that some family members would tell the truth. The lawyer seemed to be almost overcome with emotion when he spoke of his conviction that his client was innocent.

An appeal could only be based on the discovery of significant new facts or on procedural irregularities. Gaston's case had slim chances on either count. For the moment the only grounds for an appeal were that Examining Magistrate Roger Périès had issued the warrant for his arrest after the reenactment of the murders rather than immediately after Gaston's avowal, the presiding judge had not asked the accused if he had anything to say before one of the witnesses had left the stand, and the police had not removed his handcuffs when he had been taken to have a look at the car during the trial.[2] None of these factors was likely to impress the court of appeal.

On 2 December Gaston was moved to the notorious prison of Les Baumettes in Marseille, because the Digne prison did not have adequate facilities for the effective surveillance of a man on death row. He shared a maximum-security wing with an Armenian who had been condemned to death for killing a peanut vendor. They were soon joined by a soldier who had killed the adjutant of his regiment in Saigon and an informer who had denounced members of the Resistance to the Germans. They were under twenty-four-hour surveillance. A light burned in their cells day and night. They were shackled when taking exercise. They were allowed no visitors other than their lawyers.

On 8 December Gaston Dominici's lawyers, assisted by specialty lawyer André Mayer, requested that an additional inquiry be made into the Lurs murders. The atmosphere was favorable. The press generally agreed that Gaston was guilty but felt that the whole truth had not yet been revealed and that it was highly probable that he had not acted alone. Edmond Sébeille was no longer represented as the Maigret of Marseille; instead, he was seen as a hopeless bungler who had overlooked some important clues. Judge Marcel Bousquet was accused of having wanted a conviction at all costs while defending a hopelessly flawed dossier based on a shoddy investigation.

All depended on whether the court of appeals would consider Gaston's recent "revelations" to Charles-Alfred as sufficient grounds to merit a trial. First, Gustave had taken part in the murders, the motive for which had been theft. Then he claimed two other people, living within a 3-mile radius of Lurs, took part in the killings. Third, Clovis and Gustave Dominici were the joint owners of the carbine used in the crime. Next, Elizabeth Drummond was killed some time after her parents. Finally, after the murders Yvette had convened a family meeting at the Grand' Terre from which Gaston had been excluded.

None of this information made any impression on Sébeille. When he heard that Gaston was about to make a startling revelation, he merely muttered, "Don't make me laugh! Gaston Dominici won't have a chance to tell me any tall stories."[3] Meanwhile in Digne, Périès simply ignored all this chatter and quietly continued to study his files.

On 13 December, at the request of the minister of justice, Deputy Attorney General Joseph Oddou from Digne went to Marseille and interviewed Gaston in his prison cell. Oddou began by asking him to repeat what he had said to his legal team when the verdict had been delivered. Gaston, who was clearly in a bad mood, admitted that he had implicated Gustave and Zézé. He did not repeat his accusation against Jean Galizzi, the lover of Zézé's mother. When asked whether Gaston was formally accusing his son and his grandson, he replied, "They certainly had something to do with it. But I don't know who committed the crime."[4]

Gaston also repeated something he had told his lawyers that had a considerable effect on the minister of justice when he considered ordering a commission of inquiry. On 7 August 1952, two days after the crime, Gustave had lain on his bed on orders from Dr. Nalin, and after lunch Gaston had gone upstairs wearing bedroom slippers to fetch his lighter so he could have a smoke before his siesta. Once upstairs he decided to stay there and slept for about two hours. When he returned downstairs, he heard Yvette and Gustave talking in low voices. The door was ajar. They were talking about jewels. Gaston thought that Yvette wanted Gustave to buy her some as he had just received 100,000 francs ($300) for the sale of his apricots.[5] Then Yvette had asked about "the child." Gustave said that she had fainted. Yvette demanded to know who had carried her. Gustave said it was Zézé. Gaston then heard some incomprehensible talk about a handkerchief. He said then he realized that Zézé was involved in the murders, and on reflection he assumed that the jewels they had been talking about had been taken from the Drummonds. Gustave went on to talk about the carbine. He said that Clovis had often used it to shoot wild boars at a distance of 160–220 yards. He thought that the weapon had been kept at the Perrins' farm, La Serre.

Oddou reported this interview to the prosecutor's office in Marseille, and it forwarded the account to the Ministry of Justice in the Place Vendôme, Paris. Minister of Justice Jean Michel Guérin de Beaumont was a charming and astute Norman aristocrat educated at the elite Jesuit school Saint-Louis-de-Gonzague. He was a member of the Jockey Club, a former secretary of state for foreign affairs, a dog lover, and a bibliophile. He had little sympathy for a squalid old peasant like Gaston Dominici and was appalled by the adulterous adventures of his daughter, Germaine Perrin, but as a liberally minded politician with serious misgivings about the case, he promptly agreed to further investigation.[6] Fastidiously holding his nose, he passed the dossier to the Ministry of the Interior with a request that the minister organize an exploratory mission. François Mitterrand, as minister of the interior in the Mendès-France cabinet, passed the matter on to Director General of National Security Jean Mairey and Director General of the Central Directorate of the Judicial Police Henry Castaing, and gave them orders to go ahead. Never before had there been an inquiry into a case in which a death sentence had been delivered. It automatically called for a police investigation and raised the serious possibility of another trial.

Commissioner Charles Chenevier, Castaing's deputy director, was appointed to head the inquiry. He was a highly respected officer who had placed a number of prominent gangsters behind bars, among them Big Foot Paturon, Thick-Ankles Marie, Crazy Pierrot, and Walking Stick René. His most sensational case was the arrest of the train robber "Gu" Mela, who had stolen nearly 400 pounds of gold on their way to Belgium. Chenevier had used his own fourteen-year-old son to trail one of Mela's accomplices, and the tactic led to the discovery of his hiding place. For these efforts he had been awarded the Légion d'honneur. Chenevier also had been incarcerated by the Gestapo in 1943 and tortured for having arrested the assassins of Marx Dormoy, a militant socialist politician and prominent antifascist.[7] Chenevier had been one of the 11,500 French prisoners in the Neuengamme concentration camp, near Hamburg, where he contracted typhus and yellow fever. On his return to France he had weighed a mere 95 pounds. His colleagues, jealous of his successes and his fame, had intrigued against him and managed to get him placed on early retirement, but he had fought back, soon establishing an effective team that broke a number of notorious gangs that had thrived in the troubled postwar years.

A southerner hailing from Montélimar, Chenevier had already been involved in the Dominici case, having investigated a possible suspect, and was present at the trial. As a well-known antifascist, his appointment was welcomed by the communist press. Conspiracy theorists took this as further evidence for a cover-up, for the Communist Party was desperately keen to suppress any suggestion that the Soviet Union was involved in the case. Chenevier was an impressive, tough, and honest figure who had gained a national reputation for successfully smashing the gangs. The Dominici case was the first for him that was not mentioned in "The Bible," a list of the eight hundred most wanted criminals in France.

Chenevier's career was not without blemish. In 1937 Suzanne Garola had been chloroformed and murdered in a first-class sleeping car of an express train. He made a swift arrest of its conductor, Marius Paul Veyrac. A violent press campaign, led by the popular magazine *Détective*, was mounted against this hasty conclusion. The railway unions organized a defense fund. *Détective* gave a meticulous analysis of the crime, which clearly demonstrated Veyrac's innocence. Thanks to the expertise of attorney Henry Torres, Veyrac was released and returned to his job on the train from Marseille to Valence.[8] This faux pas did nothing to hinder Chenevier's advancement. He served as assistant to Inspector Jules Belin, the famous detective who had solved the case of the serial killer and embezzler Henri Désiré Landru, the model for Charlie Chaplin's film *Monsieur Verdoux*. A young Marseillais by the name of Sébeille had been on the same team. Chenevier's subsequent success rested on his resolve to avoid repeating the mistakes he had made in the Veyrac affair. He was determined to have incontrovertible proof of guilt before charges were laid to avoid the possibility of minimum sentences or of the case being dismissed for insufficient grounds for prosecution.[9] Clearly the Dominici dossier did not meet his criteria for an arrest.

Further confusion arose when Gaston leaked a story to the communist newspaper *La Marseillaise* in mid-December 1954 in which he claimed that his son Gustave and grandson Zézé Perrin, acting upon Yvette's orders, had killed Elizabeth Drummond in the kitchen of the Grand' Terre. They had carried her body to the place where it was found while

Yvette mopped up the blood-stained floor. She did not do a very good job, and it was fortunate for them that the gendarmes did not notice the stain on the floor on the morning of 5 August. Was this the reason why the Dominicis had refused to let Dr. Dragon enter the house to wash his hands on 5 August 1952? Not surprising, Yvette dismissed this tale by saying that "Pépé" had lost his mind.[10]

On 18 November 1954 Chenevier and Charles Gillard, soon to be joined by Inspectors Grisard and Goguillot, arrived in Aix-en-Provence on a fact-finding mission. Public Prosecutor Orsatelli received them with arrogant disdain. He asked what on earth they were thinking of in Paris. Did they really imagine that hints by a condemned man that he had some secrets to reveal would in fact lead to anything at all? In defiance of the minister of justice's directive, Orsatelli said that the commissioners were to restrict their investigation to questioning Gustave and Yvette, brusquely adding that he would instruct the justice of the peace in Forcalquier to arrange the meetings.

Chenevier quickly realized that he would get no cooperation whatsoever from the local authorities, who clearly thought that the presence of a well-known Parisian was both insulting and superfluous; but armed with the support of the minister of justice, he was determined not to give way. He announced that he intended to interview Gaston Dominici in accordance with his instructions. Orsatelli curtly replied that he had already been questioned by Joseph Oddou from the court of appeal at Aix-en-Provence on 13 December. Did Chenevier imagine that he would be able to learn anything new? The commissioner modestly agreed that he might well fail, but he quietly reminded the public prosecutor that the minister had given him the right to speak to whomever he wished. Orsatelli nodded in reluctant agreement.

After this less than satisfactory interview, the commissioners went to Digne, where they were received by Deputy Public Prosecutor Louis Sabatier. He was outwardly affable and courteous, but he clearly shared Orsatelli's objections to interference from on high in a case that they considered to have been conducted with exceptional professionalism and that had resulted in the unimpeachable conviction of the guilty party. Sabatier felt that the new investigation was prompted by a mixture of Parisian arrogance and political cowardice in the face of a biased press campaign. Chenevier used his considerable charm to reassure Sabatier that he had no political agenda and had no desire to get involved in an unseemly squabble between the metropolis and the provinces. Sabatier then gave the two policemen a warrant to check Gaston's statements and to pursue further investigations.

Chenevier had managed partly to overcome the obstacles that Orsatelli and Sabatier had put in his way, but clouds were on the horizon. On the day the commissioners had arrived in Provence, *France Soir* published an article in which Jacques Chapus argued they had no legal authority to question anyone laid under suspicion by Gaston Dominici. Such persons could therefore refuse to answer any questions. The commissioners' mission was simply to collect information as they had no rogatory authority. The article concluded, "It is widely felt in judicial circles in Aix-en-Provence, Marseille and Digne that Chenevier and Gillard will find it very difficult to reach a conclusion, although we can still hope that they can."[11]

Chenevier read this piece as encouraging witnesses not to cooperate. He was further outraged when Orsatelli spoke to a number of journalists in much the same vein. It was therefore with some foreboding that he and Gillard went to see Gaston in his cell at Les Baumettes, a vast white structure, backed by hills, overlooking the sea and the city. The violent criminal milieu of Marseille provides a steady stream of inmates, among whom will be found many of France's most notorious criminals.

Gaston, dressed in a drab gray prison uniform, appeared relaxed and cheerful. He had spruced himself up as much as possible for his distinguished visitors. That two of France's most eminent detectives had come all the way from Paris to visit him was evidence that he had not been forgotten and that there was at least a possibility that his fate had not been sealed. The interview began on a somewhat strange note. Chenevier asked Gaston whether he believed in God. He replied that he did, adding that his faith had diminished somewhat because of what had happened. The commissioner then asked whether he believed in heaven. Gaston, astonished at this curious line of questioning, replied in the affirmative. Changing his tone of voice, Chenevier read out a statement Gaston had made to Périès: "I am innocent, but I am sacrificing myself for my grandchildren."[12] Chenevier asked, since Gaston had procured his salvation and saved his grandchildren, why was he now changing his mind?

Gaston, disconcerted by this line of attack, muttered something about being in no great hurry to go to heaven and certainly not on someone else's account. All he knew was that he did not murder the Drummonds. In response to Chenevier's question about who was responsible, he simply said that he had already told the judge. The questioning continued for two hours, but Chenevier got nowhere. Gaston merely repeated what he had said to Oddou. Chenevier found it hard to believe that Gaston had never talked the matter over with Gustave once he had overheard his son's conversation with Yvette. Gaston replied that he hardly ever spoke to his son. Asked why he had not brought this matter up during the trial, he replied that he had not bothered because he thought that he would be acquitted. Gaston denied that the carbine had ever been at the Grand' Terre, adding that he had pointed out the shelf as the place where it had been kept because the police told him to do so. He claimed that he had made his confession when he was totally exhausted. When he came to his senses he realized the mistake he had made, but by then it was too late. Chenevier, Gillard, and two inspectors from Marseille left Gaston at six o'clock, when his evening meal was served.

They returned at three thirty the following afternoon to interview him in the visitors' room. Again they got nothing out of him beyond a garbled repetition of his familiar tale.

At five thirty Émile Pollak and Pierre Charrier, two of Gaston's lawyers, arrived at Les Baumettes. Gaston was returned to his cell for his evening meal, leaving the lawyers to discuss the case with the policemen. Chenevier told them that his talks with Gaston had revealed nothing new; consequently, there was no possibility of reopening the case. Gaston was brought back to the visitors' room at seven o'clock, where Chenevier,

Gillard, and the two lawyers were waiting for him. Pollak urged Gaston to speak out, warning him that this opportunity was positively his last chance. He had not told the truth during the trial, and if he did not do so now, all would be lost.

After this persistent urging, Gaston began a long, rambling monologue interjected with curses, denunciations of the police, reminiscences, and reflections. The gist of it all was that Gustave had brought Zézé Perrin to the Grand' Terre on the evening of 4 August 1952. They had gone out at ten minutes past one o'clock in the morning. Gaston heard shots, went down to the courtyard, and saw Gustave and Zézé walking from the campsite to the alfalfa field. Then he stopped and said, "I can't lie like this. I didn't get up." Then he added, "If I die, I die, but I won't lie." The commissioners did not seem to realize that it would have been impossible for Gaston to see the campsite or the alfalfa field from the courtyard. The ever-patient Chenevier tried to get Gaston back on track by reminding him that he had said that he had seen Zézé Perrin carrying Elizabeth Drummond. Gaston admitted that he had, but almost immediately he retracted by saying, "I was awoken by the shots. I turned the light on, but fell back to sleep until the morning."[13]

Chenevier tried to get Gaston to admit that he was at least a witness to the murders, but this approach also drew a blank. Gaston now claimed that he was the victim of a plot that Gustave and Clovis had hatched over the course of eight months. During this new version of events, Gaston claimed that when he got up at three thirty, he had found the door from the kitchen to the courtyard open, thus implying that Gustave had gone back to the scene of the crime. This frustrating session went on until eleven o'clock in the evening. The lawyers and policemen discussed these confused statements outside the prison. Chenevier was frankly mystified by the Dominicis' retractions, contradictions, and reversals and asked why they seemed to be totally incapable of cooking up a coherent story. Pollak and Charrier could offer no explanation.

This was the seventh version that Gaston had given of the Lurs murders. From 5 August 1952 to 12 November 1953, he had stuck to the story of having heard shots that he thought were from poachers, of leaving the farmhouse at five o'clock in the morning to take his goats to pasture, and of learning about the murders when he returned at eight o'clock. On 13 November 1953 his sons Clovis and Gustave had testified that their father was the murderer. Gaston had confessed on 14 November, saying that the Englishman, assuming that he was a marauder, had attacked him and that Gaston had acted in self-defense. He then changed this version to having made advances toward Lady Drummond, and that had led to a struggle with her husband. On 16 November 1953, after the reconstruction of the crime, Gaston had signed a statement that read: "I am the assassin. I was drunk. I did not know what I was doing." On 17 November 1953 he had told the prison warders at the Saint-Charles prison in Digne that he was innocent. On 20 November 1954, during his trial, he had stated that he was in bed at the time of the murders and knew nothing at all. On 29 November 1954 he had told his lawyers that he was innocent, adding that all he knew about the crime was the result of an "indiscretion." Now on 19 December 1954 he accused his son Gustave and his grandson Zézé Perrin of having committed the triple murder.

For the next couple of days Chenevier and his colleagues conducted a series of interviews with various people connected with the case. They wanted to concentrate particularly on Gaston's children Augusta Caillat, Clotilde Araman, and Marcel, as well as his nephew Léon Dominici. Thus, on 21 December Chenevier and Gillard drove to Sainte-Tulle to question Augusta Caillat, the avenging angel of the Grand' Terre, who had beaten the journalists with sticks and stones. This time she answered the policemen's questions quietly for two hours as they sat around the kitchen table. As the police left she said, "We know what we are doing when we swear upon the heads of our children that our father is innocent."[14]

The next day the commissioners went to Montfort, a typical Provençal hilltop village surrounded by olive trees on the other side of Manosque, to question Gaston's daughter Clotilde Araman, whose husband worked in a local factory. They remained there for almost four hours but learned nothing new. Gaston's sons Gaston, a lock keeper on the canal at Saint-Auban, and Marcel, a farmer from La Brillanne, were also cooperative, as was Léon Dominici. None of them had any useful information to offer.

As they were not in any way implicated in the crime, it seems odd that Chenevier should have concentrated his inquiry on them.

All the witnesses were questioned about the carbine. They all professed never to have seen it. Their anger and outrage focused on Clovis, who they claimed was solely responsible for Gaston's arrest. Gustave was portrayed as a pathetic weakling, easily influenced by his older brother. Marcel Dominici waxed particularly eloquent on the subject of his brothers. Gustave was a "manikin" who was completely under the thumb of Clovis, who in turn was "a first-class swine." Clovis had never loved his father, Marcel maintained, and only wanted to get his hands on his inheritance.

Chenevier, having completed his seemingly pointless inquiry on 23 December, handed over his report to Sabatier, the public prosecutor in Digne, who then forwarded it to Orsatelli in Aix-en-Provence. Chenevier returned to Paris to prepare a more detailed report for the minister of justice. He presented it to Guérin de Beaumont on 27 December 1954. He listened attentively to Chenevier's devastating criticisms of Edmond Sébeille's sloppy investigation, Périès's questionable handling of the case, and the seriously bungled trial. Chenevier's main objection to the proceedings was that the entire case rested on confessions, most of which were valueless, without any material evidential support. The tales that Gaston had told to the gendarme Victor Guérino, then to Commissioners Pierre Prudhomme and Sébeille, and finally to Périès differed substantially. He was also dismissive of the evidence gleaned from the reconstruction of the murders, arguing that the reenactment of the murders of Lady Drummond and Elizabeth contradicted what Gaston had previously stated, but Périès had gone ahead with the prosecution regardless.

The minister of justice, impressed by Chenevier's presentation, took precious little time to reach a decision. On 4 January his ministry issued the following communiqué: "The Minister of Justice recommends that before the Court of Appeals reaches a judgment on the case lodged with it, the prosecutor's office in Aix-en-Provence should launch an investigation against X [Unknown] for complicity in the triple crime in Lurs."[15]

It was already known that a new inquiry would be opened, a fact warmly welcomed by Gaston's defense team. Raoul Bottaï, Gustave's attorney, was less enthusiastic. He complained that a new investigation should not be allowed to begin before the high court of appeal reached a decision on Gaston's case.

This was almost Guérin de Beaumont's last act as minister. On 20 January he resigned for reasons of ill health. His successor, Emmanuel Temple, was a lawyer from Montpellier who had gone into politics as a deputy for the Aveyron. He had previously served in the Mendès-France government as the minister of defense. Temple called Chenevier and Gillard to his office and asked them to repeat their concerns about the Dominici case. Having listened carefully, he decided that the investigation against "Unknown," proposed by his predecessor, should not begin until the court of appeal had rendered judgment. After all, were the appeal successful, there would be a fresh trial, thus rendering any further investigation unnecessary. Temple therefore ordered the court of appeal to hear the case as soon as possible.

On 18 February 1955 the Supreme Court of Appeal—eleven puisne judges presided over by the chief justice, Judge Nicolas Battestini— listened to three briefs. The first was from Maurice Patin, whose duty was to give as balanced an account as possible of the relative merits of the case. He had served in the same function on the court of appeal the first time that the Dominici case had been brought before the court. Patin had examined a series of objections raised by Gaston's lawyer, André Mayer. First, the indictment had been signed by the attorney general in Aix-en-Provence, while the court of appeal had ruled that it should have been signed by his counterpart in Grenoble. Second, the advocate general's speech had been broadcast to the crowd outside the courthouse without the permission of the presiding judge. Mayer argued that the resulting tumult had seriously damaged the defendant's case. The next objection was that the Dominici family members should have all been placed under oath so that they could have been indicted for perjury had they obviously lied. Finally, Mayer argued the delay in permitting counsel to see the clerk of the court's dossier had prejudiced the appeal.

Patin dismissed Mayer's arguments out of hand and argued that the appeal could be rejected. His reasoning was the court of appeal had decided that the trial should be held in Digne; therefore, it was appropriate that the prosecutor in Aix-en-Provence should have signed the indictment. That the trial had been broadcast was a purely technical matter. A technician had turned on the loudspeakers without realizing the consequences, and as soon as Judge Bousquet had found out what had happened, he put an end to it. The judge also had been under no obligation to place the Dominicis under oath, and the matter was decided entirely at his discretion. Patin considered the question of the date at which counsel was given the dossier to be merely trivial.

André Mayer backed up his arguments with a series of precedents, but clearly he was no match for a lawyer as shrewd and experienced as Maurice Patin.[16] Advocate General Jean Dupuiche, moreover, gave his full support to Patin and launched into a diatribe against the press, which he accused of having tried to dictate to the court. Many jurists had widely shared that view ever since the trial in Digne.

The court deliberated the case for a mere two hours. The decision was foregone. The appeal was rejected on all counts. No further appeal was possible. Gaston could only now be saved by a presidential decree, which would have to be based on some new piece of evidence. He had reached the end of the road. Several of his children wrote a letter to him, calling upon him to be brave, as they claimed to be. Gaston's reactions were typical: "It's me, not them, who'll get his head chopped off. They don't give a fuck for me!"[17] He had additional reasons for concern. That month the Mendès-France government fell. The new administration under Edgar Faure seemed less likely to be favorable toward him.

Of all the Dominici clan the person who most energetically defended the old man was his nephew Léon Dominici. Orphaned at the age of fourteen, he left school and worked as a game warden in the Isle-de-France. In 1940 he returned to Provence and lived at the Grand' Terre for two years until he was shown the door. He studied beekeeping and eventually bought some land at Corbières, where he tended twenty hives. He supplemented his income from his apiary work by driving a large truck for a Marseillais hauler. He had fond memories of his childhood days at the Grand' Terre and had made an impassioned defense of his uncle during the trial in Digne. He had argued that Gaston could not possibly have committed such a dastardly crime. Waving his fist at the commissioner, he had shouted, "It's that fucker Sébeille who made a balls-up of all this!" He had a similarly low opinion of Pollak and Charrier. Convinced that they had cooked up the absurd story of Gustave, Yvette, and the stolen jewels, he urged Gaston to drop them from his defense team.[18]

Gaston's other stronger supporters among the Dominici clan were Augusta and Clotilde. But given the defection of Clovis, the Dominicis were unable to present a united front. Clovis's staunch stand and his refusal to retract were widely admired, and it was his testimony that had secured Gaston's conviction. Léon, therefore, set out to bring Clovis back into the fold. One day he visited Clovis, who was working in his vineyard with his wife, Rose. It was an awkward encounter. Léon tried to convince Clovis to accompany him to the Grand' Terre and mend fences, but for Clovis the break with his family on 13 November 1953 was definitive. He flatly refused to go to the family home, and Léon, knowing full well that Clovis was an exceptionally stubborn man, tried another tack. He suggested that the family might come and visit him, whereupon Clovis gracelessly muttered that he had not yet thrown anyone out his house. Léon immediately suggested that the meeting should take place that afternoon. Clovis sullenly agreed.

At four o'clock two cars pulled up outside Clovis's modest home in Peyruis. Léon had brought with him Gustave; Augusta Caillat; Clotilde Araman and her husband, Angelin; the younger Gaston and his wife, Marie; and Marcel and his wife, Victoria. Also in the party was Gustave's lawyer, Raoul Bottaï. Clovis was furious on spotting the latter, saying that he had only agreed to meet family members. Léon argued that they might well need his legal advice. Clovis was adamant, and Bottaï prudently retired, agreeing that this meeting was purely a family matter.

Léon pointed out that a new commission under Chenevier was about to begin work, since the appeal to the high court had failed. Therefore, it was imperative that the family work out a coordinated strategy to save Gaston. All depended on Clovis retracting his statements, but he refused to budge. The family accused him of wanting to have his father's head chopped off. They painted him as a coward. Clovis grew increasingly aggressive.

The clan went on the counterattack: "What about your gun, which you used to say that you could use to shoot rabbits 150 meters [164 yards] away?"

"You know perfectly well I never had one!"

"Liar."

"You know I'm not. I shot rabbits at 150 meters with a Russian submachine gun at the Perrins."

The Perrins indeed had a Russian submachine gun. The police had confiscated it in August 1952 when they were trying to establish the ownership of the Rock-Ola. Quite why anyone should want to shoot rabbits with a submachine gun or an M1 remains a mystery, but they soon dropped that issue to accuse Clovis of having fingered his father to shield himself. At this he leaped upon Gustave, shook him, and accused him of the murders. Léon separated the brothers. He told Clovis that Gaston had not said "*I* killed the three of them," but "*they* killed the three of them."[19] Clovis stuck to his version, whereupon he was subjected to a flood of insults and imprecations. Gustave even suggested that Sébeille had paid him a million francs to betray his father.

This accusation was altogether too much for Clovis. He picked up a chair and hurled it at Gustave, who just managed to dodge it. So ended the family gathering of the Dominicis. It was their last.

Clovis was ostracized. Even his old mother refused to speak to him. All family ties were broken. Only Germaine Perrin, who had been similarly outlawed, would speak to him. But he could not escape from his family, for they were all involved in Chenevier's second investigation. These confrontations, accusations, and recriminations were to continue under the critical gaze of the police.

With the court of appeal having rejected the case, the way was at long last open for the Chenevier inquiry to go ahead. The advocate general said that the new inquiry under the Sûreté Générale would proceed; thus, Gaston Dominici's death sentence remained suspended.[20] On 22 February 1955 Orsatelli and Calixte Rozan from the courts in Aix-en-Provence arrived in Paris to receive their marching orders from the minister of justice. This most unusual move clearly annoyed the two Provençal jurists. A somewhat humbled Orsatelli told the press that all the stories about their wishing to stop the Chenevier inquiry were absolutely false. In a case where a death sentence had been handed down, it was essential that the whole truth be revealed. He refused to speculate whether Gaston had acted alone or whether a fresh inquiry would likely shed any further light on the case.

Meanwhile, the personnel handling the case changed. In January Roger Périès was promoted to the Marseille court and was replaced by Pierre Carrias. The new examining magistrate was a tough, ambitious, and brilliant twenty-nine-year-old, who was also a passionate speleologist. He arrived in Digne in a simple Renault 4CV with his bicycle tied to the roof and took a room at the Hotel Mistre, a modest establishment in the heart of town. He was determined to make sure that Chenevier and Gillard knew their place. It was said that Carrias had colleagues but no friends, and he made it clear to the Parisians that they were his associates, not his superiors. Having discussed the affair with Périès and Sabatier and having read through the Dominici dossier carefully, Carrias reached the conclusion that the dossier made a convincing case for Gaston Dominici's culpability and that clearly he had acted alone. Thus, Carrias attributed the second thoughts of the justice minister and the Paris police to sensationalist reporting in the press.

Among the fantastic news stories circulating about the case was one in *Jours de France* claiming that a migrant worker named Antoine Llorca had two colleagues who operated a threshing machine on a farm at Pierrerue and were suspected of committing the crime. According to this story, Llorca's two companions had been absent for several days and had taken a carbine and a canvas bucket with them. When they reported to work on 5 August, they had behaved very nervously, and one of them had bloodstained shorts. On further investigation this account proved to be a pure fabrication. The two men often arrived late for work, and the other laborers would joke that the police were after them for the murders.[21]

Gustave's lawyer, Bottaï, enthusiastically embraced the Llorca tale, however, and used it as the basis for his appeal against Gaston's conviction. Bottaï appears to have been a singularly credulous man. He also accepted at face value an even more fantastic theory. According to this version a plane traveling from London to Ankara during the war that was carrying secret correspondence between Churchill and Benito Mussolini, as well as some top-secret papers belonging to the nuclear physicist Enrico Fermi, had crashed in Spanish Morocco. A Spanish secret service agent by the name of Martinez Carrera had discovered these valuable papers and tried to use them to blackmail the British Secret Intelligence Service. Drummond had been sent to France to negotiate with Carrera and had arranged a meeting on the main road by the kilometer marker near the Grand' Terre. Martinez had disguised himself as a tramp, the one who had been seen by the clairvoyant, the dowser, and the private detective Reine Ribot. Discussions over an appropriate price had turned sour, and Carrera had killed the entire Drummond family. The British consul in Marseille had taken the documents, which were left in the Hillman, and secretly kept them from the French police. It is exceedingly doubtful whether the minister of justice lent any credence whatsoever to these madcap tales.

In the paranoid atmosphere of an intensifying Cold War, it was hardly surprising that breathtaking conspiracy theories were advanced to explain what seemed to be a motiveless crime. The communist press suggested that the Americans were responsible. The right-wing papers countered by laying the blame on the Soviet Union. Others suggested that the Drummonds had been murdered by the Germans or by former members of the Resistance. To this day people in the area widely believe that Sir Jack Drummond was a British secret service agent who had chosen the Grand' Terre for an assignation while on official business. The most persistent conspiracy theory is based on the case of one Wilhelm Bartkowski, who claimed to have been the driver of a group of three gunmen who met in Frankfurt, drove to Lurs, killed the Drummonds, and then returned to Germany.

Bartkowski was a German citizen of Polish origin, who had been arrested by the police in Stuttgart on 9 August 1952 and charged with numerous burglaries and thefts, some of them armed. The German police were intrigued when he was unable or unwilling to account for his actions on the fourth and fifth of August. After several days of questioning, he confessed to having taken part in the Drummond murders.

Stuttgart had been in the American occupation zone, and the Allied military authorities still had certain residual rights. Since the crime had been committed in France, the Württemberg criminal police duly informed the French military authorities in Tübingen, who in turn referred the case to the Ministry of the Interior in Paris. Then Chenevier had sent Commissioner Gillard to Stuttgart to question Bartkowski. Gillard had received a translation of the transcript of Bartkowski's cross-examination by the German police and grilled him on several occasions, beginning in November. He had made two reports to his superior, Commissioner Chenevier. On 9 December 1952 a final report was sent to Périès in Digne.

Since the Drummonds were British citizens, the British military authorities ordered the legal adviser to the UK High Commission in Germany in Bad Godesberg to investigate the Bartkowski case.[22] An officer of the Special Investigations Branch and Public Safety Branch of the British Army of the Rhine interrogated Bartkowski, who confessed to having murdered Elizabeth Drummond and to having assisted in the murder of her parents. The officer reported to his superior in Bad Godesberg and sent a copy to the Home Office. The legal adviser at first saw no reason why this report should not be true. The High Commission suggested pursuing further investigation under strict secrecy to ensure no leaks to the press. From the outset, the Foreign Office was very skeptical, feeling that this matter should be left to the French and German police; but if the high commissioner felt otherwise, he should go ahead with the investigation.

The American authorities had already dismissed Bartkowski as a chronic liar, with paranoid delusions of having been involved in espionage work for the Russians. French Sûreté had also concluded that Bartkowski had had nothing whatsoever to do with the Drummond murders. On further investigation the Public Safety Branch agreed, reporting to the Foreign Office on 30 October 1953 that Bartkowski was a "crackpot." The Foreign Office was much relieved. Its reply to the high commissioner read: "Thank you. We have had no enquiries at all about these murders and will not volunteer any information. The story is one for the crime reporters of the press and it is unlikely that our diplomatic correspondents will be interested."[23]

That the Bartkowski affair was kept under wraps has given rise to all manner of speculation. First, William Reymond, who wrote about the murders, claims that it was because the French were anxious to avoid a diplomatic incident with Britain, fearing that it would show up the woeful inadequacy of French border security. Thus, he maintains, an innocent man was charged with the crime as part of an elaborate cover-up operation. Others suggest that in the tense atmosphere of the Cold War, it was feared that the very mention of a killer commando in the service of the Soviet Union would provide ample propaganda material both for the communists and the anticommunists, thus further poisoning the atmosphere. A third explanation is that Bartkowski was talking through his hat. Conspiracy theorists, who still cling to the idea that the Drummonds were the victims of a contract killing, complain that Chenevier was already prejudiced against the whole idea that the murders could have had anything to do with a clandestine war involving secret services.[24]

Who then was this man? Wilhelm Bartkowski was born in 1926, the son of poor Polish immigrants to Germany. His mother died in 1940, and he was alienated from the rest of his family. In the chaos of postwar Germany, like so many others, he survived by petty crime and black marketeering; consequently, he was arrested on numerous occasions and spent considerable time in jail. He claimed that in January 1951 he had gone to the French Foreign Legion's recruiting office in Cologne, where he was given a train ticket to Strasbourg. In Strasbourg he received a ticket to Marseille, where he reported to the Foreign Legion's barracks.

During his first night in the legion, he had a change of heart and decided to escape. He stole 30,000 francs ($90) or 40,000 francs ($120) from an office and a Spanish revolver of 10mm or 11mm caliber. He then jumped out of the window and hailed a taxi, which he seemed to remember was black with a yellow or perhaps red stripe. The driver wore a cap. The taxi drove him all the way to the Swiss border, using the bulk of the money he had stolen. He replenished his funds by burgling a house on the French side of the frontier. As he crossed the frontier during the night in a wooded area, he exchanged gunfire with frontier guards. Having crossed into Switzerland by train, he then traveled to Bavaria.

As a result of further investigations, Commissioner Gillard concluded that the entire story of the Foreign Legion was a fantasy. The legion did not have a recruiting office in the Federal Republic of Germany or a representative in Strasbourg. It was not possible to get a ticket across the border to Strasbourg; one could only go as far as Kehl on the German side of the Rhine River. Contrary to his previous statements, recruits were not given uniforms on their first day in the legion, and the famous white kepi was only issued upon completion of basic training in a special ceremony at the legion's home base at Sidi-bel-Abbès in Algeria. The taxi driver who had taken Bartkowski to the frontier was never found, nor was there evidence of any shooting incident with the Swiss border guards on the night in question.

Bartkowski told Gillard that he was in prison again in Hagen shortly after his fabled time in the Foreign Legion. Here he met a man by the name of Frantz, who suggested that he should work for the Soviet Union on his release from jail. The mysterious Frantz was waiting for Bartkowski at the prison gates when he was freed on 14 December 1951. He was taken to Frankfurt, where he was driven to a heavily guarded house and introduced to some Russians in civilian clothes. They put him in touch with the other members of his team.

He had given an alternative account to the German police of how he came to know the other members of the murder squad. He apparently met them in Lindau in January 1951 shortly after his escape from the Foreign Legion. Together they were involved in a series of crimes, which resulted in his being sent to jail in Hagen.

The putative killers were a motley crew. Carlo Solet (or Soled) was said to be a Greek, Roman Moesto (or Modesto) was a Frenchman of Spanish origin, and Moradis was Swiss. Much later Bartkowski claimed all three were in fact Polish, which, given their names, sounds even more improbable. (Carlo Solet or Soled is certainly not a Greek name, and Roman is neither a Spanish nor a French name.) Whatever their nationalities, the gang committed a series of petty crimes, making it seem highly unlikely that the Soviets would ever have hired such a bunch of clumsy misfits for a delicate secret mission.

Bartkowski claimed that their first serious mission was to kidnap a German and hand him over to the Czechoslovakian government. There was indeed a similar case at the time. Erich Krammer, a doctor from Sonthofen in the Allgäu, was reported missing. His body was later found in Austria near the border with Czechoslovakia. The incident was widely reported in the press, providing further material for Bartkowski's fertile imagination.

Bartkowski claimed to have set forth from the Bayerischer Hof in Lindau at about 9:00 a.m. on 4 August. This luxury hotel was an unlikely spot for a dubious group of petty criminals to choose as a meeting place, and the hotel staff had no recollection of having seen either Bartkowski or his associates. He told Gillard that he imagined that their target was a jewelry store somewhere in southern Switzerland and that they would then proceed to Marseille. They drove a lilac-colored Buick with American armed forces number plates, an unusually large and flashy vehicle for criminal purposes and for discretely crossing international borders. With Moradis at the wheel, they drove around Lake Constance, crossing into Austria at Bregenz, driving into Switzerland, passing through Zurich and Geneva, and entering France near Annecy.

Bartkowski was at the wheel when they approached the murder site. Seeing a light at shoulder level on the left-hand side of the road that looked as if it might have been a camping stove, Moesto ordered him to stop. The light was sufficient for Bartkowski to see what appeared to be a tent, but we know that the Drummonds had left their tent behind in Villefranche. At Commissioner Gillard's request, he drew a wildly inaccurate sketch of the campsite. The Hillman was shown to be parked 44–55 yards from the road and perpendicular to it. A tent was pitched to the left of the car when seen from the road.

The men then ordered Bartkowski to move up to the light, where his three associates climbed out. He moved forward about 217 yards—in other words, close to the Grand' Terre—where he waited with the doors open and the engine running. He stepped out of the car briefly to urinate. Some five minutes later he heard a single shot, followed by three or four others. He heard a woman or a child "groaning," although it must have been rather more than that to have been clearly audible at that distance. After the shots Moesto came back to the Buick with "three or four pieces of clothing," including a woman's red pullover. He then went back toward the tent. Bartkowski testified that the killers had two weapons with them—a handgun and a semi-automatic—but he was unable to give a precise description of these weapons.

The three men returned to the car after about fifteen minutes, and Bartkowski drove toward Marseille. Having driven a few miles, Moradis ordered him to make a U-turn and to hand over the driving to Moesto. When he asked his companions what had happened, he was told that it was none of his business. They returned by the same route, arriving at Schaffhausen at about two o'clock in the afternoon of 5 August. They were back in Lindau by seven o'clock. The following day they went to Stuttgart to find a fence for some jewelry they had taken from the Drummonds.

Commissioner Gillard, who was not familiar with the crime scene, had a number of Bartkowski's assertions checked and then confronted him with a host of inconsistencies and errors. At first Bartkowski stuck doggedly to his version of events. Then he broke down and admitted that he had made up the entire story. He wanted to create the impression that he was insane so he could avoid extradition, assuming that a German court would likely be more lenient with a hopeless mythomane.

Bartkowski, however, simply refused to go away and persisted in his delusional fantasies. In 1965 one J. Burton, a former warrant officer in the Special Investigations Branch attached to the British Army of the Rhine who now lived in Whitwick near Leicestershire, volunteered information on the Drummond murder. Hearing that Gustave Dominici's lawyer, Raoul Bottaï, was seeking a posthumous pardon for Gaston, Burton said that he and Lt. Gwynfor Evans from the Special Investigations Branch of the British military police had interviewed a German, Wilhelm Bartkowski, who was serving a lengthy sentence for armed robbery. Bartkowski had told them that he and three other men had taken part in an armed raid on the Drummonds' camp and committed all three murders. Bartkowski had received £65 ($182) from the money stolen from the Drummonds in payment for his services.[25]

In an interview in 2004 Bartkowski next claimed to have witnessed the assassination of Lady Diana by agents acting on behalf of Her Majesty the Queen.[26] He also discussed his difficult childhood under the Nazis, saying he was the only one of his family to survive. He had married two rich women, owned a car, and had traveled all over Europe. He denied ever having anything to do with the Foreign Legion but admitted to having been the driver during the Lurs murders. The rendezvous with "a British officer" had been arranged to collect a "large sum of money." When the Englishman had tried to swindle them out of "several millions" from money that had been designated for one Frank de Roers during the war, he had to "bite the dust." This story bears a distinct resemblance to Stanley Donen's screwball comedy *Charade*, but without Cary Grant's aging charm, Audrey Hepburn's classic Givenchy outfits, and Peter Stone's witty screenplay, it was a very damp squib.

Bartkowski was not the only crackpot involved in the Drummond case. In September 1953 the British Embassy in Dublin received a visit from one Captain Febvre, who had a tale to tell. He had been one of the 180 police commissioners in Paris during the occupation, of whom all but 60 were purged. Febvre was among those who lost their jobs after the liberation. His former colleagues told him that the communists had mistaken the Drummonds for Americans and killed them to protest the presence of American troops in Europe. Febvre was obviously suffering from paranoid delusions of a vast communist plot in France. A report to the Foreign Office described him as being pathologically anticommunist and anti-Semitic. He claimed that the murderers would never be found because the police were all communists. He suggested that Scotland Yard should send him on a special mission to France to investigate the case. The embassy curtly replied the case was outside its jurisdiction. If Febvre wanted to talk to Scotland Yard, he should do so at his own expense.[27]

The Marquess of Salisbury, at the time serving as lord president of the Privy Council, at first thought this story was all a "pipe dream," but sharing some of Febvre's fears of a vast communist conspiracy, he decided to forward the report to Scotland Yard. The Foreign Office was appalled. It stated that Febvre's story was "wildly improbable" and hoped that Scotland Yard would not be so foolish as to send him to France. Scotland Yard promptly replied that the matter was outside its jurisdiction. Nothing more was heard of Febvre and his fantasies.

11 The Case Is Closed

Having been given the go-ahead, Pierre Carrias reluctantly agreed that as a first step he would ask his distinguished colleague in Marseille Jacques Batigne to interview Gaston Dominici once again in Les Baumettes. Batigne was a controversial jurist who had been involved in a number of widely publicized cases. He was known for being ruthless with the accused and for refusing to entertain any suggestions that the police might have used somewhat rough methods of extracting confessions. In 1957 he would become notorious for his role in covering up the violent methods that the French police used against Algerian detainees in Paris. Such investigations would be boosted by the publication of both Henri Alleg's book *La Question* and Pierre Vidal-Naquet's revelations concerning the army's use of torture against the National Liberation Front in Algeria.

Batigne's mission was pointless. He had not been shown the dossier. He had gleaned all he knew about the case from the press. Did he really imagine that he would be able to uncover a truth that had been so skillfully concealed for thirty months in the course of a few short interviews and without detailed background information?

Gaston was in the prison hospital recovering from severe gastrointestinal problems. According to prison rules his lawyers were not allowed to visit him while he was in the prison ward, but Émile Pollak and Pierre Charrier asked for permission to have him examined by Professor Carcassonne, an eminent local physician from the University of Marseille. Both lawyers were convinced that Gaston had been poisoned in an attempt to put an end to the entire case. They therefore appealed to the minister of justice to order an examination of the prison's food. This request was futile, because there was no possible way of analyzing the food Gaston had eaten in the previous few days, but the minister did give the lawyers special permission to visit their client in the hospital.

They found him much recovered and in relatively good spirits but repeating his conviction that he had been poisoned. He told his lawyers that all he needed was some decent olive oil, and he would soon be well again. The next day he was much better, but the day after he had a severe relapse and developed a high fever. The prison doctor, having consulted with the prison surgeon, agreed that Professor Carcassonne should be allowed to examine their client. It seemed as if an operation was indicated, but once again the old man began to recover. A bulletin was issued indicating that Gaston was suffering from a severe bilious attack due to food poisoning. His recovery was relatively swift, but he had lost a few pounds and look very thin and weak. To dramatize Gaston's sickness, his lawyers arranged for his daughters Augusta Caillat and Clotilde Araman along with Gustave Dominici and Clément Caillat to come to Marseille. Gaston initially refused to allow any member of the Dominici clan to visit him, other than his granddaughter Marie-Claude and nephew Léon. He claimed the others were content to see him rot in prison.

Carrias still ordered Gustave and Yvette to confront Gaston at Les Baumettes under Batigne's supervision. The meeting took place during the morning of 8 March. Gaston was much recovered but still weak. Batigne listened to the stories of Gaston, Gustave, and Yvette, but hardly surprising he learned nothing new. Both Gustave and Yvette flatly denied having had the conversation concerning the jewelry that his father claimed to have overheard. Gustave repeated the statement that he had made in court: he knew nothing about the murders until five o'clock in the morning of 5 August. Gaston accused Gustave of wanting to send him to his death and claimed that he was no longer his son. He refused to bid him good-bye. Somewhat surprising, Gustave and Yvette's lawyer, Raoul Bottaï, said that the meeting had been "infinitely less sensational than might have been expected." According to him Gaston had made no accusations, and the atmosphere was "very calm, even touching."[1]

Carrias, having received a report on this worthless encounter the following day, contacted Director General of the Judicial Police Henry Castaing and asked him to send Charles Chenevier and Charles Gillard to Digne to pursue the matter further. The two commissioners were hardly entranced by the new examining magistrate's actions. They had learned from the press and not through official channels that Batigne had interviewed the Dominicis. They considered this move would further compromise their investigation.[2]

Chenevier and Gillard met Carrias for the first time on 16 March 1955. The two commissioners gave the same account of their views on the case that they had previously given to two successive ministers of justice: they argued in favor of a commission of inquiry. Their main point was that there was a strong suspicion that Gustave had been somehow involved. There was evidence that he had been outside at the time of the murders, and the persistent lying of Yvette, Zézé, and Gustave himself only made sense as an attempt to conceal the truth. The commissioners added another piece of information that they had recently acquired. While the case was still in front of the court of appeal, they had undertaken further investigations and had interviewed one Dr. Morin in Nice. He had made a statement to the Nice police in the Dominicis' defense. He was a hunter who in 1951 had camped at the Grand' Terre. He had met Gustave, who asked him to move his tent to a different spot nearer to the Grand' Terre and then invited him to join in some nighttime poaching. Afterward he was invited back the next year to hunt wild boar. Having been treated in a friendly manner by the Dominicis, he was outraged that the press was presenting them as hostile to campers.

Morin had been questioned by Edmond Sébeille and Lucien Tardieu during the initial investigation, but Sébeille had felt that Morin's memory was so vague that little could be made of his testimony. Chenevier thought that since hunters liked to talk about guns, Morin might have something to say about the Rock-Ola. Much to his surprise, Morin announced that he had probably seen it and that it was kept on a shelf in a shed near the farmhouse.

Morin's testimony presented certain problems. His recollections of the gun when he had first been shown photographs of the weapon in 1952 were very hazy, but in 1955 he no longer had any doubts. Initially he had said that the weapon was kept in a cellar; later he had said it was in a shed. There were also some discrepancies between his different versions of where this cellar, or shed, was in relation to the farmhouse.

Carrias, who clearly resented the presence of these Parisian luminaries and who felt that the whole idea of a new investigation against an "Unknown" (or "X") was an insult to the Provençal police, dismissed Chenevier and Gillard with the assurance that he would think the matter over. His stonewalling and his intent on defending the original dossier were widely seen in the press as part of a deliberate cover-up and an attempt to bury the Dominici affair.[3] In fact, his hands were tied by the court of appeal in Aix-en-Provence, as it saw no reason to open a new investigation. Carrias had ample justification for his anger at the attitude of the press, whose sensational reporting had seriously compromised the original investigation, the trial, and the subsequent inquiries. He was determined to keep the press at bay, a tactic that was taken as further evidence of a cover-up.

It was not until 15 June that Carrias recalled the two commissioners to Digne to discuss how they should approach a collaborative effort to satisfy the justice minister's request for a new investigation. Chenevier presented the judge with a detailed dossier of the witnesses he wished to see and the line of questioning he intended to adopt. This amounted to a list of 420 questions.[4] To speed up the proceedings he also had appointed two assistants. Trampling on Provençal sensibilities, he announced that he intended to work closely with Capt. Henri Albert, head of the Forcalquier gendarmerie. Chenevier implied that Albert was the only man who, during the original investigation, had shown any signs of professional competence.

Carrias listened in what Chenevier imagined was silent approval, but the next day he haughtily proclaimed that the commissioner's proposals were unacceptable on the grounds they amounted in effect to a reopening of the entire affair. Furthermore, he was constrained by the criminal section of the court of appeals in Aix-en-Provence that would not permit the granting of full rogatory competence to question whomever he wished. Carrias therefore felt obliged to reconsider the commissioners' request. He then argued that a verdict had been reached; therefore, the commission should limit itself to the examination of Gaston's recent statements. Sébeille's investigation, the trial, and the verdict were not to be put in question. Chenevier argued that such a piecemeal approach would lead to nothing. Carrias played a waiting game, saying that he needed more time to consider this difficult matter.

Gaston Dominici's nephew Léon refused to abandon the attempt to secure a retrial. As a first step he tried to see what could be done to counter Carrias's attempts to frustrate the Chenevier inquiry. To this effect he appealed to Marcel Héraud, *bâtonnier* (primus inter pares) of the Paris bar, who sought the advice of the era's probably most brilliant and certainly most expensive lawyer in Paris, René Floriot, whose law firm was known as the "Floriot Factory."[5] Héraud arranged for Léon to meet the great man.

Léon waited anxiously in the firm's minute waiting room with its sumptuous oriental carpets in the Avenue Hoche before being shown into the lawyer's gigantic office, which was in a vast rotunda with Louis XVI furniture and adorned with the works of Jean-Baptiste-Camille Corot, Édouard Manet, and Eugène Delacroix. A statue of the great jurist in a toga was on prominent display. Floriot sat amid this splendor, like the figure of a god in a sacred place of worship. Léon was ensconced in an armchair while a liveried butler offered him his choice of a wide range of drinks.

For the next two hours Floriot paced up and down, a heavily diluted whiskey and soda in his hand, while he listened to Léon's account of the case. At first he was disinclined to become involved, but finally he agreed to help, provided that Gaston Dominici personally asked him to do so. Héraud met Floriot again briefly that evening at Orly Airport shortly before the latter left for Algiers.

Héraud held a press conference on Monday morning. Such was his confidence in Floriot that he boldly announced that the inquiry would go ahead and that Carrias would give Chenevier and Gillard full rogatory authority. He was somewhat annoyed to find Léon waiting outside the room as the journalists left. He told him that he should always have his lawyers with him on any such occasion. For their part Pollak and Charrier disapproved strongly of Léon's attempt to get the entire Dominici clan declared innocent, almost certainly because were he successful, rumors of a communist assassination plot would once again circulate.

Léon was not discouraged. During the final two days of his visit to Paris, he published two articles in which he tried to prove that Gustave could not possibly have moved Lady Drummond's body. The argument revolved on a spurious question of the height of the grass in August. He somehow imagined that if he could prove Gustave was innocent, then he would also exonerate his uncle. By the same token he believed that if he could find the reason why Gustave had obviously lied about his own actions, then he would also be able to explain why Gustave had lied about his father.

Floriot ignored this nonsense but quickly went into action. On his return from Algiers he went to see Chenevier and Gillard and gained access to the dossier. On Monday, 18 July, four days after Léon returned to Provence, Floriot received a scrap of lined paper containing Gaston's handwritten request that he act on his behalf. His nephew had dictated it to him. Floriot now used his considerable influence behind the scenes to ensure that Chenevier and Gillard were eventually given rogatory power.

Floriot was convinced that Gaston was innocent.[6] His main reason for thinking so was that he considered Gaston's confession a pack of lies. He could not have watched Lady Drummond undressing because she did not undress. Her body was fully clothed. He could not have talked to her because she knew no French and he no English. The wound on Sir Jack's hand manifestly did not come from a bullet. There was no burning or any trace of powder on the wound. He accepted the dubious argument that the condition of Elizabeth's feet indicated that she had not run away, so Gaston's claim that she had was clearly false. Gaston also claimed to have killed her with one blow to the back of the head, but she had received two in the face. He also accepted Gaston's statement that he had confessed to save his family's honor.

Héraud traveled to Provence to confront the magistrates on the Aix bench. He emerged from the meeting in a towering rage, complaining that countless objections had been raised to a fresh inquiry. The magistrates announced that they refused to accept Chenevier and Gillard, but they would be prepared to accept almost anyone else. Héraud counterattacked by suggesting that they did not want to have Chenevier and Gillard on the case because they knew things that might compromise them.

A further complication arose on 13 July, when Marcel Héraud went on the attack again and published an article in which he described a visit he had made to a "senior magistrate" in Aix-en-Provence, who was generally considered to be the chief prosecutor Orsatelli. He had expressed his indignation that the minister of justice had seen fit to send two police commissioners to reexamine the Dominici case. This, he claimed, implied the minister's lack of trust in the court's proceedings and verdict. The prosecutor's office, the magistracy, and the courts—all were said to be livid that an examining magistrate had been appointed to investigate complicity in the crime. Carrias had told Héraud that he would accept anyone other than Chenevier and Gillard, to which Héraud replied that public opinion would react unfavorably to such a substitution, because it would seem that the two commissioners knew something that the Provençal authorities did not want revealed.

This ploy was a shocking breech of confidence and of normal practice, but it had an effect. One week later Carrias granted Chenevier and Gillard their rogatory commission but strictly limited it to discovering what Gustave Dominici and Zézé Perrin had done during the night of 4–5 August 1952. The Parisians were furious. All they had achieved after seven months of stonewalling was the right to examine the cases of two witnesses, both of whom were notorious liars. A further complication arose when Gustave and Yvette claimed that Examining Magistrate Roger Périès had changed the records by giving a false account of his questioning of them. This was hardly the basis for a serious investigation of a complex case.

Minister of Justice Robert Schuman had told the Aix magistrates that Chenevier and Gillard were to conduct a fully independent investigation and that they should not have any contact with the police and gendarmes who had been involved in the Dominici case. Should the two policemen decide there was a case for a judicial inquiry, they were to report directly to the ministry. The Aix magistrates had no alternative but to accept these highly unusual conditions. At long last, on 19 July 1955 Pierre Carrias reluctantly granted Chenevier and Gillard permission to collect testimony. The Dominici case could thus be reopened without necessitating an annulment of the sentence, which had simply been suspended.[7]

A fierce campaign was now fought in the press. On one side were those who argued that there had to be serious reasons to overturn a verdict that had been reached by due process and that Chenevier's mission was a deliberate insult by arrogant Parisians who questioned the professional competence of their Provençal colleagues. On the other side were those who argued that the whole case had been badly bungled and that the authorities in Digne, Aix-en-Provence, and Marseille were desperately trying to defend a wholly inadequate dossier. There was also increasing suspicion that others were involved in the crime. In such an atmosphere it was difficult to see how Chenevier would be able to achieve much, unless attitudes on both sides changed significantly. The atmosphere had become further charged with *Détective*'s publication of a series of articles by Marcel Montarron, who had interviewed the seven jurors in the Dominici trial. Although under French law jurors were permitted to ask questions during the trial, they had remained silent throughout. Now they came under fire for having returned a false judgment.[8]

Marcel-Jean Bernard, a peasant from Saumane, said that he had been disgusted by the number of barefaced lies and had not been persuaded by the arguments of Dominici's lawyers. He said that he and his fellow jurors were simple men, not lawyers, who were merely asked to answer yes or no. He had some doubts about whether Gaston had killed Elizabeth but none over the other two murders.

Jules Martin farmed at Saint-Tulle, where Gaston's daughter Augusta Caillat lived. He said that he and his fellow jurors would be relieved if the Parisian policemen could clarify a number of obscure points and bring the guilty to justice.

Marcel Aillaud, a peasant from Villemus, admitted that a number of issues had not been cleared up, but he was convinced that Gaston was involved in the first two murders. If there were accomplices, then he felt it was right to go after them.

Louis Allaincourt, a retired butcher from Château-Arnoux, had been convinced by the photographs taken during the reconstruction of the murders. He also said it would be a relief if any accomplices were found.

Paul Auzet, a peasant from Dombes, lived in a remote spot high in the mountains, where he cultivated lavender and tended his herd of goats. He said that he had been harassed for having been on the jury and announced that he wanted to have nothing to do with the new inquiry.

Télamon Sube, a peasant from Pierrerue, knew Gaston; therefore, he should have been excluded from the jury. He hoped that the full truth would be revealed. He was aware of Gaston's vile temper and violent disposition and had no doubt that he was guilty. Sube's sympathy lay with "the Sardine," whose life with Gaston had been "a Calvary."[9]

Jules Vendre, a butcher from Colmar-les-Alpes, washed his hands of the whole affair. He doubted that Chenevier's inquiry would reveal anything at all because the Dominicis were a bunch of congenital liars.

Feathers were ruffled in July when it was revealed that Orson Welles was making a documentary film on the Dominici affair for his TV series *Around the World with Orson Welles*. Minister for Industry and Commerce André Morice announced that Welles had not applied for official permission to make his film and was thus liable for prosecution. He would not permit the film to be exported from France without ministerial approval. Marcel Massot, the Gaullist deputy from the Basses-Alpes, had protested vigorously in the name of the local population about the making of the film. Massot had written to the minister in a tone of indignant outrage: "It would be scandalous if the publicity given to this sad affair were prolonged outside France by the cinema or television. . . . I am convinced that you will agree with me that, both from moral considerations and from the point of view of French propaganda, the exportation of such a film should not be tolerated."[10] Orson Welles managed to make his film, but it was a hasty and unsatisfactory collage of interviews with some of the protagonists that sheds precious little light on the affair. The film was a modest success in America but was banned in France.[11]

Commissioners Chenevier and Gillard were welcomed to Digne by Deputy Prosecutor Louis Pagès's somewhat ambiguous statement to the press that was published on the eve of their questioning of Gustave and Yvette. It read:

We have now reached an important stage in the development of the new enquiry, to be conducted by the examining magistrate and the police officers. The facts that we have already collected underline the value of the previous work done by Commissioner Sébeille as well as the Examining Magistrate Périès, without whose diligence, perseverance and devotion to duty nothing we have done and shall do could ever have been or be achieved.

Having received the advice of the lawyers and of all those involved in the case, it seemed to us to be important that before we begin the second part of our investigations, we should also hear those involved in the first inquiry, because we are determined not to overlook any of the elucidations that might be provided to whatever questions might be raised. There is a great deal of useful information available on the behavior of various people, which shows once again how conscientiously this drama and its protagonists have been studied.

We in turn shall not fail to learn from them so as to conduct our inquiry and reach a conclusion, the nature of which discretion forbids us to make any prediction.[12]

This remarkable paean to the work of Sébeille and Périès, the belittling of Chenevier and Gillard, and the implied assertion of Gaston Dominici's sole guilt was all the more remarkable because Carrias had given Chenevier instructions to maintain strict professional discretion and not to talk to the press. Carrias did not want the whole inquiry to be discussed in an open forum.

Regardless of the attitude of the authorities in Digne and Aix, Chenevier conducted a three-hour grilling of Gustave while his colleague, Gillard, questioned Yvette. Both interviews amounted to little effect beyond establishing beyond all doubt that they were both consummate liars. Nevertheless, Chenevier remained optimistic. Before returning to Paris on 12 August to await the outcome of Gustave and Yvette's charges against Périès, Chenevier put a bold face on the affair by announcing to the press that he was sure that his investigation would bring "positive results."[13]

However, Carrias did not give Chenevier somewhat extended rogatory powers until 1 October. Due procedure required that for Chenevier and Gillard to interrogate Gaston, a magistrate had to act as an intermediary. Jacques Batigne was chosen simply because he had already visited Gaston in Les Baumettes in March. They overlooked the fact that Batigne had been remarkably unsuccessful in obtaining any fresh information and that he had still not bothered to examine the dossier.

Batigne found Gaston no longer dressed in a prison uniform but in his old clothes and his trademark hat. His room look more like a hospital ward than a prison cell. When Batigne commented that he looked well and recovered from his illness, Gaston replied that his impression was a mistaken. After further attempts to humor him, Batigne suddenly said that he had a low opinion of Gustave's character, whereupon Gaston heartily agreed. In response to a series of questions, Gaston stuck to his story that he had heard Gustave and Yvette discussing the crime. He remained calm when Batigne told him that his colleague in Digne had conducted a series of experiments that indicated that he could not possibly have eavesdropped on his son and daughter-in-law. Gaston simply muttered that they were unaware that he was listening.

When Batigne asked what Gustave and Zézé had done during the night of the murders, Gaston replied he knew nothing. If he knew anything, he would be more than willing to talk. He denied having seen either Gustave or Zézé in the alfalfa field. He had not seen Zézé carrying the child. How could he have seen anything? He was in bed the whole time.

Batigne was staggered. A vast amount of time and trouble had been spent on the case. Two senior police officers had been sent to investigate. Public opinion had been aroused. The law had been set in turmoil. Now the old man had nothing to say.

Chenevier and Gillard went to Les Baumettes the next day, accompanied by Jacques Batigne. The examining magistrate opened the proceedings by saying that the two police officers had come all the way from Paris to hear his statement, but now he had withdrawn it. What did he now have to say? Gaston merely mumbled that he was innocent.

Chenevier did not allow himself to be put off by Gaston's retraction of all his previous claims. He stuck to a simple line of questioning. At what time had Zézé Perrin come to the Grand' Terre? Did he sleep at the farmhouse? Had Gaston heard Gustave talk to anyone when he arrived back home after having seen Faustin Roure on 4 August? Did Gustave go alone to investigate the landslide, or did someone go with him? Did Gustave often bring Zézé to sleep at the Grand' Terre on the several occasions when he was left alone at La Serre? Gaston refused to answer any of these questions. He could not remember anything. He knew nothing. He had seen nothing. He had nothing to say. Chenevier put an end to this pointless exercise by bidding Gaston farewell until they met again.

Among the first witnesses that Chenevier's team heard was Faustin Roure, who was now living in retirement. Had he told Gustave to go and have a close look at the landslide? Had he stopped off at the Perrins' farm to get a liter of wine, as Zézé had claimed? Roure could not remember. Chenevier had to tread very carefully for fear of overstepping the boundaries set by Carrias. He could only ask questions concerning the whereabouts of Gustave and Zézé. Little came of this line of questioning. Roure had told Gustave to keep an eye on the landslide, but it was obviously not a major concern. He claimed to have visited La Serre later that morning, but he could not remember whether he had picked up some wine.

An intensive interview with Clovis Dominici, which lasted for two days, was much more fruitful. He repeated that when he was shown the carbine for the first time, he knew that someone from the Grand' Terre was involved in the murders. He was further convinced when he noticed that the weapon was no longer on the shelf in the shed where it had been hidden. He initially thought that his brother was responsible for Elizabeth's death, because he could not imagine his old father chasing after a young girl. Furthermore, his father had not gone hunting for a number of years and had no idea how the Rock-Ola worked, whereas he imagined that Gustave had used the gun on several occasions to hunt boar. Clovis had continued to suspect Gustave even after he had pointed a finger at their father, for his brother's statements about the murders were vague and often contradictory. His suspicions were strengthened when Gustave tried to imply that Paul Maillet was involved in the crime.

It was only when he heard his father's confession that he realized that he was the murderer. Chenevier asked him whether he had perhaps misunderstood his father's dialect, but Clovis insisted that there had been no ambiguity whatsoever. When asked why he had not told other members of the family, he replied that Gaston had ordered him to keep his mouth shut, and he had respected his authority. Even though Clovis was convinced that his father was involved, he did not alter his position. Unlike Gustave he had refused to retract when confronted with his father. Chenevier suspected that Clovis was covering up for Gustave, for whom he had considerably more affection than for his overbearing father.

On the second day of interrogation in the police headquarters in Digne, using a small office with the blinds drawn to avoid the telescopic lenses of an army of press photographers, Clovis was confronted with various family members. His sister Augusta Caillat asked him why he had not told other family members of their father's confession. Clovis replied that it was Gaston's secret, not his. Marie Dominici, his brother Gaston's wife, claimed that Clovis had said that it was better for the old man to go to prison rather than a young man like Gustave. Clovis hotly denied ever having made such a statement. She then went on to categorically state that no one from the Grand' Terre was involved in the crimes. When questioned about her father-in-law's confession, she simply replied that he was an old man who could easily be manipulated. Her husband, Gaston, the lock keeper on the Manosque Canal at Saint-Auban, had accused Clovis of accepting a million francs from Sébeille during the fateful meeting they held to get Clovis to change his story, but now he flatly denied having said anything of the sort. His brother Gaston claimed that he had spent 200,000 francs ($600) on the case, whereupon Clovis had told him that he was a bloody fool because he had made money out of it. This exchange escalated into yet another family row, which the police found difficult to control.

When tempers calmed down somewhat, Yvette was the next to be questioned. She remained cool and disdainful, purposefully avoiding eye contact with Clovis. She claimed that as they drove in the police car from the Grand' Terre to Digne on 16 November 1953, Clovis had said that he had learned of his father's guilt from his confession and not from Gustave on 8 August 1952. Clovis denied this attempt to make him the first to have denounced Gaston. He insisted that Gustave was the first to have heard Gaston's confession, which had only confirmed the fears Clovis felt when Sébeille had shown him the M1 on 6 August.

Gustave was the last to be questioned that day. When asked how he had been able to show where the carbine was kept, even though he claimed never to have seen the weapon, he replied that Clovis had made a sketch for him. Clovis denied ever having done so. A series of recriminations between the two brothers followed, with policemen strategically placed to separate them should they go after one another. Gustave insisted that he had never told Clovis that their father had confessed to killing the Drummonds. He then claimed that Clovis had told him not to be "a little prick" and to say that the old man had gone hunting badgers that night; otherwise, the police would question them for a week. Clovis accused his brother once again of lying.

It was nearly midnight. Realizing that he was getting nowhere, Chenevier decided to call a halt and continue the next day by interviewing Gustave and Yvette. Gustave got off one defiantly impertinent parting shot by saying that it was up to the commissioner to prove that he was lying.

The next day's interviews brought nothing new. Chenevier pointed out that it was Gustave's and not Clovis' testimony that had led to Gaston's conviction and that Gaston was well aware of the fact. He further accused Gustave of cowardice when he begged Périès not to tell his father that he had denounced him. Chenevier tried to get Gustave to admit that he had always blamed his father when he himself was under suspicion, but he got nowhere with this line of attack, beyond Gustave's admission that he had indeed been under suspicion in December 1953. Gustave left police headquarters in Digne and returned to the Grand' Terre at about 8:00 p.m. on 25 October 1955, having escaped all Chenevier's attempts to trap him.

Gaston Dominici's favorite grandchild, Marie-Claude Caillat, a young woman of eighteen, reciprocated his affection. She made the following statement to Chenevier:

> On my last visit to Les Baumettes a week ago, my grandfather started to talk about the conversation he had overheard and blamed my mother and I for agreeing that he should die in prison in order to protect Gustave. My mother replied that it was not true and that they were doing everything possible to defend him. My grandfather said it was Gustave who did the deed, but my mother told him that that was not true.[14]

Marie-Claude repeated this statement in front of her grandfather and in the presence of Judge Batigne, adding several times that Gaston had said Gustave was responsible for the murders.

The Dominici clan rejected out of hand any suggestion that anyone from the Grand' Terre was in any way involved in the murders. They resolutely maintained that the M1 had never been anywhere near the farmhouse and that Clovis was acting out of spite toward the family, hatred for his father, and hope of personal gain. There was one exception, Marie Dominici's firstborn, Ida Balmonet. Gaston had accepted her with singularly ill grace as his own, but she had broken with the family and lived far from the Grand' Terre at a farm belonging to the Benedictine Abbey of Hautecombe in Savoy.[15] In 1953, some time before Gaston's arrest, she had visited the family home. Finding the atmosphere exceptionally tense and oppressive, she began to suspect that something was going on. She stated that having accused his father of the murders in the presence of Périès, Gustave had said upon his return to the Grand' Terre that Clovis had been the first to denounce their father and had forced him to follow suit. Gustave had lied to the entire family, with the exception of his wife and mother. Ida was Clovis's only ally within the Dominici clan.

Chenevier and Gillard returned to Les Baumettes with Judge Batigne for a final meeting with Gaston. It was as inconclusive as all the others. Gaston once again denied that he had seen Gustave and Zézé in the alfalfa field during the night of 4–5 August 1952. Chenevier reminded him that he had testified to this effect. Gaston replied that he must have been out of his mind at the time, hastily adding that it could not possibly have been so because he did not get up during the night. He stuck to his preposterous story that he had overheard Gustave and Yvette discussing the jewels. When the commissioner told him that both had denied it, he shrugged his shoulders and said that they were mistaken.

Chenevier tried to break the deadlock by bringing Gustave to the prison, but he could have saved himself the trouble. Both stuck to their versions of the story: Gaston had overheard the conversation; Gustave denied that it had ever taken place.

Clovis was also brought in to see his father. It was the first time they had met since the trial. Clovis stuck to his story that Gaston had confessed to the crime. Gaston growled that he should be ashamed of himself for making such a perfidious accusation. As Clovis was about to leave, he turned to his father, who was sitting on the edge of his bed. His parting words were:

Listen, Papa, I tell you once more for the last time that what I did was not done to harm you. If I had wanted to do that I would have spoken the first time I saw the carbine. I didn't. You told me that it was you who killed the English people. I wish it weren't true. So tell Monsieur Batigne it isn't true, that you lied to me. Tell him you didn't kill anybody, but don't say that you didn't tell me, because you did.[16]

That was the last time Clovis ever spoke to his father.

Gaston's final encounter with his grandson Zézé Perrin lacked even an iota of affection or respect. It soon degenerated into a shouting match. Zézé was in an insufferably cocky and flippant mood, taking every possible opportunity to mock his grandfather. He denied having been at the Grand' Terre on the night of 4–5 August. He claimed not to have been with Gaston when he discovered Elizabeth's body. He also cheekily inquired why Gaston had led his goats away from the direction of the campsite on the morning of 5 August, when he always took them in the other direction. Gaston yelled at him that he was a little bastard. This outburst merely prompted Zézé to taunt his grandfather by saying that if he had anything against him, he should speak up in front of the examining magistrate.

Gaston's daughter Augusta Caillat was the last of the Dominicis brought to Les Baumettes. She had always been a stout defender of the old man, but he showed her no gratitude, accusing her instead of wanting him to take the sole blame for the murders so as to protect others. Augusta angrily asked why he had not brought this up during the trial, and Gaston replied that it was because he imagined he would be acquitted. Augusta said that statement was untrue. A few days before the assizes, he had admitted to her that it was going to be extremely tough. Gaston denied having said any such thing.

Chenevier was now in a familiar bind. The Dominicis retracted their stories, invented new ones, and contradicted themselves at every turn. How was it ever possible to reach anything approximating the truth under such circumstances? Since no one had been placed under oath during the trial, he could not charge anyone with perjury, and anyway such charges would have provided grounds for an appeal and a reopening of the case. That was the last thing that anyone wanted after more than three years of hard work.

Three other issues were of considerable interest to the Chenevier commission. A roll of unexposed film was found among the Drummonds' possessions, and the police had asked Scotland Yard to find out what make of camera the Drummonds owned. They quickly discovered that it was a 35mm Kodak Retina. The Marrians were absolutely certain that the Drummonds had not left it behind in Villefranche. It had not been among the family's possessions on the campsite. Had it been stolen by the murderer or an accomplice? Did it contain compromising photographs, such as shots of family members of the Grand' Terre? Or had it simply been mislaid somewhere between Villefranche and Lurs?

Many of the same questions were asked about the family's missing canvas bucket. Chenevier assumed it had been destroyed as evidence that the Drummonds had visited the farmhouse to get water, as Zézé had consistently claimed and Gustave had confirmed. It is also possible that an item found at the murder site that was described as a "canvas bag" might have been the missing bucket.[17] Sébeille had thought it very odd that Yvette had given Zézé Perrin precise details of the bucket when she told him about the Drummonds' visiting the Grand' Terre.[18]

The only other missing item was a cheap watch belonging to Lady Anne, the loss of which seemed to the police to be of little importance. That she had taken it with her to France rested solely on the testimony of her mother, Mrs. Wilbraham, but she had suffered such a state of severe shock on hearing of the murders that she may well have been mistaken.

Even more serious was the question of the trousers left out to dry that the police had seen on the morning of 5 August. César Girolami, Sébeille's assistant, had been very concerned about this important piece of material evidence, which his superior had completely ignored. Girolami had subsequently been posted to Morocco. At the request of a magistrate in Casablanca, he sent a detailed report on the incident. During Chenevier's investigation, however, Gustave now claimed that there had never been any trousers hanging out to dry. Yvette admitted that she had washed a pair of her husband's trousers on 5 August, adding that she had a perfect right to do so. Gaston's son Aimé, then working as a market gardener at Aygalades, had read about the trousers in the press and had asked Yvette about them. She said that they belonged to her father-in-law and that she had washed them several days before the murders but had forgotten to bring them in when they had dried. This was obviously an untruth, because Inspector Girolami had seen the trousers at about 3:00 p.m. on August 5 and had testified that they were still damp. Had traces of a victim's blood been found upon them, it would have been powerful evidence for Gaston's guilt. Why Sébeille had chosen to forget this testimony remains a mystery.

Aimé Dominici's employer, Madame Bonnafous, who owned the Calarmuso farm at Eygalières, said that on 8 August 1952 Aimé and his young wife, Mauricette, had been called to the Grand' Terre, where Gustave had told them that he had heard both shots and screams during the night of 4–5 August. Aimé had shared this with Madame Bonnafous on his return to the farm. Aimé and Mauricette, having been well briefed by the clan, now vigorously denied that this had ever happened.

The Chenevier investigation ended with two epic interviews. First, Gillard tried to tackle Yvette at Forcalquier. He was familiar with the case and with his adversary, having been sent as an observer to Gaston's trial. By now Yvette had three children, and a fourth was on the way. She had lost none of her feisty determination to defend her father-in-law, to remove all suspicion from her husband, and to denounce the traitors within the clan. During thirteen hours of cross-examination, she did not blink an eyelid, make one false move, or fall into Gillard's carefully prepared traps. At 12:30 a.m. Gillard finally gave up.

Chenevier confronted Gustave in the law courts in Digne. He arrived on the bus at 9:00 a.m. They sparred with one another until 1:00 p.m. and then went to lunch together, taking the 250-franc (73-cent) menu, washed down with a local rosé. They then returned to the fray, with the session lasting until the next morning. During this mammoth session, they sometimes took a break. Standing by the window, quietly smoking, they watched the crowds below. Gillard arrived at 1:15 a.m. to tell his superior that he had lost "the battle of Forcalquier." By 3:00 a.m. the few remaining onlookers abandoned the scene. At 4:00 a.m. the lights went out, and Gustave was driven back to the Grand' Terre. As it was already light he took a pitchfork and went to work, without having slept a wink.

Chenevier emerged from the courthouse and told the waiting journalists in an indignant tone that Gustave had accused Périès of being a swindler and a liar. He could do so with impunity because of the technical impossibility of making an investigating magistrate a witness in his own investigation. Only the investigating magistrate in an eventual supplementary inquiry could do that.

Chenevier and Gillard had exhausted their 420 questions and gained precious little. Although familiar with the criminal underworld of the nation's capital, they had been outfoxed by the wily Provençal peasants, whose mentality they had failed to comprehend. They had not realized that the Dominicis' tactic was based unwittingly on Churchill's premise that "in wartime, truth is so precious that she should always be attended by a bodyguard of lies." Zézé Perrin was the master of this tactic. He claimed to have bought milk from a man who had died three years before. He frequently withdrew his statements. When asked why he had lied, he simply said that he had no idea. That was the ultimate lie. He knew the reasons full well.

The main question was whether Zézé had spent the night of 4–5 August at the Grand' Terre. He was known to be childish and beset with all manner of anxieties. Some claimed that he refused to go to the cinema in Peyruis on his own and that he insisted on his mother going with him to the outhouse to make sure no stranger was there. Would he have dared sleep alone in La Serre? Jean Galizzi, his mother's lover and with whom he was on good terms, said that when he worked at the farm at Pont Bernard belonging to Daniel Garcin, the mayor of Ganagobie, he always spent the night there. That night Garcin had suggested that Galizzi go to La Serre and keep Zézé company, but he had refused, saying he was too tired. Zézé mostly claimed to have slept alone at La Serre on 4 August, but at other times he said that he had gone to his parents' new farm at La Cassine at 9 p.m. His mother, Germaine, testified that this was so, but she had no means of proving it. Another witness claimed that he had arrived at the Pont Bernard farm late at night. He appeared to be in a state of shock and had to be given a cordial to revive him. Daniel Garcin stated categorically that Zézé had not spent the night of 4–5 August at his farm and that he had not worked on the farm on 4 August. Zézé claimed that he first heard of the crime when Faustin Roure came in the morning of 5 August to La Serre to buy some wine, but Roure had been unable to say with any confidence whether this was so.[19]

The commissioner and his associates returned to Paris to prepare their report for the minister of justice. They had heard a hundred witnesses, had asked ten thousand questions, and had traveled nine thousand miles. Their report was nine hundred pages long. Although they had gleaned a mass of material, they had precious little in the way of hard facts. On 25

February 1956 Chenevier submitted it to his superior, Director General of the Judicial Police Castaing. His conclusion was that the investigation against "Unknown" should be continued. He suggested that the next phase should begin with a confrontation between Gustave and Périès to establish whether he would continue to denounce as false the record of the interrogation that a respected examining magistrate vouched to be true.

Pierre Carrias took nine months to reply to Chenevier's request to continue the investigation. He was a man of exceptional probity, open-mindedness, and sound judgment. His reticence was due to his disgust at the role the press had played in the entire affair; to his concerns about Chenevier's detestation of Sébeille, the reason for which he was unable to discover; and to his concern for due procedure. He also began to have some doubts about the case. He established that Gaston could not possibly have seen Gustave and Zézé in the alfalfa field if he had been standing in the courtyard as he claimed. Carrias was also worried about the lack of a credible motive for the crime. The contradictions in the Dominicis' testimonies were glaringly obvious. He asked himself why Gaston claimed to have fired only one shot at Lady Drummond and why he said that he had hit Elizabeth just once with the butt of the M1. He was astonished that the essential clue of the trousers left hanging out to dry on the morning of the crime had not been pursued. Furthermore, as he wrote in his reflections on the case: "The shadow of the resistance and the liberation hung over the enquiry."[20] But none of this, nor anything in Chenevier's report, persuaded him that anything could be gained from another hunt for accomplices. Gustave was obviously a liar, but in the magistrate's view none of his lies had established any connection with the crime.

Carrias was contemptuous of Chenevier's approach, accusing him of bias. He charged him for failing to accept Sébeille's explanation of the photograph showing Gaston pointing to the upper shelf, rather than the lower one, where Gustave and Clovis had clearly shown that the carbine had been placed. Sébeille had said that the police had been obliged to take several pictures. Gaston had grown impatient and had waved his cane too high in the air. Carrias also dismissed the notion that the pool of blood near the sump indicated that Elizabeth had been killed there and then carried to the bank of the Durance. Sir Jack had been shot in the liver and had bled profusely, so he had been virtually drained of blood by the time he collapsed on the other side of the road. Carrias remained convinced that the evidence of the trousers drying in the courtyard was further indication of Gaston's guilt. He felt that the dossier also served to exculpate Zézé, whose insolent attitude toward his grandfather and Uncle Gustave was evidence that he did not fear any damaging revelation on their part. He suspected that Gustave might have been involved, but the evidence against him was not strong enough to open a further investigation.

The public prosecutor's office in Digne concluded on 30 October 1956 that there was insufficient evidence that anyone aided Gaston in his crime, so there was no reason to pursue the case.[21] On 13 November 1956 Carrias signed a document dismissing the case against "Unknown."[22] This judgment of nonsuit confirmed Gaston's guilt. The Dominici case was thus closed. Only a confession by a guilty person could now overthrow this final judgment.

The Times summed up this strange case: "It was not merely that the victims were distinguished or that the crime was so senseless and mysterious. There was also the dark background of a region of France where life is still primitive and passions are unchecked." The article paraphrased Jean Giono, who said of the region: "One of long-settled, much in-bred immigrant stock, living in a primitive world with its harsh simplicities and savage hatreds, incapable of telling the truth, many of these people seem a survival from another age." It was a region where sons accused fathers, who in turn execrated their sons. Statements were withdrawn, denied, contradicted, or altered, apparently without a second thought. The article ended on an understandable note of puzzlement: "Any ordinary English reader studying the evidence that was published day by day could well be excused for feeling that he would never know where the truth lay."[23]

In 1957 President Coty commuted Gaston's death sentence to life imprisonment. In March 1960 the journalist Jacques Chapus, who had covered the case for *France Soir*, and a television crew visited Gaston at Les Baumettes to make a film titled "Dominici: To Die in Prison."[24] The program attracted a large audience, which tended to sympathize with the decrepit old peasant. A number of newspapers now argued that he should be released, regardless of whether he was innocent or guilty. On 14 July that year, at eight thirty in the morning, on President de Gaulle's instructions, Gaston was released from prison.[25] Despite widespread public protests against his returning to live in the Basses-Alpes and although French law did not permit a convicted murderer to reside in either the department where the crime was committed or any adjacent department for five years, he was allowed briefly to stay with his favorite daughter, Clotilde Araman, in Montfort, where her husband was now a level-crossing keeper.[26] *The Times* reported that he appeared to be in reasonably good health for an eighty-three-year-old. The writer added, "His cantankerous nature tended to add to the mystery and to give a general atmosphere of dark intrigue."[27]

The local people were up in arms when they heard of Gaston's release and that he was once again living in the Basses-Alpes. They made various attempts to have him banished. Most of his family wanted nothing to do with him. The people in Lurs voted to boycott him. Local councilors intimated that at the next meeting of the Council of the Basses-Alpes they would ask why, contrary to the law, he was allowed to return to the area where he had committed such a terrible crime.[28]

Poor Clotilde found life with her parents intolerable, because Gaston's temper was as vile as ever and he still treated his poor wife in an insufferable manner. Clotilde felt obliged to move to a smaller house so that they could no longer live with her. Gaston then moved to a retirement home in Digne, where, prompted by the clairvoyant Reine Ribot, he unsuccessfully launched an appeal against his conviction.

Miss Ribot, who styled herself as a private detective, was one of the most persistent rumormongers, insisting that she had a photograph in her possession showing Sir Jack Drummond giving the secret Maquis sign that involved placing three fingers on a lapel. She clinched her argument by saying that the Maquis in the Basses-Alpes was known as "Drumont," a French pronunciation of "Drummond." The lady was a mythomane well known to the Paris police and to the mental health services in the capital. Incorrigible conspiracy theorists took the fact that she was not called as a witness at the trial, even though mention was made of the raincoat she had found at Lurs railway station, as proof that the British government did not want the link between Sir Jack and the Resistance to be so clearly established.[29]

Gaston died on 4 April 1965. He lies buried in Peyruis. Gaston's wife, Marie, died on 2 January 1967. Yvette and Gustave divorced in 1967. She was reputed to have been having an affair with a gendarme at the time of the investigation, and Pollak attributed it to the machinations of Captain Albert, who hoped thereby to extract some inside information. Yvette remains a staunchly outspoken champion of her former father-in-law's innocence and is always ready, for a consideration, to make yet another revelation to a hungry press.

12 Reception

One of the most fascinating aspects of the Dominici affair is the marked change in public opinion regarding Gaston. At the time of his arrest, journalists outdid one another in vilifying the "wild boar of the Basses-Alpes," thus enflaming the public and making a fair trial almost impossible. Once he was convicted, the security police had to be called in to save him from a lynching. Even though people had serious misgivings about the police investigation, the way in which the confessions were obtained, and the conduct of the trial, only those who subscribed to the most fantastic conspiracy theories felt that he was not guilty. The question then was simply whether he had acted alone. Meanwhile, the Dominici family was totally ostracized, the Grand' Terre was cut off from the rest of the community, and the region was traumatized by the horrific events that had brought it into such ill repute. As a child Gustave's son Alain lived like an animal in the zoo but with people throwing rocks at him rather than peanuts. He claimed that he later was refused a place at the high school in Digne because of his name.[1] As noted previously, widespread protests arose on Gaston's release from prison in 1960 because he had been allowed, contrary to established practice, to reside in the department that he had disgraced.

The Grand' Terre was an accursed place that was soon left abandoned. One Monsieur Belmont tried to tend the fields, but as he was constantly bombarded with questions and insulted by passersby, he gave up the attempt. One enterprising soul tried to run the place as a restaurant, but it was not a success. It has now been transformed into a charming family home, with the violent past having been exorcised and the owner building anew on the century-long association with the monastery at Ganagobie.

Gradually attitudes began to change. A 1973 film *L'affaire Dominici* (*The Dominici Affair*) starring Jean Gabin as Gaston Dominici and the young Gérard Depardieu as Zézé Perrin painted Gaston in a more favorable light. The 2003 television film starring Michel Serrault was based on conspiracy theories, which had gained new currency as the details of the affair faded and explanations, however fantastic, were sought to explain this senseless crime. These theories were fanned by Gustave's son Alain, who is still seeking to absolve his grandfather. He is supported by William Reymond, who has managed to convince himself that the Drummonds were the victims of a murder squad in which Wilhelm Bartkowski was involved.

The rehabilitation of Gaston Dominici, at least in terms of local opinion, must be seen within the context of profound changes within French society during what the economist Jean Fourastié called *les trente glorieuses* (the glorious thirty)—that is, the thirty years of astonishing economic growth between 1945 and 1975 that resulted in a revolutionary transformation of French society.[2] This was the culmination of a lengthy process. For two hundred years progress in France meant the gradual elimination of the peasantry.[3] If France were to continue exporting agricultural goods to maintain a positive trade balance, then peasant farming à la Grand' Terre would have to disappear and make way for large-scale agribusiness. It was a brutal process in which some three-quarters of the peasantry had to adapt to a different way of life. The peasantry was demoralized and confused, unable to support any one political party, and less likely to become involved in electoral politics than other occupational groups were. It was a situation that the Communist Party sought to exploit to its advantage.

At first sight this seems extraordinary. Karl Marx wrote of the "idiocy of rural life" and in volume 3 of *Das Kapital* predicted that small farms would be gobbled up by large capitalist estates. This was confirmed in a letter on the agrarian question written by Friedrich Engels to the French communists. In referencing policy changes and innovation, the French Marxist Jules Guesde's aphorism that "the only way to make peasants fecund is by rape" was widely quoted. But the French Communist Party succeeded in gaining considerable support in the countryside among the peasantry, as can be seen in the Dominicis' immediate entourage and the support that the party gave them in the early stages of the police investigation.[4] After World War I, in a major rupture with orthodox Marxism, the French communists reconsidered their policy toward the rural population by suggesting that smallholdings might prove to be centers of resistance against capitalism and that an alliance between the peasantry and the industrial proletariat might be feasible. This policy shift was ideologically suspect and did nothing to overcome the antagonism of the industrial working class toward the peasantry, whom the former regarded as petit-bourgeois reactionaries who were largely responsible for the high cost of food.

Provence had always been an area of radical peasantry. Its people supported the radical republican Montagnards in 1849, went with the socialists in the Section Française de l'Internationale Ouvrière (French Section of the Workers' International) and the Partie Communiste Française in the 1930s, and helped maintain the communists' share of the vote between 1947 and 1952. Theirs was essentially a protest vote without any ideological underpinnings. No one thought of quoting Marx's musings about whether the Russian village commune offered an alternative route to socialism, in which he overlooked the awkward fact that the mir was little more than a form of collectivized serfdom.

The victory of the Popular Front in the 1936 came as a profound shock to the French bourgeoisie. Some sectors reacted by moving to the extreme right, adopting slogans such "Better Hitler than Léon Blum."[5] The more considered response was the attempt to kill two birds by one stone by means of corporatism on the Italian fascist model. They hoped thereby to overcome the class struggle in the industrial sector as well as ending cutthroat competition between enterprises. As far as the peasantry was concerned, a host of writers chanted eulogies to the eternal verities and values of rural life, conjuring up a vision of a France frozen in a romantic past. It was a popular literature, aimed at a broad audience and widely disseminated. The most eloquent of the theoreticians of this corporatist vision was Jacques Le Roy Ladurie, a militant Catholic syndicalist who saw Marxism as a direct result of unbridled economic liberalism and as a mortal threat to the peasantry as the pillar of rural civilization. He preached a form of rural corporatism, defending the peasants against the encroachments of neo-feudalism. He served as the minister of agriculture in the Vichy government until he resigned in protest when the Germans forced French workers into labor service. He then joined the Resistance but remained true to his corporatist ideals until his death in 1988.[6]

Le Roy Ladurie had a redoubtable amanuensis in Henri d'Halluin. Known as Dorgères, d'Halluin was an appalling rural fascist and strident demagogue who preached a form of peasant racism, denounced the system that was oppressing the people, and gave them a sense of empowerment. Distancing himself from the wealthy farmers, he developed a kind of rural poujadism, which he spiced with such slogans as "Civil servants are your enemies" (*Le fonctionnaire, voilà l'ennemi*) and denouncements of the typical village teacher as the agent of an alien world, serving the "school of deracination" (*l'école du déracinement*). This pied piper of Vichy corporatism had some success in the Vaucluse, but the neighboring Basses-Alpes with its radical tradition remained largely immune.[7]

Vichy's "National Revolution" harped at length on the agrarian theme, with Philippe Pétain styled as the "peasant marshal." In one of his first speeches as head of state, he proclaimed, "The earth does not lie. It is your recourse. It is an embodiment of the motherland. A field that lies fallow is a part of France that dies. Fallow land that is cultivated is a part of France that is reborn." For Pétain the peasant was the docile and obedient infantryman at Verdun, the embodiment of an eternal, preindustrial France. The Communist Party stoutly resisted the reorganization of French agriculture along corporatist lines. The clandestine newspaper *La Terre* published the following appeal: "French peasants! You have sacred duties towards the motherland! . . . Slow down thrashing and hide your harvests for Frenchmen. Do not give the Boches anything, get rid of the controllers . . . hide, help and arm the youths who refuse to be deported. . . . Take part together with the working class in the armed struggle against the invader." The response to this appeal was particularly strong in southern France.[8]

In 1945 all European economies were in ruins. The French gross domestic product was a mere 40 percent of its prewar level. The Provisional Government of the French Republic under the chairmanship of Charles de Gaulle was fully committed to a policy of forced industrialization and economic growth. It was able to do so because of a strange marriage of convenience resulting from wartime alliances. The Communist Party, styling itself with breathtaking hyperbole as "the party of the 85,000 shot" in the struggle against fascism, was allied with the socialists in the Section Française de l'Internationale Ouvrière and Georges Bidault's Mouvement Républican Populaire, a Christian democratic-republican alliance. The two other main parties, the Radical-Socialistes (Radical Socialists) and the conservative Alliance Républicaine Démocratique (Democratic Republican Alliance), were discredited for their pusillanimous prewar policies and their support for the Vichy regime. Across the board it was agreed that only a determined cooperative effort and massive state intervention could put the country back on its feet. Management accepted that it would have to make short-term sacrifices to attain long-term goals. The trade unions in the Confédération Générale du Travail (General Confederation of Labor), supported by the Communist Party, outlawed strikes. Maurice Thorez, the communist leader, announced that the government's aim was to "win the battle of production."

The provisional government took advantage of this truce in the class war that had raged in the prewar years to nationalize entire sections of the economy. In part, as in the case of Renault, this was punishment for having collaborated with the enemy, but as with the nationalization of the coal industry, it was done mainly in the interests of forced economic growth. But the way ahead was blocked by massive debts, the shortage of capital, and the "dollar gap," or the lack of foreign exchange. The situation was made all the worse because the Vichy government had handed over France's foreign exchange reserves to the Germans. In 1946 Léon Blum, who had taken over the chairmanship of the provisional government, went to the United States to negotiate the annulment of at least part of France's wartime debt, hoping that the Americans would be able to recover some of the foreign exchange that had gone to Germany. Blum was successful, but in return he had reluctantly agreed to open the French market for Hollywood movies, a concession that many in France saw as a direct assault on the very foundations of their national culture. In December 1945 Jean Monnet was appointed head of the Plan de Modernisation de l'Équipement (Modernization Plan). In January 1946 this organization was greatly expanded to become the Commissariat Général du Plan (General Planning Commission). Monnet's appointed task was to coordinate the public sector so as to achieve the maximum rate of economic growth.

Announced in 1947, the first five-year plan had two aims—by 1950 attain the level of production of 1929, which was the highest in the prewar years, and by 1952 surpass it by 25 percent. The plan's emphasis was on coal, electricity, steel, cement, and tractors. It concentrated on the industrial north, where the most fertile land was amalgamated to increase the production of cereal crops. Sugar beet production was intensified and dairy farming encouraged. Southern France was largely neglected, so small peasant holdings were doomed. It was an imaginative and comprehensive scheme, but it was difficult to see how, given the parlous state of French finances, these ambitious goals could possibly be achieved. Salvation was achieved chiefly by means of the Marshall Plan, through which France received about $2.5 billion. This was enough to plug the dollar gap and to maintain the value of the franc, which had steadily lost value since 1945 due to both an alarming rate of inflation caused by a tripling of nominal wages between 1945 and 1948 and a decline in purchasing power by a third. These problems were further compounded by the successful reorganization of northern agriculture. It led to a bumper wheat harvest in 1948, resulting in overproduction and a sharp decline in agricultural prices as the glut replaced scarcity before bottoming out in 1951.

The Marshall Plan marked the break with the Communist Party and the real beginning of the Cold War. The times were difficult. As elsewhere in Europe, employees were called upon to work long hours for wretched wages. Thorez and four other communist ministers were expelled from the provisional government. Some of this backfired. The Communist Party posed as champions of French culture, which the party claimed was under attack from sneaking Americanization, thanks to Hollywood and the Marshall Plan. Initially this stance brought the party some additional support, but in the long run the Stalinist toady Thorez, who had endorsed the Molotov-Ribbentrop Pact and who had deserted to Moscow during France's greatest danger, could hardly pose as the savior of France's cultural independence. Nor were the communists able to form an independent peasant movement despite all their appeals for an alliance between the peasantry and the working class. Sharp divisions on the land among agricultural entrepreneurs, independent peasants like Gaston Dominici, sharecroppers such as Paul Maillet, and agricultural laborers were compounded by the industrial workers' innate aversion to the peasantry.

Yet despite all these problems, France had made significant progress. By 1949 wages were rising faster than prices and rationing was abolished.[9] By 1952 the goals of the five-year plan had been largely met. The problem of inflation remained severe, but in 1952 the center-right government of Antoine Pinay began to get the situation under control by drastically cutting back public investment. The government was also helped in that since 1950 the United States paid 80 percent of the cost of its proxy war in Indochina.

From 1945 to 1973, when the world economy was shattered by the oil crisis, industrial production in France rose 4.5 times, or at an annual rate of 5.9 percent. France had ceased to be essentially an agricultural country, with 40 percent of the population classified as "farmers and peasants," and was now an industrial society with a mere 8 percent working on the land. Agricultural prices steadily declined relative to those in industry. The drop had begun in the 1870s with the mass influx of grain and meat from the Americas and was further exacerbated until prices were offset by the subsidies of the European Commission's Common Agricultural Policy (CAP), which was agreed upon in 1960 and came into force two years later. CAP sustained moribund sectors of the agricultural economy at enormous expense and with dubious political and ethical consequences.[10] Prime Minister Georges Pompidou made no bones about the role of the CAP in restructuring the French economy. The Treaty of Rome initially only created a common market for industrial goods that left France unable to compete with the overwhelming superiority of German industry. CAP offered compensation, whereby subsidies from other member states provided remunerative outlets for French agriculture. The state was thereby relieved of the burden of supporting the farming sector and could concentrate on lightening the burden weighing on industry.[11]

The world of Gaston Dominici was doomed by the forces of modernity. A smallholding such as the Grand' Terre, which sat between a main road and a railway and would soon be joined by an expressway—all signifiers of the forces that were to destroy it—could not possibly survive. Capital for mechanization and modernization, subsidies, tax relief, and price supports were only lavished on the big sugar beet and grain producers of the north. Peasants such as Gaston Dominici also could not compete with the wine, fruit, and olive oil producers of southern France, where the market was already glutted. Small peasant farmers were thus barely able to struggle on at the subsistence level. Agriculture still exists in the region because the European Union provides subsidies and the French government wants to avoid other violent protests against its proposals to further rationalize agriculture, a program that involves closing down uneconomical farms.

French society was being rapidly transformed at a time when the country was to face a series of humiliations and defeats. The ignominy of 1940 was hardly offset by the exaggerated contribution of the Resistance, whose 160,000 members—most of whom were very late arrivals—roughly equaled the full-time collaborators. The year of Gaston's trial, 1954, also saw France's defeat in Indochina and the beginning of the Algerian revolt, which would lead to a shattering humiliation and leave the country on the brink of civil war. The Suez crisis of 1956 was a further embarrassment but was overshadowed by the Battle of Algiers that began that same year. The lesson that de Gaulle drew from Suez was that France's future lay not with a close relationship with *les Anglo-Saxons* in Britain and America but in Europe, where the country could aspire to leadership. Thus, from 1958 he began his quixotic schemes to restore to *la grande nation* something of its former glory.

The modernization of French society bore a high price tag. The average citizen was better off and enjoyed the benefits of a consumer society, but the gap between rich and poor grew ever wider. The movement from the countryside to urban centers caused overcrowding and a severe pressure on essential services. With the Algerian war ending in a crushing defeat, France was faced with the integration of the Harkis, or those Algerians who remained loyal to France, as well as the colonial French Pieds-Noirs (French citizens of Algeria). Immigration from North Africa and the former French colonies created further problems that the government addressed inadequately. Violence and racism spiraled. Mounting social tensions placed an intolerable pressure on the generous French model of the welfare state, while entrenched interests made any fundamental reform an intractable problem.

In such an atmosphere, it is hardly surprising that there was a widespread hankering after the good old days when it appeared that life was simpler, values more secure, and people more honest and authentic. The search began for a mythical *France profonde* (Deep France), otherwise known as *la douce France* (sweet France), *la bonne vieille France* (good old France), or *la France éternelle* (eternal France). "Peasantism" and "agrarianism," two widely used if inelegant neologisms, are deeply engrained in France, a country where people are exceptionally proud of their peasant ancestry; and that sensibility served to make their adjustment to the industrial age all the more difficult. As Nobel Laureate François Mauriac put it, France is a country where "Cybele has more disciples than Christ." There was a lingering feeling that there was something in the physiocrat François Quesnay's dictum that "the earth is the sole source of wealth" and that the peasantry was the only truly productive class.[12] Once this transformation became irreversible a sentimental attachment to the rustic, both on the left and on the right, began to express itself in terms of a search for "authenticity," the "natural," and "community." In time of uncertainty and change, the appeal of a sentimentalized version of a rural past is hard to resist. It can be found in Oliver Goldsmith's "The Deserted Village" (1770), Matthew Arnold's "Scholar Gypsy" (1853),

Alfred Lord Tennyson's "Locksley Hall Sixty Years After" (1886), and Jacques Brel's "C'est comme ça" (1954) to name but a random few.

This romanticized vision of French rural life was far removed from the brutal depictions of the peasantry by Balzac and Zola. Even the peasant world as presented in the popular works of Émile Guillaumin—a man who had five years of schooling, farmed 3 hectares (7.4 acres), and won the Prix Goncourt in 1904—was fearful, superstitious, and wretchedly subjected to harsh treatment by the more fortunate. Gradually the vanished world of the clog maker, the charcoal burner, the hedger and ditch digger, the itinerant worker, and the tinker was seen as embodying inestimable human values, and its loss was the cause of much that was wrong with the modern world. This distorted vision was reinforced by the myth that the French Revolution had led to a radical redistribution of landed property that, in turn, made the peasants the heirs of the republic, the embodiment of the essence of France.

Nouville: Un Village Français, the first of many books that awoke a renewed interest in a way of life that was rapidly disappearing, was written by two outstanding ethnologists Lucien Bernot and René Blanchard in 1952. The next year saw the publication of a collection of papers on rural and urban life edited by the sociologist Georges Friedmann. Laurence Wylie's study of a village in the Vaucluse, published in 1957, soon became an established classic and was widely read in France.[13] The 1960s witnessed a growing interest in social history, cultural studies, and popular culture. In 1967 Henri Mendras published his study of the demise of the French peasant.[14] This interest led in the following decade to the astonishing international success of Emmanuel Le Roy Ladurie's *Montaillou*; the publication of Georges Duby and Armand Wallon's multivolume history of rural France, whose last volume of is titled *La Fin de la France paysanne* (The end of peasant France); as well as Michel Foucault's analysis of medical, legal, and national discourses on language, rurality, and state power as illustrated by the parricide case of Pierre Rivière. Foucault's work was greatly influenced by Jean Giono's meditations on the Dominici trial and by Roland Barthes's semiological approach to the case.[15] There was much talk in such intellectual circles of violence as a dialectical response to the imperialism of language and as the sole means by which the voice of the dispossessed could gain a hearing. Was Gaston Dominici's violent character the means by which a barely literate person, unable to express himself in intelligible and unambiguous French, an expression of revolt against a capitalist economy that was gradually strangling him? Was not his position analogous to that of the developing world's peasantry, whose violent struggle against imperialist exploitation was fervently endorsed by the intellectual left?

The sentimental attachment to rural France—encouraged by environmentalists, local politicians on the lookout for juicy subsidies, peasants struggling to make ends meet, and the wealthy concerned about the bucolic surroundings of their holiday homes—has had some strange results. Most noticeable is the extraordinary tolerance displayed in the face of violent manifestations of rural discontent. Roads are blocked with burning tires, streets are barricaded with surplus fruit, tractors bring traffic to a standstill, and the easily aroused Frenchman shrugs the whole business off with a tolerant reference to the hard lot of *les paysans*.[16]

The most astonishing example of such forbearance was the popularity of José Bové, a California-bred draft dodger, former hippie, and prankster, who bears a striking physical resemblance to the comic book character Astérix. He led colorful campaigns to smuggle Roquefort cheese into the United States, to outlaw genetically manipulated crops, to legalize marijuana, and to protest globalization and agribusiness. He achieved international fame in 1999 when he led a group of protestors who demolished a McDonald's restaurant at Millau, an act that he compared to the storming of the Bastille. He received a very modest sentence for this action.

Bové's half-baked ideology—a potent mixture of undifferentiated anti-Americanism, French chauvinism, and protectionism disguised as anti-globalization and anticapitalism—ensured him widespread popularity that was symptomatic of a fundamental change in attitudes toward the countryside and the peasantry since the 1950s.[17] When Gaston Dominici repeatedly said during his trial, "Je suis franc z'loyal. Je suis un bon

Français," he was reacting to the stereotype of the French peasant as sly, sneaky, secretive, and unpatriotic.[18] With the critiques of the capitalist state, anti-imperialism, Third World liberation, ecology, subsidiarity, regionalism, and the discovery of the countryside as an oppositional space, the typical peasant was increasingly seen as a frank, loyal, and good French person. The "wild boar of Lurs" became the victim of the colonization of the countryside, a hapless being living in a world saturated by signification but with no access to meaning and trapped at the intersection of disparate discourses.

In the interwar years, successive French governments faced the intractable problem of how to address the issue of the peasantry. Should the system be preserved in the interests of social stability or drastically modified to increase productivity, lower costs, and ensure increased exports? The problem was essentially one of the distribution of land. In 1929 there were one million dwarf farms of less than 1 hectare (2.5 acres) and three million farms of less than 10 hectares (25 acres), into which category the Grand' Terre would have fallen. Another statistic showed that 10 percent of farmers owned half the agricultural land, and the remaining 90 percent of farmers tended the other half. Even as late as 1975, 62 percent of French farms were still less than 20 hectares (49 acres).[19] Eighty-eight percent of peasants owned the land on which they worked.

Farmers, great and small, did well during the war and the immediate postwar years due to food shortages, rationing, and a thriving black market. But agricultural prices collapsed in 1948. Production barely increased compared with 1938, whereas industry had grown by 40 percent. Only 5 percent of public investment was earmarked for agriculture, most of which went to large estates. The country faced a "scissors crisis," where industrial prices rose ever higher than those in agriculture, resulting in widespread discontent on the land.

The peasantry was renowned for its hostility toward the authorities in Paris, an attitude known as *incivisme* (lack of civic-mindedness). Many lived a wretched life of heavily indebted penury and were never able for lack of capital to rise above the subsistence level. They were resentful of bureaucratic regulations and others' apparent lack of concern with their plight. It was a situation that the Communist Party skillfully exploited. Once the Germans invaded the Soviet Union in 1941, the party had adopted the slogan of "Democracy, peace, and France" and posed as champions of the antifascist struggle. With the onset of the Cold War and the expulsion of the communists from the government, the party placed renewed emphasis on the class struggle. A quote from Stalin was unearthed that provided highest sanction for a bid to win support among the peasantry within a new political situation. As the Soviet dictator prepared to send millions of peasants to their deaths in his collectivization program, he had cynically announced that the aim of his policy was "to transform the peasantry from the reserve of the bourgeoisie into a reserve and ally of the working class." This sounded well and good in theory, but there was little chance of it ever working in France. It was highly unlikely that a *fétishisme paysanne* (peasant fetishism) would soon match the party's *fétichisme ouvrière* (factory worker fetishism). Industrial workers regarded peasants, even the most wretched among them, as "egoists," "rich men," and culturally backward. In turn, peasants thought of industrial workers as having a "soft life" as a result of "coddling" by indulgent governments eager to win their support.[20]

A grand alliance between the proletariat and the peasantry was thus never in the cards, as rural society was characterized more by internal conflicts than by cooperation. But the communists pointed to the gross inequalities in the distribution of land and fanned resentment against agribusiness and government inaction in the face of a mounting crisis. Slogans such as "There is land to distribute" and "The land belongs to those who cultivate it" found widespread resonance. The peasantry had no desire for a Soviet France or for being herded into collective farms, but the people saw the communists as useful allies against a government that showed little concern with their plight. They agreed that the Marshall Plan had done nothing to help agriculture, they saw the Council of Europe's agricultural plan as a direct threat in that it removed protective barriers between member states, and many felt a strong affective attachment to a Communist Party that seemed to be upholding the traditions of peasant radicalism. The peasantry had deep feelings and resentments that were not carefully analyzed, but the Communist Party was able to articulate them clearly and without ideological obfuscation. Party cells in rural areas provided a sense of community, cooperation, and purpose that was otherwise lacking, and the rigid Stalinist party hierarchy ensured that they were not troubled with ideological or political decision-making. Peasant communism was thus affective rather than intellectual. It provided a means of expressing their wounded pride, their jealousy, their mistrust, and their ambitions. Some French intellectuals dreamed that an alliance between the peasantry and the industrial working class could be forged, one that would lead to a new society, but the divisions between the two factions and among themselves, compounded by the profound individualism of the peasants, rendered such a dream utopian.[21]

The philosopher Raymond Aron, writing roughly at the time of the Drummond murders, argued that the conservatism of French politics was due to the votes of women and peasants, and the maintenance of a strong agricultural population was a necessary barrier to communism and Marxism. Within twenty years this barrier was lowered by more than 50 percent, and the Left increased its representation correspondingly. Thus, the dwindling of the peasantry strengthened the Left. This may very well be true in aggregate, but the case of the Dominicis proved different. We saw how successful the Communist Party was in specific areas of rural France and how the party supported the family members until they were finally denounced by the local party secretary, who in turn was dropped when he was compromised by the police. By that point, only the Italian communists still championed the Dominicis, with their party newspaper, *L'Unità*, cooking up the outlandish tale that the Drummonds had been assassinated on orders from the U.S. government.

The discourses of the occupation of France and the Resistance were intertwined with that of the Dominicis to the point that the Communist Party initially stylized the police attack on them as an attack on the antifascist struggle, a desecration of the memory of the "85,000 shot," and a sinister shift to the right. Once it could no longer be denied that the Dominicis were at least implicated in the crime and when the local party organization became seriously compromised, the party no longer openly supported them. The Dominicis' defense team, however, comprised prominent communist lawyers, and the party did everything it could to counter the conspiracy theories suggesting that the Drummonds were the victims of a Soviet-instigated assassination. Gaston's claim to be *franc z'loyal* and the association of the Dominicis with the Resistance are part of the reason why his reputation underwent a sea change from sadistic brute to maligned patriarch.

The radical politics of certain areas of rural France stem in large part from opposition to Paris rather than any carefully considered ideology. Thus, at the time of the Dominici trial, the communists, with 28.8 percent of the popular vote in the 1946 election, were the largest party. They were popular first and foremost because of their close association with and significant role in the Resistance after 22 June 1941. Even in 1951 they dropped only 2.8 percentage points and were still the largest party due to their stand against the Americanization implied in the Marshall Plan, the North Atlantic Treaty Organization, and the rearming of Germany. The party's quixotic stand against modernity had much appeal in backward and declining areas such as Lurs. Little attention was paid to the party's bizarre denunciation of refrigerators, washing machines, dishwashers, and vacuum cleaners as dehumanizing, because such key items in the new consumer society were unknown in rural France. The drug-addicted, alcoholic novelist, playwright, and essayist Roger Vailland, who joined the party in 1952, gave literary expression to this view but delighted in driving around in a Jaguar in pursuit of libertinage. Similarly, the party's robust antifeminism and the denunciation of birth control as "bourgeois" were perfectly acceptable in this chauvinist and fecund society. Party leader Maurice Thorez, an unabashed Stalinist who was denounced Nikita Khrushchev for his 1956 speech attacking the great man and who in the same year spoke of "Hungarian fascism," was a serious, intelligent, cultured, charming, and immensely popular figurehead.

As the Communist Party ossified and went into steady decline, it lost all attraction as a locus of inchoate protest. Its place was taken by such disparate movements as the ultra-right Front National (National Front) or various fringe groups of Trotskyites, Maoists, and ecologists. Anticommunism played precious little role in local politics. There were matters of more pressing concern such as the ukases from Brussels on the types of birds hunters were no longer permitted to slaughter, the closing of a local post office, or the building of subsidized housing for homeless Maghrebis. The association of the Dominicis with the Communist Party was thus no impediment to their rehabilitation. Gaston could be seen as yet another victim of Parisian arrogance and of the typically disdainful attitude of those on high who were utterly ignorant of his milieu. His world had disappeared and was now regarded with romanticized affection.

Meanwhile, cases such as that of Gaston Dominici that have not been fully explained provide rich humus for conspiracy theories, but even those that have been investigated still give rise to paranoid fantasies. Thus, the murders of John F. Kennedy, Martin Luther King Jr., and John Lennon have spawned all manner of exotic explanations. A horror as complex as the Shoah is explained away as never having happened. Delusional theories such as that of the world Jewish conspiracy or of a Masonic mafia are still afforded widespread credence or are transformed into an all-embracing anti-Americanism that serves to explain everything that is wrong with the world. These ideas are not simply the obsessions of tyrants such as Adolf Hitler or Stalin; they can also be the product of exceptional minds. The eminent Austrian orientalist Baron Joseph von Hammer-Purgstall wrote a paper for the Austrian Academy in 1855 uncovering the Templars as a powerful secret society, thus providing rich material for further wild speculation and literary invention. Conspiracy theories provide fruitful material for the sensationalist press and radio talk shows, Hollywood movies, pseudo-scholarly books, best-selling novels, and even election campaigns.

This paranoid attitude of mind was deliciously satirized by George Farquhar in his play *The Beaux' Stratagem* of 1707 in which Squire Sullen's servant Scrub exclaims:

First, it must be a plot because there's a Woman in't; secondly, it must be a plot because there's a Priest in't; thirdly, it must be a plot because there's French Gold in't; and, fourthly, it must be a Plot, because I don't know what to make on't.[22]

Then, of course, for some, there is always the lingering suspicion that Humpty Dumpty was pushed.

In this case, for a conspiracy theory to have any credence whatsoever, Sir Jack Drummond—the distinguished scientist whose work was all in the public domain—had to be given a new persona. That he had worked at the government's Porton Down Experimental Station on the decontamination of foodstuffs subsequent to a gas attack, about which he published a pamphlet, was converted into the fiction that he did extensive work developing poison gas. That a factory near Lurs had once been involved in manufacturing poison gas was taken as proof that he had been involved in negotiating a deal involving this weapon. That a British officer had parachuted into southern France during the war and had met with the Resistance was rewritten so that Drummond was the man in question. That he had gone behind enemy lines in Holland in the war's final stages was evidence that he was in league with the Nazis. That Drummond had worked in Germany on nutritional problems was seen as proof that he had worked for Operation Paperclip, the secret recruitment of German scientists to work for the United States. (Paperclip was in fact a uniquely American operation that had been organized by the U.S. Office of Strategic Services, which created a Joint Intelligence Objectives Agency as an operational staff for the program. It was not in the least interested in questions of nutrition and did not require Jack Drummond's expertise.) That the British government formally denied Drummond was ever an intelligence agent was taken as proof that he was indeed deeply implicated in clandestine operations. Secret agents are, after all, kept secret.

The most persistent of the conspiracy theories involved Bartkowski. His story fit the bill perfectly. Outsiders committed the crime. The perpetrators were in the service of the Soviet Union. British authorities hampered the police inquiry with their reluctance to admit that Drummond was in France on official business.

It is now hotly denied that a French peasant was capable of committing such a terrible crime as the Drummond murders. It must have been the work of outsiders. Once again this belief is contrary to some singularly unpleasant facts. In 1973, shortly after the movie *L'affaire Dominici* starring Jean Gabin opened in Paris, an Englishman and his son went camping at Pélissanne near Salon-de-Provence, where the father was hacked to death with an ax. His son, the poet Jeremy Cartland, was seriously wounded but survived the attack. This case provoked outrage in Britain.[23] The French police suspected patricide, but the case was eventually dropped for lack of evidence. Again, unfounded rumors circulated that the sixty-year-old John Cartland had been a Special Operations Executive operative who had betrayed members of the Maquis.

In 1977 two Britons were shot while camping in a remote area in the Forêt des Maures near Saint-Tropez. The following year two Britons in Cannes were killed by savage blows to the head. Despite these appalling crimes, the myth of a peaceful and placid Provence lives on, and Gaston Dominici is now seen as the victim of a gross injustice, as a typical peasant, and as a member of a class still perceived as forming the moral foundation of eternal France. His life is now seen as reminiscent of Tennyson's "Tithonus": "Man comes and tills the field and lies beneath."[24]

Notes

INTRODUCTION

1. *Times* (London) said Elizabeth was "about twelve" (hereafter *Times*). She was in fact ten years old.
2. For an excellent discussion of this complex issue, see Quintard-Morénas, "Presumption of Innocence."
3. Truche, "Rappport au président."
4. Sagnes, *Le midi rouge.*

1. A FATAL JOURNEY

1. Rations were as follows:
   1 ounce (28 grams) cheese (about enough to fill one sandwich)
   2 ounces (56 grams) tea (roughly twenty teabags)
   2 ounces (56 grams) jam spread
   4 ounces (113 grams) bacon or ham
   8 ounces (226 grams) sugar
   1 shilling's worth of meat (20 shillings = £1)
   8 ounces (226 grams) fats, of which only 2 ounces (56 grams)
   could be butter
   Later sweets and tinned goods could be had on a points system. Bread was not rationed until 1946.
2. *Paris Match*, 30 August–6 September 1952, reprinted a section of Jack's dotingly affectionate diary.
3. The exchange rate was roughly 1,000 anciens francs (10 nouveaux francs) for £1, or $1.22. The allowance had been increased from £5 in sterling and £10 in foreign currency ($6.08 and $12.17, respectively).
4. Wages for lower-paid workers in mining or the railways were £5 per week. A salary of £1,000 a year would guarantee an affluent standard of living, even with extremely steep marginal rates of income tax. Sir Jack earned £4,000 ($4,866) a year.

5. The department was renamed the Alpes-de-Haute-Provence in April 1970.

6. The rates in 1952 were between 400 and 1,300 francs. Meals were within the same range. Although very cheap, the Drummonds' currency allowance would have soon been depleted even at such low rates.

7. The official designation was "un grand gala taurin avec tournoi de toro ball."

8. There is some doubt about the price of this ticket. Chenevier, *De la combe aux fées*, 15, claims that they cost 507 francs; but Guerrier, *L'affaire Dominici*, 163, puts the figure at 750 francs. Seats in the sun and the shade could explain the difference.

9. According to Valerie Marrian's testimony on 12 December 1953. Digne Archives.

10. Maximilien Vox was the pseudonym of Samuel Monod. The meetings, known as Les Rencontres internationales de Lure, are still held every August. Monthly sessions are also held in Paris.

11. The name "Ganagobie" is of Celtic origin and means "hill of light."

12. Marque's testimony can be found at "Le témoignage du gendarme Marque" (The testimony of Officer Marque), 11 April 2003, https://www.samuelhuet .com/fr/affaire-dominici/53-lursfacts/410-temoignage-marque.html. It was not made until 19 March 1953. The later date may account for some minor discrepancies, such as the color of Jack Drummond's jacket, which was dark blue rather than black.

13. The factory was founded during the First World War to produce chlorine. It was then run by various companies: Péchiney-Saint-Gobain, Rhône-Poulenc, Elf Atochem (1992), Atofina (2000), and Arkema in October (2004). After 1918 it produced a wide range of standard products. Saint-Auban was incorporated into the community of Château-Arnoux to become Château-Arnoux-Saint-Auban in 1991.

14. Absolutely nothing is known about Saint Donat. He may well never have existed, but he is much revered in Provence.

15. The road is now the D4096. An autoroute, the A51, now runs parallel along the banks of the Durance.

16. The money was equivalent at that time to $336 and $303.

17. Fines were calculated at 1,000 francs (about €1.85 or $1.95) per minute of delay, a substantial sum in those days. Guerrier, *L'affaire Dominici*, 195. The small trains were "michelines," equipped with pneumatic tires.

18. That they went to the farm to ask for water was asserted by Zézé Perrin, who had heard it from Gaston and Marie, and his mother, Germaine, had heard it from Yvette. Yvette had ordered Zézé not to say anything about it.

2. THE MURDER

1. Archives Départmentales Digne, 1182 W 1, part 1. Also, the N96 route is now known as the D4096.
2. Archives Départmentales Digne, 1182 W 1.
3. Gustave said the body was that of a female (*une morte*).
4. Guerrier, *L'affaire Dominici*, 245. Autheville wrote for communist dailies *La Marseillaise* and *L'Allobroges*.
5. Judt, *Postwar*, 33.
6. The Gras was an adaptation of the old breech-loading chassepot army rifle, adopted in 1874. It fired a single 11mm round. A powerful and accurate weapon, it was widely used by guerrilla fighters and was later adapted for use as a hunting rifle.
7. Domènech, *Lurs*, 82.
8. This is somewhat curious, as the socialists, or French Section of the Workers' International (Section Française de l'Internationale Ouvrière), had been formally allied with the communists since the liberation. The alliance later fell apart due to the pressures of the Cold War.
9. Ernest Hemingway paints a singularly unflattering portrait of Marty in *For Whom the Bell Tolls*, where he appears as the character André Massart. He was a ruthless man obsessed with rooting out "fascist-trotskyite spies" and establishing rigorous communist orthodoxy, but he hardly deserves his nickname of "the butcher of Albacete."
10. Quoted by Warwick Charlton in *Picture Post*, October 1952.
11. Quotes from Burrin, *France under the Germans*, 351.
12. Archives Départmentales Digne, 1182 W 1, part 1, *procès-verbal* (PV) 13 May 1953.
13. It is characteristic of the amazingly shoddy police work in the case that neither the bus driver nor the passengers were ever questioned. Roure also must have crossed paths with Ricard on the main road, but again neither was asked this obvious question.

14. Archives Départmentales Digne, 1182 W 1, part 1, PV 15 August 1952.

15. Archives Départmentales Digne, 1182 W 1, part 1. The conversation between Yvette and Gaston was witnessed by Roure, who had just at that moment returned to the Grand' Terre. It is not clear whether he went out of curiosity or to fetch Clovis, who should have been working at the Lurs station. Roure stated that Gaston had shown surprise when told of the murders, but it cannot be established whether this was indeed the case or whether, if true, the surprise was genuine. Gaston later testified that Gustave had told him about the crime but then retracted his statement.

16. Archives Départmentales Digne, 1182 W 1, part 1.

17. *Paris Match*, 16–23 August 1952.

18. According to article 14 of the Code of Criminal Procedure, the *police judiciaire* (judicial police) are "charged with confirming infractions of criminal law, to collect proof thereof and to discover the perpetrators."

19. Sébeille, *L'affaire Dominici*, 31.

20. Laborde, *Un matin d'été à Lurs*, 99.

21. Sébeille, *L'affaire Dominici*, 290.

3. THE POLICE INVESTIGATION

1. Sébeille claimed that the wound was on the left hand, but he is clearly in error.

2. "Infortunés Drummond: Rapports d'autopsie" (Unfortunate Drummond :Autopsy reports), 20 August 2010, https://www.samuelhuet.com/fr /affaire-dominici/54-lursdocs/361-autopsies-drummond.html.

3. See Deniau and Sultan, *Dominici*.

4. This is suggested by Guerrier, *L'affaire Dominici*, 359, having consulted a traumatologist.

5. National Archives, Kew, MEPO 2/9393.

6. The Sten was a primitive 9mm automatic developed in 1941 and was supplied to the Maquis in large numbers. The name comes from the initials of its inventors, Reginald V. Shepperd and Harold J. Turpin, plus the first two letters of Royal Small Arms Factory in Enfield.

7. *L'Humanité*, 30 August 1952.

8. Guerrier, *L'affaire Dominici*, 325, claims that this is nonsense since Elizabeth had been sleeping in the Hillman and would not have gone anywhere near the mulberry tree as she tried to escape. The map of the crime scene in plate

35 of his book, however, clearly shows that she would indeed have passed directly by the tree.

9. *Combat*, 6 August 1952.

10. Yet in a statement made to the gendarmes on 8 August, Olivier said that Gustave "had made a sign for me to stop." Perhaps Olivier was already stopping when Gustave made the sign. There is also confusion about where exactly he came to a halt.

11. Sébeille, *L'affaire Dominici*, 86.

12. Archives Départmentales Digne, 1182 W 1, part 1.

13. Gaston had said, "Vaï te coutcha!"

14. *L'Humanité*, 8 August 1952.

15. Domènech's book on the case, *Lurs: Toute l'affaire Dominici*, is one of the best contemporaneous accounts and contains some interesting photographs taken by the author.

16. *Combat*, 19 August 1952.

17. *L'Humanité*, 12 August 1952.

18. As mentioned elsewhere, Drummond was granted permission to go behind enemy lines and help provide food for the starving Dutch.

19. *L'Humanité*, 19 August 1952.

20. National Archives, Kew, FO 369/4924, Reilly to Patrick Dean at the FO, 22 December 1953. Also in FO 369/5032.

21. The full extent of Sir Jack's involvement in "secret" work is described in chapter 6, in the section on his career.

22. *Paris Match*, 23–30 August 1952.

23. Sébeille, *L'affaire Dominici*, 89.

24. *L'Humanité*, 28 August 1952. The paper referred to this new witness as "M. Panconi" and said he was "an electrician from Nice."

25. Sébeille, *L'affaire Dominici*, 91.

4. GASTON DENOUNCED

1. National Archives, Kew, MEPO 2/9393.

2. *Paris Match*, 4–11 October 1952. Hopefully the well was disused, but the record contains no such indication, simply mentioning "the well at the farm."

3. Archives Départmentales Digne, 1182 W 5, 28.4.1956. It was a .30 carbine (7.62 x 33 mm), the standard ammunition for the M1.

4. *Ce Soir*, 4 September 1952.

5. *L'Humanité*, 5 September 1952.

6. *Combat*, 6 September 1952.

7. Laborde, *Dominici Affair*, 117.

8. Pollak was a fervent opponent of the death penalty, but five of his clients were executed, including the last person in France to receive the death penalty, Hamida Djandoubi, who was executed on 10 September 1977. He also defended the notorious Marseille Unione Corse family Guérini, who organized the so-called French Connection that supplied the heroin trade to New York. See Pollak, *La parole est à la défense*.

9. Archives Départmentales Digne, 1182 W 2. The name in the archives is incorrectly spelled. Stansfield was an outstanding operative and was awarded the Commander of the Most Excellent Order of the British Empire and the Military Cross for his services in the Aveyron.

10. Archives Départmentales Digne, 1182 W 7.

11. *L'Humanité*, 6 September 1952.

12. Under a paragraph in the penal code introduced by the Vichy government on 28 November 1943 and signed into law by de Gaulle on 25 June 1945.

13. As in a number of instances, there is some confusion in the record regarding the spelling of this family's name. It sometimes appears as "Barthe," but "Barth" is the most common.

14. One set was taken by the gendarmes; the other, by the technical and scientific police.

15. *Times*, 21 November 1952.

16. The mythical "second Hillman," seen by the Lurs postman and by two road menders on the main road near Ganagobie, was almost certainly that of the Drummonds. The second car, which a gendarme saw in Digne on the evening of 4 August, might well have been British but not a Hillman.

17. National Archives, Kew, MEPO 2/9393.

18. *Daily Express*, 18 October 1952.

19. *L'Humanité*, 28 August 1952.

20. National Archives, Kew, mepo 2/9393.

21. Guerrier, *L'affaire Dominici*, 304.

22. Guerrier, *L'affaire Dominici*, 121.

23. See, for example, *Ce Soir*, 4 September 1952.

24. Speaking in dialect, Paul Maillet had said, "Mai mount érès?" Gustave replied, "A qui devans." Guerrier, *L'affaire Dominici*, 464–65.

25. In December 1953 Maillet admitted that before Yvette returned, he had asked where Gustave was. Gustave replied that he was "in front."

26. He was minister of justice from 20 January 1952 to 18 June 1954 in the governments of Edgar Faure, Antoine Pinay, René Meyer, and Joseph Laniel.

27. Sébeille, *L'affaire Dominici*, 160.

28. Roure was accompanied by Clovis and Boyer.

29. *Le Parisien Libéré*, 13 November 1953.

30. Guerrier, *L'affaire Dominici*, [page?].

31. Gaston spoke in dialect: "Ai paù de dégun! Es ioù qu'aï fa péta leis Inglés!" There is some debate about the precise meaning of these words. Guerrier (*L'affaire Dominici*, 495) suggests that there is an ambiguity in the expression "fa péta," in that it could imply that he had someone else to do the deed. That this is far-fetched can be seen by the repetition of the phrase in the next paragraph, "I killed all three of them."

32. The Gras was the French Army's standard single-round 11mm rifle, which was introduced in 1874. It was a modified version of the famous Chassepot, using metal rather than paper cartridges. It was replaced by the Lebel in 1886.

33. "Leis aï fa péta toutéi très." Guerrier, *L'affaire Dominici*, 496.

5. CONFESSION

1. Laborde, *Dominici Affair*, 235.

2. There seems to be some confusion about when mention is first made in official papers of the carbine being kept on the shelf in the shed. See Guerrier, *L'affaire Dominici*, 491.

3. *Combat*, 2 September 1952.

4. See, for example, *Times*, 14 November 1953.

5. *Le Parisien Libéré*, 20 November 1953.

6. Archives Départmentales Digne, 1182 W 1, part 1.

7. By the time of the Dominici trial, Sabatier had been promoted to staff sergeant (*chef de brigade*).

8. Guerrier, *L'affaire Dominici*, 504, makes much of the fact that Gaston spoke of "the rifle" in one version of this exchange with Guérino and said "my rifle" in another. Also, he spoke of a "rifle" and not a "carbine." The second distinction is hardly relevant, because whoever used the weapon did not realize that it was an automatic.

9. Archives Départmentales Digne, 1182 w 1, part 1.

10. Archives Départmentales Digne, 1182 w 1.

11. Archives Départmentales Digne, 1182 w 1.

12. It will be remembered that the magazine held fifteen rounds.

13. Archives Départmentales Digne, 1182 w 1.

14. Archives Départmentales Digne, 1182 w 1.

15. Guerrier, *L'affaire Dominici*, 522.

16. Gaston had spoken in dialect: "Lei aï fa péta toutéi très. Sè nin faù faïre péta encore, lou farai péta." Archives Départmentales Digne, 1182 w 1. Notice the slight difference in the wording (aï fa péta) from his account of the incident as mentioned in chapter 4, note 31.

17. "Je vous remercie, monsieur Gustave." Archives Départmentales Digne, 1182 w 1.

18. "Au moment des faits." Archives Départmentales Digne, 1182 w 1.

19. Guerrier, *L'affaire Dominici*, 533.

20. *Times* (London), 17 November 1953.

21. *Le Figaro*, 17 November 1953.

22. *Daily Express*, 17 November 1953.

23. The work of Jean Meckert, Jean Laborde, and Jean-Charles Deniau and Madeleine Sultan are in broad agreement. Domènech supports the official version.

24. In dialect: "Aguès pas paou, ti piqueraï pas." Guerrier, *L'affaire Dominici*. 540.

25. Archives Départmentales Digne, 1182 w 1.

26. Archives Départmentales Digne, 1182 w 1.

27. William Reymond, *Dominici non coupable*, 89, claims that it was "the family"; Domènech, *Lurs*, 209, says it was Marie Dominici; and for Pollak, *La parole est à la défense*, 237, it was Gustave.

28. *Le Figaro*, 17 November 1953.

29. *Le Figaro*, 11–12 September 1953 and 17 November 1953.

30. *Le Figaro*, 16 September 1953.

31. *Le Parisien Libéré*, 14 November 1953.

32. *Le Parisien Libéré*, 16 and 17 November 1953.

33. *News Chronicle*, 18 November 1953.

1. Details on Drummond's life can be found in National Archives, Kew, MAF 256 and 256/4; and in his obituary by F. G. Young, "Jack Cecil Drummond, 1891–1952," *Obituary Notices of Fellows of the Royal Society* 9, no. 1 (November 1954): 98–129. See also Fergusson, *The Vitamin Murders*.

2. In 1929, together with Christiaan Eijkman, he was awarded the Nobel Prize for work establishing the association between beriberi and the consumption of decorticated rice.

3. See Drummond's article in the *Biochemical Journal* 14 (1920): 660.

4. Boyd Orr, *Food, Health and Income*.

5. Friend, *The Schoolboy*.

6. Drummond and Wilbraham, *The Englishman's Food*.

7. Dorothy Hollingsworth tried to bring the book up to date in 1957, but her changes were minor and do not meet present-day concerns about dairy products, which Drummond championed. See the edition published by Pimlico in 1994.

8. Ministry of Food, *Food and Its Protection*.

9. Kingsley Wood had served as minister of food in Baldwin's third term.

10. In 1942 the Ministry of Food demanded 12.4 million tons but only received 11.4 million tons. There were no unmanageable shortages. Taylor, *English History, 1914–1945*, 546. The prewar importation of foodstuffs averaged 22 million tons per annum, according to the ministry.

11. Roughly seven U.S. cents.

12. Sir Wilson Jameson was the chief medical officer at the Ministry of Health and the architect of the National Health Service. Sir John Boyd Orr was a feisty champion of nutrition and a brilliant scientist who was awarded the 1949 Nobel Peace Prize for his work in the field. See Lasker Foundation, "Group Awards: 1947—The British Ministries of Food and Health," http://www.laskerfoundation.org/awards/show/historical-awards/.I.

13. Malta was the most heavily bombed area in the entire war.

14. Council of British Societies for Relief Abroad, *Nutrition and Relief Work*.

15. Chapman, *Jesse Boot*, 201.

16. Boots Annual Report, 1949–1950, Boots UK Limited Archives. Schering, founded in 1841, was taken over by Bayer in 2006.

17. National Archives, Kew, MAF 256/4. Evans was a professor of physiology at University College, London, and he worked at the Chemical Defence Experimental Station at Porton Down, Wiltshire. He was a specialist in gas contamination, and Drummond consulted him when writing his paper on decontamination.
18. National Archives, Kew, MEPO 2/9393
19. On 30 December 1952.
20. CID to Sûreté, 26 January 1953, MEPO 2/9393.
21. As noted previously, the department was renamed the Alpes-de-Haute-Provence in April 1970.
22. "La famille de Gaston et Marie Dominici," Affaire Dominici—Triple crime de Lurs (forum), 13 October 2008, http://www.affairedominicitriplecrimedelurs.com/t54-La-famille-de-Gaston-et-Marie-Dominici.htm.
23. For further reference, it is also known as *Livre des secrets sur les vertus des herbes, des pierres et de certains animaux*. Better known as Albertus Magnus (1206–80), Albert le Grand was a distinguished scholar and scientist who did much to promote Aristotle and Avicenna and thus was a great influence on Saint Thomas Aquinas. He dabbled in alchemy, magic, and the occult, for which he was roundly denounced. He was canonized by Pope Pius XI in 1931.

7. DOMINICI AWAITS HIS TRIAL

1. Guerrier, *L'affaire Dominici*, 573.
2. Meckert, *La tragédie de Lurs*, 231; and Laborde, *Dominici Affair*, 282.
3. "Aï pou de dégun. Naï fa péta très . . . naï fara uncap éta sin fau." Guerrier, *L'affaire Dominici*, 549.
4. Archives Départmentales Digne, 1182 W 1, Minutes, PV, 5 December 1953.
5. Archives Départmentales Digne, 1182 W 1, PV, 7 December 1953.
6. Archives Départmentales Digne, 1182 W 1, PV, 7 December 1953.
7. Archives Départmentales Digne, 1182 W 1, PV, 17 December 1953.
8. Archives Départmentales Digne, 1182 W 1, PV, 18 December 1953.
9. *Figaro*, 21 November 1953.
10. Archives Départmentales Digne, 1182 W 1, PV, 28 December 1952.
11. Archives Départmentales Digne, 1182 W 1, PV, 30 December 1953. The year before Roure had put the time at about 7:45 a.m.
12. Marshal François-Achille Bazaine had fought with great distinction in the Crimea, at Solferino, and in Mexico. He was the commander of the French

forces trapped with 170,000 men in Metz during the Franco-Prussian War. There he made the famous remark, "We are in a chamber pot, and they'll shit on us!" He capitulated on 27 October 1870. Widely seen as a traitor, he was condemned to death by a court martial, but the sentence was commuted. In 1888 he died in obscurity in Madrid.

13. Archives Départmentales Digne, 1182 w 1, PV, 4 February 1954.
14. Pollak, *La parole est à la défense*, 275.
15. Gustave said this was on 13 November, but this is clearly a mistake.
16. Archives Départmentales Digne, 1182 w 1, PV, 23 February 1954.Archives.
17. Départmentales Digne, 1182 w 1, PV, 23 February 1954.
18. Laborde, *Dominici Affair*, 253.
19. Archives Départmentales Digne, 1182 w 1, PV, 20 March 1954.
20. Archives Départmentales Digne, 1182 w 1, PV, 24 February 1954.
21. Clotilde would have been ten years old at the time.
22. Archives Départmentales Digne, 1182 w 1, PV, 24 February 1954.
23. Archives Départmentales Digne, 1182 w 1, PV, 8 March 1954.
24. No such statement by Gaston can be found in the written record.
25. Laborde, *Dominici Affair*, 269.

8. THE TRIAL OPENS

1. As noted in chapter 6, a santon is a small nativity figurine and popular in Provence. A traditional Provençal crèche has fifty-five individual figures representing various characters from Provençal village life. The *Images d'Épinal* were prints of military subjects, storybook characters, and other folk themes, and they were hugely popular throughout the nineteenth century. They were usually backed by wood or metal.
2. Giono, *Notes sur l'affaire Dominici*, 86.
3. National Archives, Kew, FO 369/5032.
4. Unless otherwise noted, for all quoted passages from the trial, see the transcript in Enquêtes criminelles diverse, Art. 2–3: Affaire Dominici (suite), 1952–56, Archives Nationales, Paris.
5. Pollak mistakenly dated this as 17 December 1953.
6. In a French court the jury is the judge, whereas the judge acts as a president. As is shown in the case of Gaston Dominici's trial, the president acts not as an impartial judge but very much as a prosecutor.

7. Scize, *Au grand jour des assises*, 305. A similar verb—*maronner*—is standard French, meaning "groan." The verb is formed from the slang noun *marron*.

8. For example, see Jean Thiery-Doyen in *Voilà: Europe Magazine*, 5 December 1954.

9. See Birdwhistell, *Kinesis and Context*.

10. Barthes, "Dominici," in *Mythologies*, 43–46. The original article is reprinted with comments in *La Vie Judiciaire*, 17–23 December 1990, 7–8. He cites the example of Gaston being asked, "Êtes-vous allé au pont?" (Did you go to the bridge?) He replied: "Allée? Il n'y pas d'allée; je le sais, j'y suis été." (A path? There is no path; I know, I've been there!) *Allé* means "gone", *allée* is "path." Dominici also used *suis été* rather than *ai été* for "been." *Mythologies* was first published in Paris in 1957.

11. National Archives, Kew, MEPO 2/9394 report of 20 July 1955.

12. Archives Départmentales Digne, 1182 W 8.

13. Vincent, *L'affaire Dominici*, 236.

14. Scize, *Au grand jour des assises*, 307.

15. Sébeille said Gaston used the term *péché d'amour*.

9. THE VERDICT

1. Unless otherwise noted, for quoted passages from the trial, see the transcript in Enquêtes criminelles diverse, Art. 2–3: Affaire Dominici (suite), 1952–56, Archives Nationales, Paris.

2. "Ah! Cette petite!"

3. "Quelle garce!" The term means "what a bitch" or "what a slut."

4. Clovis had used the term "occupation" instead of "incarcération" when referring to Gustave's jail term.

5. "N'aï péta très! N'en pourrié faïre péta un aoutré!"

6. Scapel was a former *bâtonnier* and a member of the *conseil d'ordre* of the Marseilles barristers. *Bâtonnier* is an office that does not exist in British or American law. The title is attached to the president of lawyers attached to a particular court; in other words, the person serves as the leader of the bar. On Scapel's arrival in Digne, he had said, "I hope to remain a silent witness throughout the trial." *Combat*, 24 November 1954.

7. Quoted in Dumarcet, *L'affaire Dominici*, 73.

8. *France Soir*, 26 November 1954, wrongly described Roger Perrin as Gaston's brother-in-law.
9. *Le Figaro*, 28 November 1954.
10. Unlike court procedures in the United States, in French law the civil suit is heard at the same time.
11. *News Chronicle*, 18 November 1954.
12. National Archives, Kew, FO 369/5032. The original letter was written in December 1953. The letter was translated into French and given to Delorme by Geoffrey Meade, the British consul general in Marseille.
13. Giono, *Notes sur l'affaire Dominici*, saw Yvette as a product of the new world of consumerism, a *paysanne travestie* (a tarted-up peasant).
14. *France-Soir*, 19 December 1954.
15. *Le Dauphiné Libéré*, 30 November 1954.
16. This was subsequently changed to a jury of nine jurors and a panel of three judges: the president and two associate judges. On appeal there is a jury of twelve jurors and three judges. Terrorism and major drug trafficking cases are tried in a special court with seven active justices in the first hearing and nine on appeal. There are no jurors. The system remains inquisitorial rather than confrontational.
17. *Daily Express*, 29 November 1954.
18. *News Chronicle*, 23 November 1954.
19. *Times*, 5 February 1955.
20. See the useful summary of press reactions in France and Britain in a dispatch from Gladwyn Jebb in Paris to Foreign Secretary Anthony Eden, dated 20 December 1954, in National Archives, Kew, FO 369/5032.
21. *Le Figaro*, 8 February 1955.

10. THE CHENEVIER INQUIRY

1. This translation does not convey all the grammatical and syntactical faults of the original. Archives Départmentales Digne, 1182 W 1.
2. *Manchester Guardian*, 29 November 1954.
3. Guerrier, *L'affaire Dominici*, 612.
4. Chevenier inquiry papers in Enquêtes criminelles diverse, Art. 2–3: Affaire Dominici (suite), 1952–56, Archives Nationales, Paris.
5. For an apricot crop in 1952, $300 seems a great deal of money.

6. His full name was Jean-Michel Guérin du Boscq de Beaumont. He came from a distinguished Norman family, had joined de Gaulle in London during the war, was sent to New York as consul for Free France, and subsequently had a distinguished career, holding several cabinet positions. As foreign minister he helped pave the way for French acceptance of German rearmament, and as minister of justice he played a major role in Pierre Mendès-France's campaign against excessive alcohol consumption, summed up in the slogan "Never more than one liter of wine per day!"

7. A street and a metro station are named after Marx Dormoy in the eighteenth arrondissement. The assassins were former "cagoulardes," or members of La Cagoule, a right-wing extremist group active in the 1930s.

8. *Constellation*, March 1955, 36–40.

9. Known in French as *non-lieu*.

10. *France Soir*, 17 December 1954.

11. *France Soir*, 18 December 1954.

12. Chevenier inquiry papers in Enquêtes criminelles diverse, Art. 2–3: Affaire Dominici (suite), 1952–56, Archives Nationales, Paris.

13. Chevenier inquiry papers in Enquêtes criminelles diverse, Art. 2–3: Affaire Dominici (suite), 1952–56, Archives Nationales, Paris.

14. Guerrier, *L'affaire Dominici*, 682.

15. Chevenier inquiry papers in Enquêtes criminelles diverse, Art. 2–3: Affaire Dominici (suite), 1952–56, Archives Nationales, Paris.

16. Maurice Patin would have a very distinguished career. He went on to become president of the court of appeal and head of the committee of public safety in Algeria. In 1959 President de Gaulle nominated him to serve on the Constitutional Council.

17. Archives Départmentales Digne, 1182 W 4.

18. Archives Départmentales Digne, 1182 W 4.

19. Archives Départmentales Digne, 1182 W 4.

20. *Times*, 18 February 1955.

21. Archives Départmentales Digne, 1182 W 8.

22. National Archives Kew, FO 369/4924.

23. National Archives Kew, FO 369/4924.

24. Guerrier, *L'affaire Dominici*, 611.

25. *Times*, 21 June 1965.

26. Deniau and Sultan, *Dominici*, 275.

27. National Archives, Kew, FO 369/4924.

11. THE CASE IS CLOSED

1. *Times*, 9 March 1955.
2. Chenevier, *De la combe*, 181.
3. See, for example, *Populaire Dimanche*, 3 July 1955.
4. Laborde, *Dominici Affair*, 341.
5. For information about *bâtonnier*, see chapter 9, note 6.
6. Floriot, *When Justice Falters*, 98–117.
7. *Times*, 20 July 1955.
8. See *Détective*, 15 August 1955.
9. Sube meant that her life had been a terrible ordeal.
10. *Times*, 26 July 1955.
11. *Times*, 20 October 1955. The ban was subsequently lifted, and the short film is now on DVD.
12. Enquêtes criminelles diverse, Art. 2–3: Affaire Dominici (suite), 1952–56, Archives Nationales, Paris.
13. *Times*, 11 August 1955.
14. Chenevier, *De la combe*, 203–4.
15. The abbey closed in 1992. The remaining monks then moved to Ganagobie.
16. Enquêtes criminelles diverse, Art. 2–3: Affaire Dominici (suite), 1952–56, Archives Nationales, Paris.
17. Archives Départmentales Digne, 1182 W 1, part 1.
18. Archives Départmentales Digne, 1182 W 1, part 1.
19. Archives Départmentales Digne, 1182 W 3.
20. Vincent Carrias, "Pourquoi je le crois coupable," http://vincent.carrias .pagesperso-orange.fr/dominici.htm.
21. "Qu'il a pas lieu à suivre en l'état." Archives Départmentales Digne, 1182 W 3?
22. Archives Départmentales Digne, 1182 W 4.
23. *Times*, 5 August 1954.
24. As part of a television series titled *Cinq colonnes à la une.*
25. This was not a pardon, simply a *remise de réclusion* (released from prison).
26. See the protests in *Dauphiné Libéré*, 26 August 1960.
27. *Times*, 15 November 1957.
28. *Times*, 28 July 1960.

29. *Daily Telegraph*, 29 November 1954.

12. RECEPTION

1. Reymond, *Dominici non coupable*, 7.
2. Fourastié, *Les Trente Glorieuses*. The expression was a modification of *les trois glorieux*, or the three days in July 1830 that brought down Charles X, who was replaced by Louis-Philippe, *le roi bourgeois* (the bourgeois monarch).
3. Zeldin, "Destruction of the Peasants."
4. Ehrmann, "French Peasant and Communism."
5. Blum was the socialist leader of the Popular Front government.
6. Le Roy Ladurie, a tall, stolid, royalist Norman and inheritor of a vast estate, was the father of the historian Emmanuel Le Roy Ladurie.
7. Paxton, *French Peasant Fascism*.
8. Duby and Wallon, *Histoire de la France rurale*, 4:449.
9. This was six years before rationing was finally ended in Britain.
10. The CAP consumes about half the European Union's budget at a cost of about €50 billion (about $53 billion).
11. *Le Monde*, 29 July 1965. Thanks to the European Economic Community, between 1959 and 1975 French agricultural production rose by 61.3 percent in volume and by 228 percent in value.
12. Quesnay wrote, "La terre est l'unique source des richesses," and spoke of the peasantry as the sole *classe productive* (productive class).
13. Bernot and Blanchard, *Nouville*; Friedmann, *Villes et compagnes*; and Wylie, *Village in the Vaucluse*.
14. Mendras, *La fin des Paysans*.
15. Le Roy Ladurie, *Montaillou*; Duby and Wallon, *Histoire de la France rurale*; and Foucault, *Moi, Pierre Rivière*.
16. The French concept of *paysan* is far less archaic and pejorative than the English word "peasant" and is still in common everyday usage to describe both farmers and laborers. A "peasant" is a hayseed; a *paysan* is a highly respected and hardworking member of the community.
17. Bové managed to get 1.32 percent of the popular vote in the 2007 presidential election with 483,008 votes. He is now a member of the European Parliament.
18. There is some doubt as to what he meant by *franc z'loyal*. Did he mean "frank," or did he mean *français* (French)?

19. Ministry of the Economy, *Annuaire statistique de France*, 159.
20. Ehrmann, "French Peasant and Communism," 34. A 1972 survey showed that 41 percent of workers and only 19 percent of peasants could identify Jean-Paul Sartre. This was considered a shocking example of the latter's cultural backwardness.
21. See, for example, the article by Faure, "Ouvriers et paysans."
22. Farquhar, *Beaux' Strategem*, act 4, scene 1.
23. Innocenzi, *L'enigme de Pélissanne*.
24. Alfred Lord Tennyson, "Tithonus," Poetry Foundation, https://www.poetry foundation.org/poems-and-poets/poems/detail/45389?.

Bibliography

ARCHIVAL SOURCES

Archives Départementales Digne-Les-Bains
   1182 W 1–8.
Archives Nationales, Paris
   Enquêtes criminelles diverses: Rapports de police, procédures judiciaires,
   documents photographiques, et coupures de presse:
      Art. 1: Affaires Attia, Buisson, Dominici (crime de Lurs), 1927–72.
      Art. 2–3: Affaire Dominici (suite), 1952–56.
      Art. 4: Affaires Dominici (suite), Girier et Loutrel (Gang DIT des "trac-
      tions avant"), 1945–68.
Boots UK Limited Archives, Nottingham, England
   Boots Annual Report, 1948–9150.
National Archives, Kew, England
   Foreign Office, Consular Department (FO) 369/4924: Murder of Jack
   Drummond, British scientist, and family in France, 1953.
   FO 369/5032: Trial of Gaston Dominici for the Murder of Sir Jack Drum-
   mond, Lady Drummond, and their daughter, Elizabeth, 1954.
   FO 371/107475: Various requests concerning memorials in France in honour
   of the murdered Jack Drummond, 1953.
   FO 943/422: Austrian wheat supplies: wheat, flour, biscuits, pulses, 1946–47.
   Metropolitan Police, Office of the Commissioner (MEPO) 2/9393: Murder
   of Sir Jack Drummond and family at Lurs, Basses Alpes, Southern France,
   on the Night of 4/5 Aug. 1952.
   MEPO 2/9394: Murder of Sir Jack Drummond and family at Lurs, Basses
   Alpes, Southern France, 1953–60.
   Ministry of Food and Ministry of Agriculture (MAF) 256/4: Sir Jack Drum-
   mond, Scientific Adviser to Ministry, 1939–46.

PUBLISHED SOURCES

Barthes, Roland. "Dominici, or the Triumph of Literature." In *Mythologies*, 43–46. Translated by Annette Lavers. New York: Farrar, Straus and Giroux, 1972.

Bernot, Lucien, and René Blanchard. *Nouville: Un village français*. Paris: Institut d'Ethnologie, 1952.

Birdwhistell, R. L. *Kinesis and Context: Essays in Body Motion Communication*. Philadelphia: University of Pennsylvania Press, 1970.

Boyd Orr, John. *Food, Health and Income: Report on a Survey of Adequacy of Diet in Relation to Income*. London: Macmillan, 1936.

Burrin, Philippe. *France under the Germans: Collaboration and Compromise*. New York: New Press, 1996.

Carles, Émilie. *Une soupe aux herbes sauvages*. Paris: Pocket, 1977.

Chapman, Stanley. *Jesse Boot of Boots the Chemist: A Study in Business History*. London: Hodder and Stoughton, 1974.

Chapus, Jacques. *Cinquante ans de journalisme*. Paris: Anne Carrière, 2001.

Charrier, Pierre. *Affaire Dominici, le dernier témoin*. Marseille: L'écailler du Sud, 2003.

Chenevier, Charles. *L'affaire Dominici: Vingt ans après le drame de Lurs, toute la vérité*. Paris: Productions de Paris Noé, 1973.

———. *De la combe aux fées à Lurs: Souvenirs et révélations*. Paris: Flammarion, 1962.

Council of British Societies for Relief Abroad. *Nutrition and Relief Work: A Handbook for the Guidance of Relief Workers*. 2nd ed. Oxford: Oxford University Press, 1945.

Deniau, Jean Charles, and Madeleine Sultan. *Dominici: C'était une affaire de famille*. Paris: L'Archipel, 2004.

Domènech, Gabriel. *Lurs: Toute l'affaire Dominici*. Forcalquier: Charles Testanière, 1956.

Drummond, J. C., and Anne Wilbraham. *The Englishman's Food: A History of Five Centuries of English Diet*. London: Jonathan Cape, 1939.

Duby, Georges, and Armand Wallon. *Histoire de la France rurale*. 4 vols. Paris: Seuil, 1975–77.

Dumarcet, Lionel. *L'affaire Dominici*. Paris: De Vecchi, 1999.

Ehrmann, Henry W. "The French Peasant and Communism." *American Political Science Review* 46, no.1 (March 1952): 19–43.

Farquhar, George. *The Beaux' Strategem*. London: J. M. Dent, 1898.

Faure, Marcel. "Ouvriers et paysans." *Esprit* 227, no. 6 (June 1955): 1050–1063.

Fergusson, James. *The Vitamin Murders: Who Killed Healthy Eating in Britain?* London: Portobello Books, 2007.

Floriot, René. *Les erreurs judiciaires*. Paris: Flammarion, 1968.

———. *When Justice Falters*. Translated by R. Heppenstall. London: George G. Harrap, 1972.

Foucault, Michel. *Moi, Pierre Rivière, ayant égorgé ma mère, ma soeur, et mon frère: Un cas de parricide au XIXe siècle*. Paris: Gallimard, 1973.

Fougeron, Marie. *En marge du procès de Gaston Dominici: Mon doute en face de la conviction Sébeille*. Cannes: Devaye, 1955.

Fourastié, Jean. *Les Trente Glorieuses: Ou la révolution invisible de 1946 à 1975*. Paris: Fayard, 1979.

Friedmann, Georges, ed. *Villes et compagnes: Civilisation urbaine et civilisation rurale en France*. Paris: Armand Colin, 1953.

Friend, G. E. *The Schoolboy: A Study of His Nutrition, Physical Development, and Health*. Foreword by Prof. J. C. Drummond. Cambridge: W. Heffer & Sons, 1935.

Giono, Jean. *The Horseman on the Roof*. New York: North Point Press, 1982.

———. *Notes sur l'affaire Dominici*. Paris: Gallimard, 1955.

Guerrier, Eric. *L'affaire Dominici: Expertise du triple crime de Lurs*. Paris: Cheminements, 2007.

Guillaumin, Émile. *La vie d'un simple*. Paris: Le Livre de Poche, 1977.

Innocenzi, Paul-Claude. *L'enigme de Pélissanne: L'Affaire Jeremy Cartland*. Paris: J'ai lu, 1999.

Jacob, Madeleine. *À vous de juger: Pauline Dubuisson, Dominici, Sylvie Paul, Abbé Desnoyers, Maître Jaccoud*. Paris: Les yeux ouverts, 1962.

Judt, Tony. *Postwar: A History of Europe since 1945*. New York: Penguin, 2005.

Laborde, Jean. *The Dominici Affair*. New York: W. Morrow, 1974.

———. *Un matin d'été à Lurs: 5 août 1952*. Paris: Robert Laffont, 1972.

Le Roy Ladurie, Emmanuel. *Montaillou: Village Occitan de 1294 à 1324*. Paris: Gallimard, 1975.

Meckert, Jean. *La tragédie de Lurs*. Paris: Gallimard, 1972.

Mendras, Henri. *La fin des Paysans*. Paris: SEDEIS, 1967.

Ministry of Food. *Food and Its Protection against Poison Gas*. SO No. 70-9999. London: His Majesty's Stationary Office, 1940.

Ministry of the Economy. *Annuaire statistique de la France, 1979*. Vol. 84., no. 26. Paris: Institut national de la statistique et des études économiques, 1978.

Mossé, Claude. *Dominici innocent*. Paris: Rocher, 1993.

Ollivier, Jean-Paul. *Le massacre de Lurs: Qui est l'assassin?* Lille: Janicot, 1953.

Paxton, Robert O. *French Peasant Fascism: Henry Dorgères' Greenshirts and the Crises of French Agriculture, 1929–1939*. Oxford: Oxford University Press, 1997.

Pollak, Émile. *La parole est à la défense*. Paris: Robert Laffont, 1975.

Quintard-Morénas, François. "The Presumption of Innocence in the French and Anglo-American Legal Traditions." *American Journal of Comparative Law* 58, no. 1 (2010): 107–49.

Reymond, William. *Dominici non coupable: Les assassins retrouvés*. Paris: France loisirs, 1997.

Russell-Young, Gordon. *Valley of Silence: The Mystery of the Drummond Murders*. London: Robert Hale, 1955.

Sagnes, Jean. *Le midi rouge, mythe et réalitié: Études d'histoire occitane*. Paris: Anthropos, 1982.

Scize, Pierre. *Au grand jour des assisses*. Paris: Denoël, 1955.

Sébeille, Edmond. *L'affaire Dominici: La vérité sur le crime de Lurs*. Paris: PLON, 1970.

Taylor, A. J. P. *English History, 1914–1945*. Oxford: Oxford University Press, 1965.

Teyssier, Jean. *Mémoires et souvenirs d'un journaliste provincial*. Digne-les-Bains: Haute-Provence, 1989.

Tindall, Gillian. *Célestine: Voices from a French Village*. New York: Henry Holt, 1997.

Truche, Pierre. "Rapport au Président de la République de la commission de réflexion sur la justice." La documentation Française, 1997. http://www.ladocumentationfrancaise.fr/rapports-publics/974072100/index.shtml.

Vincent, Jean-Louis. *L'affaire Dominici: La contre-enquête*. Paris: Vendémiaire, 2016.

Wylie, Laurence. *A Village in the Vaucluse*. Cambridge MA: Harvard University Press, 1957.

Zeldin, Theodore. "The Destruction of the Peasants." *New York Review of Books*, Nov. 24, 1977.

———. *France, 1848–1945*. Oxford: Clarendon Press, 1973.

Index

Batigne, Jacques, 240, 241–42, 250, 255
Battestini, Nicolas, 227
Les Baumettes, 217, 222
Bazaine, François-Achille, 156, 292n12
The Beaux' Stratagem (Farquhar), 279–80
Becker, Jacques, xviii–xix
Belin, Jules, 220
Benedictines, 139
Bernard, Marcel-Jean, 247
Bernard-Aubert, Claude, xviii
Bernier, Commandant, 26, 27, 45, 89, 98
Bernot, Lucien, 273
Besnard, Marie, 211
Beucherie, Gaston, 62–63
Biochemical Studies of Nutritional Problems (Drummond), 126–27
Blanc, Marceau, 67–68, 179
Blanchard, René, 273
blood at crime scene, 40, 42, 86, 117, 161, 178
Blum, Léon, 266, 268–69, 298n5
Bocca, Joseph, 101, 102, 187
bodies being moved, 30–31, 34, 40, 87, 90, 181
Bonino (Léon Dominici's cousin), 202
Bonnafous, Madame, 257–58
Bonnaire, Mr. (Noël), 17, 21
Boot, Jesse, 134
Boots Pure Drug Company, 1, 55, 132–33
Bottaï, Raoul, 227, 229, 232, 238, 241

Bouchier, Raymond, 25–26
Bourgues, Albert, 25
Bousquet, Marcel: appearance of, 206; bringing Roger Périès to stand, 196; communication style of, 170, 172; Communist Party meeting and, 184; concluding trial, 206–7; dossier and, 168, 184, 217; Edmond Sébeille and, 186; on Gaston Dominici, 169–70; on Gustave Dominici, 193; looking at Hillman stand-in, 196; loudspeaker incident and, 228; misgivings about, 210, 212, 217; oath issue and, 185, 189, 228; questioning Dominici family, 173–74, 176–77, 188–91, 193–94, 196–98, 200; questioning Zézé Perrin, 191–92; refusing to follow procedure, 197; sentencing Gaston Dominici, 207
Bové, José, 274, 298n17
Boyer, Marcel, 15–16, 89–90
bridge over railway, 11, 12, 13, 15, 16, 30, 35
British Empire Cancer Campaign, 134
British Medical Association, 126
"British Restaurants" (nonprofit communal organization), 130
bullets as evidence, 62–63, 92, 178
bullfight, comic. See *charlotade* (comic bullfight)
Burton, J., 238
Burton, Norman Henry, 74–75

La Cagoule, 296n7

Caillat, Augusta: answering questions, 225; as bad-tempered person, 78, 80, 100; birth of, 138; confronting Clovis Dominici, 252; Gaston Dominici and, 207–8, 215, 229, 241, 256; laundering clothes, 36; testifying, 199

Caillat, Clément, 199

Caillat, Marie-Claude, 100, 241, 254

Calas, Jean, 206

camera, missing, 256

Cancer Hospital Research Institute, 123

canvas bucket, 13, 86, 183, 190, 192, 231, 257

CAP (Common Agricultural Policy), 270–71, 298n10

carbine: American troops supplying, 99, 102, 110, 161, 175; Clovis Dominici and, 51, 77, 95–97, 151–52, 159, 190, 194–95, 251–52, 255; disposal of, 109, 175; Dr. Morin and, 242–43; as evidence, 44–45, 178–79, 226; Gaston Dominici and, 102, 104–6, 108, 116, 173, 174, 188, 209–10, 253, 289n8; Gustave Dominici and, 93, 99, 111, 114, 151, 155, 157, 159, 160, 161, 162, 187–88, 218, 223; identification of, 42–43; patched, 44, 149–50, 199, 200; splinter of wood from, 173; storage place of, 98, 100, 108, 116, 149–50, 155, 253, 260; uncertain possession of, 44, 119, 164–65, 199, 201, 217; Yvette Dominici and, 153. *See also* murder weapon

Carcassonne, Professor, 240–41

Carrera, Martinez, 232

Carrias, Pierre: Charles Chenevier and, 231, 241–44, 246–47, 249, 250; Charles Gillard and, 231, 241–44, 246–47; concerns about Dominici case, 260–61; evidence and, 35; personal characteristics of, 231; press and, 231, 260; starting investigation, 240

Cartier family, 21–22

Cartland, Jeremy, 281

cartridges, 34, 63, 92–93, 94, 105, 109, 112, 178, 181, 209, 289n32

La Cassine, 88, 183, 259

Castaing, Henry, 241, 260

Castaing, René-Marcel, 42–43

Chaillan, Fernand, 82

Chaillan, Louis, 82

Chaillan, Marcel, 80, 82

Chapman, Stanley, 134

Chapus, Jacques, 222, 262

Charles-Alfred, Léon, 168, 187, 194, 196, 205, 215–16

charlotade (comic bullfight), 4, 7, 10, 58, 287n8

Charrier, Pierre: anticipating Gaston Dominici case, 116; defending Gaston Dominici, 181, 183–84, 188, 205, 207; defending Gustave Dominici, 70, 71; Dominici family and, 119, 245; dossier and, 168; frustrated with case, 194; at Grand' Terre, 80–82; visiting Gaston Dominici in prison, 223–24, 240–41

Chastel, Henri, 67
Château-Arnoux (Provence), 8, 284n13
Chauffeurs de la Drôme, 49
Chauve, Joseph, 44, 150
Chemical Defence Experimental Station (Wiltshire, England), 292n17
chemical factory at Saint-Auban, 8–9, 284n13
Chenevier, Charles: background and career of, 219–20; Bartkowski case and, 233; beginning inquiry, 221–22; gaining rogatory power, 245, 250; on Gaston Dominici's trial, 198; Louis Pagè on, 249; Pierre Carrias and, 241–44; questioning Dominici family, 224–26, 250–52, 253–55, 258; reports completed by, 226–27, 259–60
Chenevier inquiry, 217, 218, 219, 231, 244, 248, 256
Chirac, Jacques, xiii
Churchill, Winston, 1, 211
civil case, 182, 185, 202, 207
civil law, xiv
Clemenceau, Georges, 48
Cluny Abbey, 139
Cold War, xv, 232, 234, 269, 276, 285n8
collaborators, xii, 17–18, 19, 271
Combas, Roger, 210
Combat (newspaper), 46, 135
Combat (resistance group), 19
Commissariat Général du Plan, 269
Common Agricultural Policy (CAP), 270–71, 298n10

common law, xiv
Communist Party, 264–65, 267–70, 276–79. *See also* PCF (Partie Communiste Française)
Confédération Générale du Travail, 268
Conil, Henri, 67, 143
conspiracy theories, xv–xvi, 211, 220, 265, 279–80. *See also* Bartkowski, Wilhelm; speculation about crime
Constant, Fernand: on conspiracy theories, 178; crime scene reconstruction and, 119; Edmond Sébeille and, 68, 83, 84; Gustave Dominici on, 64; making announcements, 63, 67; methods and style of, 69; "Opération Bergerie" and, 80–81, 82; pursuing leads, 71, 80; questioning Gustave Dominici, 63–64; questioning Marie Dominici, 70
contraband money, 2, 5
contraband weapons, 24, 44
Cornox, 134
corporatism, 266–67
Coty, René, 214, 262
Coudouing, Jean-Claude, 62–63
Council of British Societies for Relief Abroad, 132
Council of Europe, 276
courts of appeal, 148, 165–67, 227, 243
Crespy (gendarme), 27
crime scene: compromising of, 34; not sealed off, 26, 27; reconstruction of, 63, 89–90, 115–19, 205

Dominici, Gaston (*cont.*)

Edmond Sébeille and, 45–46, 51–52, 55, 58, 67, 70, 75–76, 83–84; fighting Mr. Giraud, 142–43; Gustave Dominici and, 19, 93–94, 192, 197–98, 241; incarceration of, 148; marriage of, 138, 262; "medical knowledge" of, 140; as midwife, 140, 174; overhearing conversation, 218; personal characteristics of, 137, 139–40, 145; as poacher, 139; press and, 120–21, 208, 209–10; in prison, 217; relationship with rest of family, 11–13, 142, 143–44, 146–47; release from prison, 262; representing struggling peasantry, 274; requesting René Floriot's assistance, 245; Roger Périès and, 107–8; "saving" family honor, 102–3, 107, 115, 198; sentence of, 103, 207, 231, 262; speaking in dialect, 289n31, 290n16; stomach problems of, 240–41; as suspect, 67, 77, 84–85; testifying, 172–74, 224–25, 250–51; verdict, 207; violence of, 143; wedding night of, 138; wood splinter and, 35; writing letters to family, 215–16; Yvette Dominici and, 241, 263; Zézé Perrin and, 164, 174, 182–83, 192, 218, 220, 224, 255–56. *See also* trial of Gaston Dominici

Dominici, Gaston (son), 138–39, 159, 225–26, 229, 252–53

Dominici, Germaine. *See* Perrin, Germaine

Dominici, Gilbert, 88, 145

Dominici, Gustave, xii; alone with another witness, 97; answering Charles Chenevier's questions, 249, 253; answering Edmond Sébeille's questions, 52–53, 55–56, 63, 90–92, 93–94, 99, 156; answering Émile Pollack's questions, 258; answering Fernand Constant's questions, 63–65, 69; answering Noël Mével's questions, 63–65; answering Roger Périès's questions, 82, 92–94, 113–14, 149–50, 151, 155, 157–62; appearance of, 192–93; appendicitis of, 147; aware Elizabeth Drummond still alive, 69, 94; in bed with doctor's note, 54–55; birth of, 141; Clovis Dominici and, 200–201, 252–53; collapsing during inquest, 156; court appeal of, 215–17; during crime scene visit, 90; on day before murder discovery, 12–13; on day of murder discovery, 25–27, 46–47, 297n10; divorce of, 263; Edmond Sébeille on, 67; Émile Pollak on, 205–6; family's opinion of, 201–2; at Feast of the Assumption, 59–60; in FTPF (Francs-Tireurs et Partisans Français), 17, 19, 79; Gaston Dominici and, 11–12, 113, 145, 147, 157, 217–18, 241; guns and, 24, 42–43; marriage of, 70, 83–84; mentioned in trial proceedings, 168, 174, 180–81, 183–84, 186, 187–88, 189–91; as outcast, 216; overheard conversation of, 218; personal characteristics of, 162; press and, 65, 120–21; returning home from jail, 78; revealing information, 84, 93–94; sentence of, 103; as suspect, 67, 96–97; testifying, 192–94, 197–98; trial and sentence of, 71–72; trousers and, 36–37; in young adulthood, 146–47. *See also* trial of Gustave Dominici

Dominici, Léon (brother), 136–37, 146

Dominici, Léon (nephew), 146, 201–2, 207, 225, 228–30, 241, 244–45

Dominici, Marcel (grandson), 207

Dominici, Marcel (son), 16, 35, 140, 145, 225–26, 229

Dominici, Marie, 11; answering questions, 54, 70, 76–77, 150, 153, 188–89; during crime scene visit, 90; death of, 263; disliking sister-in-law, 146; Gaston Dominici on, 75–76; Jo and, 80–82; keeping Henri Dragon outside, 31, 221; before marriage, 137–38; marriage of, 143; turning off water, 12; wedding night of, 138

Dominici, Marie (daughter-in-law), 201, 229, 252

Dominici, Mauricette, 258

Dominici, Rose, 51, 100, 145, 195

Dominici, Victoria, 229

Dominici, Yvette: answering questions, 100–101, 249, 253;

appearance of, 189; on carbine, 117; Charles Gillard and, 258; on day of murder discovery, 25, 26–27; divorce of, 263; at Feast of the Assumption, 59; Gaston Dominici and, 263; Gustave Dominici and, 64; Jean Giono on, 295n13; knowing what to say, 76–77; marriage of, 70, 83–84; "Opération Bergerie" and, 82; overheard conversation of, 218; riding bicycle while pregnant, 25, 47, 111; staying at parents, 70–71; testifying, 152–53, 189–90; wet trousers and, 36, 37; in Zézé Perrin's testimony, 182

Dominici family, xii, 11; Communist Party helping, 277–78; on day of murder discovery, 46–48; discord among, 78, 148; education of children of, 141; guns of, 164–65; during inquiry, 90; Maillet family and, 78–80, 144–45; normal interval for, 89; and Perrin family, 285n18; reacting to verdict, 207–8; relationships among, 113; violence of, 24

"Dominici: To Die in Prison" (Chapus), 262

Dorgères, Henri. *See* Halluin, Henri d'

Dormoy, Marx, 219, 296n7

dossier: in appeal decision, 227; Charles Chenevier and, 220; closing of, 165; in French law, 28; omissions in, 184; Pierre Carrias and, 231, 261; "on trial," 168, 202, 205, 217, 243, 247

Drac, Roger, 15

Dragon, Henri, 30–31, 34, 41, 70, 71, 89, 177–78, 221

Dreyfus, Alfred, 57, 206

Drummond, Anne: Claude Delorme on, 202; on holiday, 3, 4; meeting and marrying Jack Drummond, 126; rumors about, 58, 75; stomach contents, 40

Drummond, Elizabeth: blows to head of, 30, 41–42, 175, 177, 245; Calixte Rozan mentioning, 204; condition of feet of, 30, 41–42, 177, 203, 245; Gaston Dominici and, 118; holiday plans of, 1–2, 3, 4; rigidity of body of, 30, 41, 178; speaking French, 3, 13–14; time of death of, 41, 70–71, 94, 177, 217

Drummond, Jack: in advisory capacity, 128–32; *Biochemical Studies of Nutritional Problems*, 126–27; childhood of, 123; C. Lovatt Evans and, 292n17; criticism of, 124–25; *The Englishman's Food*, 126, 291n7; estate value of, 135; as father, 10; hand wound of, 38–39, 179; health problems of, 1, 123; holiday plans of, 1–2; honors bestowed upon, 131, 132, 291n2; interests of, 134; legacy of, 133; marrying Anne Drummond, 126; obituary of, 131; passing through German lines, 132; personal characteristics of, 124–25, 133, 134–35, 176; rumors about, xv–xvi, 58–59, 66, 214, 232–33, 262–63, 280–

81; salary of, 133, 283n4(ch.1); stomach and bladder contents, 39; traveling, 126, 131–32; work life of, 5, 124–28, 132–33

Drummond family: camping, 14; at *charlotade* (comic bull fight), 7; Claude Delorme on, 202; discovery of bodies of, 15–16; funeral of, 55; missing one and a half hours, 3; obtaining water from Dominici farm, 13, 86, 91, 182, 183, 192, 257, 285n18; possible detour of, 6–7; reputation of, 75; road trip, 3, 4, 5–6, 9–11

Duc brothers, 67

Dupuiche, Jean, 228

Duralumin band, 44, 150, 199

Durance River, 11, 37, 42, 109, 204

Duron, Madame, 175

East Surrey Regiment, 123

Emmanuelli, Mr., 17

Engels, Friedrich, 265

English families, rumored, 8

The Englishman's Food (Drummond), 126, 291n7

Escudier, Émile, 69, 150–51

Estoublon, Henri, 26, 140

Estrangin, Benoît, 139

European Commission, 270

European Convention on Human Rights, xv

European Court for Human Rights, xiii

European Economic Community, 298n11

monetary allowance for travel, 3,
283n3(ch.1), 284n6
money changing hands, 80
Monnet, Jean, 269
Monod, Samuel. *See* Vox, Maximilien
Montarron, Marcel, 247
Moradis (Swiss killer), 236
Morice, André, 248
Morin, Dr., 242–43
Moro-Giafferi, Vincent de, 56–57
motive, xi, xii, xv; as important in
French investigations, 26, 37;
lacking, 77–78, 83, 122, 212, 232;
possible, 32, 59, 106, 114, 175, 203,
217, 224
motorcycle with sidecar, xi, 27, 52, 53,
108, 111, 157
Moulin, Jean, 19
Mouvement Républicain Populaire,
268
Moynier, Joseph, 179
Mucha, Stephan, 48
mulberry tree, 45, 63, 88, 105, 108,
188, 286n8
murder weapon: bullet from, 63;
Clovis Dominici and, 92, 186, 195,
202, 205; disposal of, 37, 42; as evidence, 46; Gaston Dominici and,
92, 110; Robert Sébeille and, 49,
50, 186; splinter of wood from, 35,
42, 173, 209; uncertain possession
of, 43, 50, 79–80, 150, 205. *See also*
carbine
Muzy, François, 19–20
Muzy, Mrs., 20, 141, 170

Nalin, Paul, 38–39, 177–78
National Health Service, 291n12
"national loaf," 130–31
National Police. *See* Sûreté National
News Chronicle, 121, 214
Ninth Mobile Brigade, 32
Nobel Prize, 291n2, 291n12
Notes sur l'affaire Dominici (Giono),
295n13
Nottingham Playhouse, 134
Nouville: Un Village Français
(Bernot and Blanchard), 273

oath issue, 185, 189, 212, 227–28, 256
Oddou, Joseph, 218–19
oil for guns, 164–65, 178–79, 194
Olivier, Jean-Marie: on day of
murder discovery, 15, 24–25, 47–
48, 287n10; in Gustave Dominici's
testimony, 53, 64–65, 94, 158;
during inquiry, 89–91; at scene
reconstruction, 63; testifying, 180
Ollivier, André, 61, 63, 178–79
"Opération Bergerie," 81–83
Orr, John Boyd, 125, 131, 291n12
Orsatelli (public prosecutor), 64,
221, 222, 231

Pagè, Louis, 249
Pagnol, Marcel, xvi
Panayotou, Aristide, 60–61, 71, 169,
179–80, 287n24
Le Parisien Libéré, 120, 135
Paris Match, 31, 73
Parliamentary and Scientific Com-
mittee, 127

photographs/photography: as evidence, 71, 116, 182, 242, 248, 260; needed, but lacking, 38, 117; during trial, 168

Pieds-Noirs, xvii, 272

Pinay, Antoine, 270

Plan de Modernisation de l'Équipement, 269

poaching: Gustave Dominici and, 183, 192, 242; as part of Gaston Dominici persona, 110; Paul Maillet and, 76, 192; in peasant life, 139, 154, 194; in psychic's vision, 62; Zézé Perrin and, 180, 183, 192

police, British, 73–74, 75

police, French: Algerians and, 241; British press on, 58, 121; carelessness of, 61–62, 71, 100; criticism of, 212–14; gendarmes and, 32, 34; Gustave Dominici on, 64; local residents and, 65, 85; methods and role of, 26, 27, 33–34, 116; PCF (Partie Communiste Française) and, 17–18, 19, 45, 56. *See also* judicial police; Sûreté National

police dog, 31

Pollak, Émile: clients of, 288n8; in court, 169, 174–75, 176, 178–79, 182, 184; Dominici family and, 119; dossier and, 168; eager to take Dominici case, 116; Edmond Sébeille and, 186; frustrated with case, 159, 192, 194; Gaston Dominici and, 205–6, 223–24, 240–41; Gustave Dominici and, 65, 70, 71, 155–56; on inconsistencies in court case, 187, 188, 205–6; Léon Dominici and, 245; in motor accident, 148; oath issue and, 185, 189; protesting rogatory power, 88; questioning Clovis Dominici, 194–95; requesting dismissal of case, 165; style of, 174; visiting Grand' Terre, 80–81; Zézé Perrin and, 191

Pompidou, Georges, 270

Popular Front, 266

Porton Down Experimental Station, 127, 280, 292n17

Postes, Télégraphes et Téléphones, 16

potato transaction, 84

press, British, xii, 58, 68, 121, 211, 214

press, French, 68, 120–21, 212, 231–32, 247

Le Provençal, 115

Provençal mentality, 48, 49–50, 65, 167, 258–59

Provence (France), xv, 4, 14, 154, 261, 266, 281

Provisional Government of the French Republic, 268–69

Prudhomme, Pierre, 101–4, 106, 175, 188

psychics, 62–63, 175–76

psychology, 121, 171–72, 176

Puisssant, Pierre, 20

Quesnay, François, 272

Queyrel, Adrien, 72

Queyrel brothers, 21

Radical-Socialistes, 268

Sten guns, 43, 286n6

Stigny, Commissioner, 22

Straw, Mabel (later Drummond), 123, 135

Sube, Télamon, 248

submachine gun, Russian, 230

Suez crisis, xviii, 271

Sunday Dispatch, 58, 61

Supreme Headquarters Allied Expeditionary Force, 132

Sûreté National, 72–73, 74–75, 135, 234. *See also* judicial police; police, French

Tardieu, Lucien, 33, 161, 185

Temple, Emmanuel, 227

La Terre, 267

Thompson, May Rebecca, xii

Thorez, Maurice, 23, 72, 268, 270, 278

Tillon, Charles, 22–23

The Times, xi, 71, 116, 213, 261, 262

Treaty of Rome, 270–71

les trente glorieuses, 265, 298n2

trial of Gaston Dominici: civil suit component of, 182–84, 202; closing procedures of, 203–8; consequences of, 208–14; inspection of similar Hillman during, 196; language problematic during, 170, 172, 294n7, 294n10, 298n18; loudspeaker incident during, 203, 223; opening procedures of, 167–70; postponed, 166; proceedings of, 172–75, 176–82, 184–85, 186–96, 196–202; psychological aspects of, 171–72

trial of Gustave Dominici, 71–72

Triumph sports cars, 74

trousers, 36–37, 114, 188–89, 257

Truche report, xiii

Ughetto, Joseph, 48

uniform, legionnaire's, xi, 46

University College London, 124, 132, 292n17

urban-rural differences, xvi, 171, 273, 275

Vailland, Roger, 278

Vendre, Jules, 248

Veyrac, Marius Paul, 220

Vichy government, 18, 71, 210, 267–68, 288n12

Vidocq, François, 48–49

von Bollstädt, Albert, 140, 292n23

Vox, Maximilien, 5–6, 167

watch, missing, 257

Welles, Orson, 248

Wilbraham, Anne. *See* Drummond, Anne

Wilbraham, Mrs., 2–3, 202, 207, 257

woman in black, rumored, 8–9

women, attitudes toward, 143, 168, 176

Wood, Kingsley, 128–29, 291n9

Woolton, Lord, 128, 131

world news during Dominici affair, xi, 68, 89, 211

World War II, 1–2, 18, 20, 131, 276, 291n10

Wylie, Laurence, 273

X (unknown accomplice), 214, 226, 243, 260–61